Digital Food

Contemporary Food Studies: Economy, Culture and Politics

Series Editors: David Goodman and Michael K. Goodman
ISSN: 2058–1807

This interdisciplinary series represents a significant step toward unifying the study, teaching, and research of food studies across the social sciences. The series features authoritative appraisals of core themes, debates and emerging research, written by leading scholars in the field. Each title offers a jargon-free introduction to upper-level undergraduate and postgraduate students in the social sciences and humanities.

Kate Cairns and Josée Johnston, *Food and Femininity*
Peter Jackson, *Anxious Appetites: Food and Consumer Culture*
Philip H. Howard, *Concentration and Power in the Food System: Who Controls What We Eat?*
Terry Marsden, *Agri-Food and Rural Development: Sustainable Place-Making*
Emma-Jayne Abbots, *The Agency of Eating: Mediation, Food, and the Body*
Henry Buller and Emma Roe, *Food and Animal Welfare*

Digital Food

From Paddock to Platform

Tania Lewis

BLOOMSBURY ACADEMIC
LONDON · NEW YORK · OXFORD · NEW DELHI · SYDNEY

BLOOMSBURY ACADEMIC
Bloomsbury Publishing Plc
50 Bedford Square, London, WC1B 3DP, UK
1385 Broadway, New York, NY 10018, USA

BLOOMSBURY, BLOOMSBURY ACADEMIC and the Diana logo are trademarks
of Bloomsbury Publishing Plc

First published in Great Britain 2020

A catalogue record for this book is available from the British Library.

A catalog record for this book is available from the Library of Congress.

ISBN: HB: 978-1-3500-5510-0
        PB: 978-1-3500-5509-4
        ePDF: 978-1-3500-5511-7
        ePub: 978-1-3500-5512-4

Typeset by Integra Software Services Pvt. Ltd.
Printed and bound in India

To find out more about our authors and books visit www.bloomsbury.com
and sign up for our newsletters.

For Fred and Chloé

Contents

List of Figures

Acknowledgments

This book began its life in Tasmania. In 2016, fellow media studies scholar Michelle Phillipov held a conference on The New Politics of Food and the Australian Media in the coastal city of Hobart where I had the pleasure of sharing keynote duties with Mike Goodman. Speaking as I did on the topic of food and the digital, Mike in his wisdom thought it would make a good book length topic and encouraged me to write a proposal for his and David Goodman's Contemporary Food Studies series with Bloomsbury. Three years down the track I am supremely grateful for Mike's early encouragement and for his and David's generous shepherding of the project from go to whoa. One couldn't wish for better critical but supportive readers when it comes to Mike Goodman and David Goodman. Thanks also to Miriam Cantwell and Lucy Carroll at Bloomsbury for their highly professional guidance and support.

I am indebted to the generosity of a number of academic colleagues who gave me feedback on the manuscript including Ramon Lobato, Edgar Gómez Cruz, Kelly Donati, Kathleen Lebesco, Jonatan Leer, Daniel Palmer and Yolande Strengers. Thanks to the American University of Paris for hosting my research leave in Paris in 2018 and to my always supportive boss, the Dean of my School Lisa French, for recognizing my need to take leave to complete this book. I would also like to thank my wonderful colleagues in the Digital Ethnography Research Centre (DERC), and in particular the leadership team in DERC—Co-Director Ellie Rennie and HDR Director, Ramon Lobato, and the other members of the DERC executive, Anne Harris, Anna Hickey-Moody, Jaz Choi and Rowan Wilken, all of whom kindly took turns to run the Centre during my absence in 2018, supported by Melody Ellis, Else Fitzgerald and more recently Yee Man Louie. Thanks to Larissa Hjorth, Robert Crawford, Ralph Horne and Julian Thomas for their collegiality and wisdom. I'm also grateful for the support of Melody Ellis who was a kindly critical guide and one-woman personal cheer squad with this project! Thanks also to Andrew Glover for research support and to Allister Hill who did some early literature review work for the book. I'd also like to express my thanks to the various people—from food Instagrammers, bloggers and YouTubers to food activists and producers—who kindly permitted me to use their photos in this book.

Finally, I wouldn't have gotten through the research and writing process without my partner Frédéric Rauturier. While I was writing about affective labor and the gender divide in the kitchen, he was doing all the cooking and cleaning while also juggling nappies, baby bottles and a new-ish baby. As a French-born millennial male and avid media consumer, he also offered a helpful "alternative perspective" to my antipodean-shaped, Generation X worldview. Lastly, to the ever delightful (now toddler) Chloé—thanks for regularly bringing me down from my writing cloud.

Why Digital food?

This book is about the intersection between food and the digital realm. The phrase "digital food" tends to conjure up visions of a futuristic automated present in which restaurant goers are served by robots, smart fridges order our groceries, 3D printers produce perfectly sculptured delicate culinary creations, and wearables monitor and anticipate our personal dietary needs. For most of us though the daily realities of how food and the digital world come together is much more mundane. The key images that probably best sum up today's engagements with the culinary in a digital era are the home cook using their (bacteria laden) smartphone in the kitchen to check for recipes, the restaurant goer painstakingly trying to capture the best image of their meal to post to social media, the tourist using a GPS-based restaurant app to find a good local café for breakfast or the time-pressured parent ordering dinner for the family from an online restaurant service (a middle-class parent recently complained to me that their teenager's concept of "cooking for the family" essentially involved ordering Uber Eats).

Digital Food is a book about food and everyday life in a world in which digital devices and digital content have become not only central to much of what we do but are also largely invisible and taken for granted. Digital is in some ways now just a shorthand term for the contemporary moment. In other words, for better or for worse, it has become a thoroughly normative concept to the point where it is hard to imagine a future that doesn't involve complete connectivity and the automation of every aspect of our daily lives.

At first glance then the topics of food and the digital might seem like odd bedfellows. When we think of pressing contemporary food issues we tend to think of big picture concerns around public health, sustainable agriculture, food safety and security, and geopolitics and the future of global food systems. Or the emergence of critical counter-movements to a technologized future as reflected in the now-worldwide Slow Food (*cittaslow*) community and the rise of strongly localized approaches to food production and distribution, such as urban farming, backyard permaculture, community-supported agriculture and the revitalization of small-scale agrarianism.

Meanwhile the key themes circulating in discussions about the digital realm—automation, AI, blockchain, big data, copyright, privacy, trust and data security, identity and digital citizenship and inclusion, e-waste, and the monitoring, surveillance, and monetization of digital connectivity through algorithmic processes—seem a world away from our daily engagements with grocery shopping, cooking, and eating. As I show in this book, however, our everyday food practices and experiences have become thoroughly entwined with the wider ethics and politics of digital media and technology.

Over the past decade the world of food, from grocery shopping and home cookery to restaurant going, and food politics, has been quietly colonized by the digital (see Figure I.1). Meanwhile, the realm of the digital has been invaded by all things food related. Indeed, it is hard to imagine social media platforms such as Instagram without the highly stylized and curated images of home- and restaurant-cooked meals that circulate daily through our feeds, while for many

Figure I.1 Digital devices are increasingly making their way into people's kitchens [Credit: Jeff Sheldon].

of us, going out to eat now habitually involves assessing a café or restaurant's ratings and reviews on Yelp and related apps. Similarly, YouTube would not be what it is today without its huge array of cooking and food channels, from creative food hacks and how-to cookery shows shot in people's homes around the world, to the live, interactive broadcasts (or *mukbang*) popular in South Korea and beyond where the video's "host" noisily ingests large amounts of food for our viewing pleasure. Alongside porn, celebrity selfies, and cute animals, food content reigns supreme on many digital platforms.

The digital turn in the lives of many people on the planet has triggered a huge amount of critical commentary on what has been variously characterized as "data colonialism," "the digital condition," the "platform society," and "the data revolution" (Couldry and Mejias 2019; Kitchin 2014; Stalder 2017; Van Dijck et al. 2018). In academia, a number of major accounts have now emerged examining the digitization of work, society and politics, governance, democracy, and citizen engagement (Chayko 2016; Fuchs 2010; Miller 2011; Miller and Slater 2000; Papacharissi 2010; Van Dijck 2013). Similarly, there is growing amount of more fine-grained work on the specific role of the digital in various aspects of everyday life—from work that understands the *digit*-al quite literally in terms of touch and "manual media" (Moores 2018) or "haptic media studies" (see Parisi et al. 2017) to books that engage with specific social media platforms such as Facebook and YouTube (Burgess and Green 2018; Miller 2011). These critical scholarly literatures sit alongside a huge amount of media commentary and marketing research on digital lifestyle trends and the elusive digital consumer.

Food meanwhile has become the topic on everyone's lips, so to speak. Hipster food and restaurant culture is booming around the world, from Rio to Mumbai (Halawa and Parasecoli 2019). Cookbooks are the new bestsellers while chefs, it seems, are the new rock stars. Growing numbers of people now identify as "foodies" despite associated connotations of class and cultural snobbery while arguably the average person on the street, from India to New Zealand, has a greater food literacy and awareness of food politics than ever before (see Johnston and Baumann 2010, for a book-length discussion of this tension between "distinction" and "democracy" in the culinary world). Central to this explosion of interest in all things gastronomic has been the role of food media and in particular the global popularity of food television. When I spent time with lower middle and "middling" middle-class households in Mumbai some half a decade ago talking to them about reality TV, I was somewhat surprised to learn that the Australian version of *MasterChef*—despite an Indian version airing at the time—was a popular primetime show (Lewis et al. 2016).

Internationally franchised shows like *MasterChef* have arguably contributed to changing the way we think about and do cooking in the home—"plating up" and "croquembouche," for instance, have become regular household terms post the *MasterChef* phenomenon (Lewis 2011). Yet, despite this widespread interest and engagement with food culture and food media, there has been surprisingly little written in the academic world on the growing entanglements between the digital and the world of food (for exceptions to this see Rousseau 2012; Choi et al. 2014; De Solier 2013, 2018; Lupton 2018; Schneider et al. 2018; also see Lewis and Philipov's special issue 2018).

This book aims to contribute to and shape the new and emerging field of what I am calling "digital food." The culinary realm I suggest offers a particularly generative space through which to understand the complex evolution and impact of the digital in our everyday lives and associated, emergent public and political cultures more broadly. On the one hand—much like our everyday digital use—buying, cooking, and eating food is tied to the habits, rituals, and rhythms of daily life and is therefore both ordinary and invisible. On the other hand, our daily engagements with both food and with the digital have become politically contested and sources of much cultural anxiety or "gastro-anomie"

Figure I.2 Customers use touchscreens to order meals at a Yum China Holdings Inc. KFC restaurant in Shanghai, China, on March 19, 2019 [Credit: Getty Images/ Bloomberg].

as French sociologist Claude Fischler puts it (1979). In a much-quoted quip, American celebrity farmer-activist Wendell Berry (2009) argues that "eating is an agricultural act," speaking to the fact that what we put on our plates today is linked to a wider politics of animal welfare, sustainability, food security, the plight of producers in developing nations in the face of globalizing agri-business as well as questions of food safety, health, and risk.

Similarly, our everyday digital practices are embedded in wider political issues. The seemingly banal habit of checking one's smartphone fifty times a day or posting on social media triggers a complex array of data privacy, economic, environmental, and governmental concerns. Where traditional media institutions, both public and commercial, are bound to some degree to governmental and professional regulation, the brave new world of (largely commercially driven) digital connectivity has rapidly brought us into a twenty-first-century communications era that is surprisingly lacking in regulation and transparency. This is at a time when households around the world are becoming more and more digitized and data-driven, underpinned by a governmental and commercial fervor for "smart" cities and homes and a "connected" citizenry.

Approach

How we live our daily lives then is increasingly entangled in the politics and ethics of food (from sourcing to sharing) while our growing habituation to connected technological devices and practices is embedded in a broader, albeit not necessarily visible, digital politics. This book uses the realm of food as a way of grounding and materializing these growing daily engagements with digital media. One of the first book-length treatments of the rise of the digital culinary cultural economy, it covers a wide range of content from the forms of digital food that are now part of our everyday lives, as in the case of food images on YouTube and Instagram, to corporate domination of digital food space and activist efforts to counter this commercial influence. In order to approach a critical overview of this complex and shifting terrain, I examine a large range of examples of practices that occur at the intersections between digital and food and have sought to draw my examples from a range of countries. There are of course limitations with such an approach; having such a wide coverage means that the book doesn't necessarily delve as deeply as it might into key concerns, such as the growing impact of automation in society for instance. Further, while I have sought to broaden the cultural focus of the book, with examples of digital food practices from India to South America, the book—written in English, published in the UK, and researched while the author was based in France and Australia—is primarily an Anglo/Euro-American contribution but with an antipodean flavor.

While this book is aimed at a broad readership—from media studies students to food policy professionals and indeed anyone interested in the implications of digital media for our daily lives—it draws upon a range of concepts and theories drawn from academic scholarship. My aim here has been to approach theory with a light touch and to draw upon useful concepts and frameworks from across a range of fields, from food studies, sociology and cultural geography, to feminist studies and philosophy. The book is primarily situated, however, at the crossroads of cultural studies and media studies, with a particular focus on understanding digital food within the broader context of lifestyle and consumption. As a piece of cultural studies research, it draws upon a long tradition of scholarship on everyday life (in relation to class, gender, and race) and on the importance of the household as a site for understanding not just social and cultural practices but also shifting and emergent political and economic practices. The chapters in this book on the growing meal-sharing economy and the role of gendered domestic labor in the so-called collaborative economy, and on the rise of everyday forms of digital apptivism and ethical consumption, speak directly to the home as an important space of political and economic activity.

Digital Food also owes many of its concerns and concepts to media studies. However, rather than using analyses of everyday life to confirm particular theories about the sharing capacities of platforms or the data-driven limits of communicative capitalism, the book examines how "technologies are used and engaged with in practice, as opposed to in idealised ways" (Giraud: 142). As such, the book draws on a large range of approaches to understanding media and technology. The chapter on online masculinities for instance borrows from fairly conventional media studies traditions around the politics of representation and asks what the rise of hipster "bros" cooking on YouTube might mean for the politics of domestic labor. By contrast, the opening chapter on social media, food, and photography draws on *post*-representational theories of images as data-laden interfaces rather than as seeing them in symbolic or meaning-making terms. Meanwhile the chapter on online food videos draws on understandings of media engagement as a form of "making," taking into account the embodied domestic and online labor involved in producing cookery videos (Gauntlett 2018; Moores 2014). This chapter also employs social practice theory and non-media-centric approaches to conceptualize the role of online streaming videos in practices involving people cooking, eating, and socializing "together" while located in dispersed domestic spaces. Finally, the chapter on food politics speaks to some of the more immaterial or invisible aspects of digital media culture, including the role of algorithms, questions of data ownership and governance, and tensions between a cooperativist or commons-based approach to digital activism and engagement versus the growing impact of commercial logics in shaping digital culture. The book thus draws on a wide variety of critical approaches, reflecting the fact that no one theoretical apparatus can capture the constantly evolving and increasingly unbounded world of digital media.

While this book is not concerned with offering a meta-theory of digital food, there are some recurrent themes and concerns that emerge in relation to food, digital media, and everyday life: first, the *presence* of digital media, as quasi-companions or family members in households. The laptop in the kitchen for instance is not just another kitchen appliance (though as I discuss in the conclusion the smart kitchen starts to blur the boundaries between "white goods" and ICTs) but offers a portal into the rich space and practices of online culinary advice culture. Secondly, on the other hand, digital media are remarkably invisible despite their centrality to daily life. Focusing on food-related practices enables one to *materialize* the often-routinized practices that accompany the introduction of new technologies. For instance, recent media concerns about the need to wash one's hands when using a digital device in the kitchen also forces us to recognize the many hundreds of times we touch these devices within a day and the intimate relationships they have with our bodies and daily routines, often spending time with us in bed and when we go to the toilet. Thirdly, the practices of digital culinary culture where many householders engage in complex assemblages of food preparation, styling, photography, videoing, editing, and sharing emphasizes the centrality of the role of *creativity* and *labor* to our digital media worlds. Given the degree of technological know-how and engagement in content creation that now accompanies media use, does it make sense to refer to us as digital media consumers anymore given the implications of relative passivity that consumption has tended to hold?

This point brings us to the other key framework or body of work that this book draws upon—that is, scholarship on lifestyle, lifestyle media, and related forms of consumption. *Digital Food* makes various connections between contemporary digital food practices and non-digital lifestyle media forms and practices foregrounding the need to move beyond old/new media distinctions. As Graeme Turner argues in *Reinventing the Media* (2016), there is a tendency for digital media scholarship to exhibit an historical amnesia in relation to earlier media forms. By contrast, I show that both the world of food and the realm of digital media are thoroughly ensconced in a broader lifestyle culture with online food videos and food photography, whether amateur or professional, sharing strong links with recent historical and contemporary lifestyle media, such as cooking shows, cookbooks, and food and lifestyle magazines. Key theorists of the rise of lifestyle culture in late modern societies, David Bell and Joanne Hollows (2005), argue that the notion of lifestyle as it is presented on lifestyle television and in magazines is underpinned by a consumer-driven conception of the self where people, their homes, and their ways of living are seen as sites of an array of consumption choices, and as such, as spaces of transformation and improvement. Relatedly, as I discussed in *Smart Living: Lifestyle Media and Popular Expertise* (2008), central to the idea of lifestyle in late modernity is the notion that ordinary people themselves can (and should) become experts of a sort in the art and aesthetics of everyday living. The much maligned yet poorly defined figure of the hipster—a kind of "super" or uber consumer or prosumer (producer/consumer) who shapes and creates taste cultures on a daily basis through food, fashion, and other lifestyle choices—can be understood in part as emerging out of this context. As we will see, this sense of one's self and lifestyle, at least as it is presented to the world, as being a site of (constant potential) improvement, creativity, and optimization, is alive and well in the DIY spaces of online culinary culture.

How to read this book

I've written this book in such a way that the reader can read individual chapters as stand-alone pieces. The book however does have an overall logic. As it moves from chapters on food photography, and on cultures and economies of online videos and meal sharing, to chapters on ethical consumption and food politics—it pans out, as it were, from a close-up focus on the personal, small scale and the everyday to a wider frame, with the later chapters tackling larger ethical and political issues in relation to life politics, food movements, corporate domination and "surveillance capitalism" (Zuboff 2019), "algorithmic culture" (Striphas 2015), and digital activism.

Chapter 1 discusses that product of the intersection between daily life, food and the digital that we're all probably most familiar with: the food photo. In a pre-camera phone era, taking pictures of food was something we tended to do as part of a special occasion, with the person behind the camera usually focusing on capturing images of people and much as the meal. Today the food itself is the star of the show with most of us—whether or not we consider ourselves keen amateur photographers—engaging regularly in the process of documenting our eating and sometimes cooking practices. Chapter 1 discusses the role of ordinary members of the public in creating much of the shared content that shores up digital communities on social media. The amateur photographer in restaurants for instance has been credited with both single-handedly revolutionizing and ruining the restaurant industry. The chapter argues that the huge popularity of food images on a range of social media platforms is not just due to shifts in technology—in particular the ubiquity of the camera phone—but also needs to be understood in terms of broader developments over the past couple of decades in lifestyle, media, and consumer culture. Here I argue that high-end "foodies" on Instagram for instance have become key influencers or tastemakers and shapers in culinary culture with an emphasis not just on the quality of cuisine but on the style and aesthetics of restaurants and their offerings, in terms of food as well as interior design and the dining "experience." Beyond the realm of aesthetics and the transmission of meaning, taste and cultural values via curated forms of social media food imagery, the chapter also discusses the role of food photographs as functioning in non-representational ways. For instance, the sharing of ordinary food images on Facebook or via food memes can be understood as having a purely phatic or conversational function. An increasingly common practice is to employ food images as interfaces containing embedded data, such as QR codes or barcodes. As I argue, here the food photograph sheds its symbolic qualities and shifts us into "an internet of things" where the parties "communicating" are not people but are instead encoded images, devices, and objects. Finally, the chapter raises the critical issue of the role of our everyday digital practices in what Shoshana Zuboff terms "surveillance capitalism" (2019), a theme that we will return to throughout the book. If the creative "work" we do when we trace and record our own daily lifestyles through social media has become primary economic fodder for the immensely powerful digital corporate players that now dominate the internet, what does this mean for us as food citizens and critical media users?

The large and eclectic world of amateur online food and cooking videos—a "genre" that exemplifies digital media engagement as a labor-intensive, creative, often community-oriented practice—is the focus of Chapter 2. In the first part of the chapter I view the rise of home-based cookery videos and YouTube "how-to" advisors and food hackers in terms of the concept of "ordinary expertise" (Lewis 2008a). The ordinary expert is, I argue, the product of a broader turn in contemporary culture and lifestyle media over the past couple of decades in which domestic skills and knowledge have been embraced and aestheticized—from the art of tidying, Marie Kondo style, to cooking and home renovation. In the second section of the chapter I discuss the (for the most part) highly convivial culinary advice culture enacted via food videos as an example of the participatory "cultural economy" of platforms such as YouTube, which started out life as user-driven spaces of DIY content production, collaboration, and sharing (Burgess and Green 2018). The third part of the chapter focuses on the growing monetization of the culinary communities on platforms like YouTube through the rise of professionalized cookery channels and branded cooks, a process which is part of what Stuart Cunningham and David Craig usefully describe in their book of the same name, as "social media entertainment" (2019).

The fourth section shifts gear to consider the issue of genre and content. In this section, and in the conclusion, I examine whether the video sharing world is becoming more like mainstream commercial media. The chapter suggests that, despite the symbiotic relationship between commercial lifestyle media and amateur video making, the interactive and participatory dimensions of elements of food video culture (such as the popularity of live shared "broadcasts" of people eating) also require new conceptions of media beyond conventional notions of media production and reception. For instance, I discuss the growing popularity of sound- and sensory-based food video experiences such as "Autonomous Sensory Meridian Response" or ASMR videos, a genre that represents a far cry from Jamie Oliver-style cooking videos. Revisiting the argument made in Chapter 1 about food images as post-representational, the chapter concludes by examining how we might understand these kinds of online food videos in terms of what has been termed "non-media centric" understandings of the role of digital media, as reflected in concepts such as of "ambient media" or media that is ever present but in the background of daily life.

Chapter 3 takes us into the online world of "meatrosexuals," foodie "dadpreneurs," food hackers, and Epic Meal Timers and asks, what are the cultural politics at play in masculine representations and practices around food and cooking online today. Examining Instagram and YouTube as two sites where men are increasingly engaging with food culture, the chapter examines trends around the dominant images and practices of food and masculinity online in the face of claims that men are increasingly embracing the role of family cook. Setting the scene for the discussion of food and masculinity online, the first section of the chapter maps the changes (or in some cases lack thereof) that have occurred in men's cooking practices in the home in recent decades. I then turn to a discussion of the shifting role of men in the kitchen on television from the late 1990s onwards, followed by an examination of dominant representations of culinary masculinity in food media more broadly. As we will see, the world of online food masculinity has strong historical (and ongoing) links to food television and in particular the figure of the celebrity chef. Compared to the relatively conservative, white, and heterosexual world of cookery television, in both the world of Instagram and YouTube there appears to be considerably more diversity and space for more progressive (as well as more reactionary) depictions of men and food. Does this flourishing of online masculinities suggest a transition to a relatively post-gendered culinary culture?

Speaking to Nancy Fraser's claim regarding late capitalism's "crisis of care" in post-welfare societies, the chapter interrogates the politics of online food masculinities, discussing how the emergence of foodie fathers on Instagram and millennial cooking "bros" on YouTube might be understood in relation to pressures and expectations in late modern capitalist societies around gender, domestic labor, and home cooking.

Continuing this focus on food, labor, gender, and the home, Chapter 4 examines the rise of digital meal sharing, from small-scale apps that enable local amateur chefs to invite guests into their own kitchen to the burgeoning market of online restaurant delivery services such as Deliveroo and Uber Eats. The chapter discusses some of the key issues raised by this food-based example of the "sharing," gig-based economy. Discussing the politics and practices of sharing, the chapter examines the increasingly domestic location in which both digital practices—such as setting up profiles on apps and producing associated blogs—and food production and consumption practices—from preparing meals in one's own home as a paid host for a group of strangers to making extra lunches for neighbors in need—occur. While meal sharing extends domestic and community-based practices of collaboration and caring into the digital sphere, at the same time it also sees domestic space become a site of publicity, economics, value, and potential exploitation in a range of new and emergent ways. The chapter focuses on a wide range of empirical examples of meal sharing using digital technology including those concerned primarily with economic profit, which we might see as part of the "uberization" of domestic food production and consumption. On the other hand, it also examines the communitarian, social enterprise end of the meal sharing spectrum, where the distribution of food and conviviality is driven by a social justice and equity agenda that has been in part enabled by social media technologies. In doing so it asks a range of questions about this emerging domestic digital food ecology. What kinds of practices are involved in these collaborative domestically based initiatives? Why do people seek to share as hosts and participants and who is involved in this emerging and evolving meal sharing ecology? What do these developments mean for the changing role of the private, domestic sphere in social, community, and economic life?

Chapter 5 discusses the growing practice of ethical food consumption online, including the emergence of apps and platforms that enable consumers to shop for food products they see as more socially, ethically, or environmentally responsible, such as Fair Trade coffee or groceries sourced from local farmers. Examining the broader context for this relatively recent development, the chapter outlines the key role played by mainstream media in the Global North, in particular documentaries and food television, in paving the way for the recognition of the consumer-citizen as an important social actor. My argument is that the practices and politics of today's online food citizen—while articulated to contemporary issues and tied to particular digital affordances—can be seen to have a range of connections to, and ongoing links with, a broader process of media mainstreaming of ethical and political consumerism that has occurred over the past three decades.

The ubiquity of digital technology in many people's daily lives has extended upon these media genealogies and added a further range of tools to the arsenal of the ethical consumer, with apps and platforms tending to enable and shape certain kinds of practices. While there are major limitations to the kind of privatized "lifestyle politics" enabled by consumer-driven apps, a critical development within the space of political consumerism has been the media's focus on *connecting* consumer-citizens with various "others," both human and non-human—the environment, producers, farmers, workers, material goods, both distant and local. Furthermore, the rise of forms of platform cooperativism through open source ventures such as the Open Food Network exemplifies an evolving digital space in which producers, consumers, retailers, and other community groups are able to come together to potentially build alternative food systems. These kinds of commons-driven ventures—like the social enterprise models that have emerged out of the meal sharing space—suggest that the intersections of digital and food need not necessarily be tied to profit-oriented, capitalist modes of platform connectivity.

Extending on from many of the concerns of Chapter 5, Chapter 6 asks what it means to do "food politics" today in a digital era. This chapter examines a range of examples of digitally enabled civic or public modes of political engagement around food. Using these examples to touch upon some of the key themes and concerns facing food citizens, producers and activists in a digital age, the chapter interrogates what Bennett and Segerberg (2012) have called "connective action." How can platforms enable large numbers of people who may not belong to any formal political group or movement to connect and collectivize around key food concerns such as animal welfare or GMO food? What might be the limitations of civic practices of connectivity that are dependent on essentially commercial infrastructures, such as Facebook? What do we mean by "transparency" in relation to food markets in an era characterized by increasingly complex and often hidden practices of data management and access, where software codes and algorithms are attuned to PR and market-oriented rather than the communicative logics of "open sourced" modes of online deliberative democracy? And finally, if a key concern of the alternative food movement is with reconnecting with the origins of food—with where and how it is grown—how do digital infrastructures and software logics enable these kinds of "hands on" modes of material and embodied connection?

Examining these broad questions through concrete examples of "online food politics" the first section of Chapter 6 uses the example of Permablitz, the Australian household-based permaculture movement, to discuss the role of online platforms in organizing and scaling up the activities and "civic" food politics of individual households concerned with developing alternatives to supermarket and agribusiness-driven food provision. The second section discusses what might be seen as more conventional forms of collective political engagement, such as anti-GMO street marches, that are nevertheless organized and enacted through online petitions and blogs, and via social media sites such as Facebook. The third section then moves on to a discussion of the case of corporate social media strategy, focusing in particular on the timely example of Monsanto.[1] It outlines on the one hand Monsanto's use of social media as part of a supposedly open dialogue with the community and on the other hand revelations regarding their use of behind-the-scenes digital tactics to cover up links between cancer and glyphosate, the chemical used in their trademark herbicide RoundUp. The chapter concludes with a discussion of the affordances and limits of connectivity and tropes of visibility and transparency within increasingly commercially managed digital platforms, pointing to the growing need for alternative cooperativist or commons-based platforms, practices, and models of digital connectivity.

In the concluding remarks to the book, I return to the opening theme of the sci-fi imagery often evoked in media and marketing discourse around digital food—where techno-utopian futures are invariably embedded in consumerist visions of slick hermetically sealed households populated by "smart" kitchen appliances and intelligent gadgets, houses where dirt, compost, and chickens are invariably nowhere to be seen. What might be the not-so-smart aspects of the energy-hungry futures imagined in these digital future-present scenarios? What are the limits not only in terms of e-waste and environmental burden but also in social, political, and communitarian terms of such a privatized imaginary? Developments like the Open Food Network I suggest offer a rather different example of the potential for "smart," connected digital food futures. In my conclusion I discuss the need to draw on the sharing, collaborative dimensions of online alternative food movements to imagine a range of counter scenarios, including imagining an alternative food and data sharing ecology based on a post-capitalist ethos of the commons, drawing on peer-to-peer cooperative forms of production, labor, and creativity in order to build forms of "social" media that genuinely support collective and collaborative models of digital sociality.

Note

1   As of June 7, 2018, Monsanto is now owned by Bayer, one of the largest pharmaceutical companies in the world.

From Culinary Aesthetics to Phatic Food: Food Photography on Instagram and Facebook

In many of our field sites, posting on social media is overwhelmingly visual. The growing popularity of platforms such as Instagram and Snapchat has shown that social media can work effectively where the core content is photographic and text is relatively peripheral.

Daniel Miller et al., *How the World Changed Social Media* (2016: 155).

It is no exaggeration to say that the rise of amateur digital photography on social media has and is playing a revolutionary role in shaping contemporary food culture, one that has occurred in a relatively short space of time. Back in 2010, for instance, when the photo-sharing Web site Flickr reigned supreme, the *New York Times* was marveling over the fact that the number of pictures with the tag "food" had increased tenfold to more than six million within two years while one of the largest and most active groups, called "I Ate This," included more than 300,000 photos produced and shared by 19,000 followers (Murphy 2010). Fast forward to 2017 and Flickr is now rocking in the wake of the rise of social network Instagram which as of June 2018 now has 1 billion monthly active users (Carmen 2018). As per Flickr, food photography represents a significant part of the traffic on Instagram with *Business.com* in an article on the "Food Photo Frenzy: Inside the Instagram Craze and Travel Trend" noting that at the time of writing (February 2017) "there were 168,375,343 posts on Instagram for #food and 76,239,441 posts for #foodporn" (McGuire 2017).

As *Forbes India* observed in 2017, while food photography has a long history, today "photographing food has assumed a proportion that has perhaps never been seen before, thanks to the ubiquitous camera phone" (Banerjee 2017). This apparently global food photo "frenzy" has of course gone hand in hand with a broader embrace of photographic practices—with many of us now habitually engaging in styling, shooting, editing, and sharing images via social media, whether of our latest meal, our pets, human loved ones, or travel pictures. While people's social media practices globally vary significantly across cultures, social groups, gender, generations, and classes, it seems the photographic image links us all, or many of us at least—with the over 65s also increasingly using photos to keep in touch with family (Foster 2016).

In *How the World Changed Social Media* (2016), a book coming out of a major global anthropological project headed by British anthropologist Daniel Miller looking at social media practices around the world with a particular focus on social media use in poorer communities, one of the rare generalizations he and his co-authors make—attentive as they are to the plurality of social media practices around the world—is that social media is dominated by photographic content rather than text. On the one hand this may seem like an obvious and perhaps banal observation, but the shift not only to photographic ubiquity but more importantly to photographs taken and shared for the most part by ordinary non-professionals is a highly significant one. Despite the technological capacities of smartphones and platforms to enable people to create and share sophisticated multimedia offerings of all kinds, *photographs* are still the visual media of choice, overwhelmingly dominating social media. Small manageable file sizes, easy sharing and readability across sites, and platforms and software that have democratized editing processes have all ensured that photos remain supreme when it comes to posting and sharing (Gunthert 2014), aided and abetted by the fact that small photogenic screens are increasingly for many the main route to engaging with social media and the internet more broadly. As French visual historian André Gunthert argues, while the digital camera was meant to usher in the death of photography quite the opposite has in fact happened, with photographic images remaining by the far the most shared content on the internet (Gunthert 2014). Meanwhile, employing a range of systems and platforms that streamline and normalize photographic modes of communication, micro-blogging and social media have further boosted the centrality of the photographic image, with Snapchat perhaps best embodying the photo-centric nature of networked communications (Gunthert 2014).

Along with diminishing newspaper budgets and general cuts in staff, one of the reasons for the dwindling numbers of professional photographers at newspapers is the growing impact of social media, mobile technology and amateur digital photography in breaking news (Anderson 2013). This is just one of the many developments that have also put into question the divisions between professionalism and amateurism in the context of the relative democratization of access to mobile technology and networked social media. In the food space, photography as a contemporary cultural technology tied to networked mobile phones (see Gómez Cruz 2012) has impacted in a range of areas from restaurant reviewing to high-end microblogging platforms such as Instagram where DIY photo editing and geo-tagged images are key to the role of "influencers" in the world of food and beyond (Hjorth and Hendry 2015; Rousseau 2012). For instance, while figures like celebrity chef Jamie Oliver continue to function as old school lifestyle gurus through TV shows, public health campaigns, and cook books, Oliver also has a very active Instagram account with a huge following and has accordingly managed to win the hearts of the social media generation. But Oliver is now joined by a host of other food Instagram influencers, some of whom are chefs, food stylists, and "professional" food photographers but also many of whom are people whose day jobs have nothing to do with food. At a more everyday level, food photography and sharing food images are now something that many of us engage with, often without thinking and sometimes on a very regular basis. A study conducted in Beijing shows that over 85 percent of young Chinese urbanites have shared food photographs on social media (Peng 2017) while, according to a 2016 survey of all supermarket use by UK supermarket Waitrose (Smithers 2016), one in five Britons had shared a food picture in the previous month.

Why are people who in the past may have had little interest in photography now engaging in the practice of sharing food imagery? The popular embrace of food photography has led to a frequently heard lamentation, echoed by the press, that "Instagram is ruining food" (First 2017) while the Independent tells us "How Instagram Has Ruined Restaurants" noting that "69 per cent of millennials take photos of their food before eating" (Petter 2017). But this kind of culinary purism tells us little about the specific role of food imagery in the digital realm. Food and photography have of course had a long and intimate relationship. In a pre-smartphone, analogue era, however, food close-ups were largely the domain of professional photographers while in Bourdieu's study of amateur photography in 1960s France, *Photography: A Middle Brow Art* (Bourdieu et al. 1990), more everyday forms of photography tended to be largely tied to a conventional, "family function," i.e., food might be incidentally captured in snapshots of family events such as weddings and birthday parties. Today, amateur food photography has taken on a much more prominent social, cultural, and economic role while, around the world, culinary culture and food aesthetics have become a much more prominent feature of cultural life. As the Waitrose report mentioned above also states almost half of people surveyed say they take more care over a dish if they think a photo might be taken of it, and nearly 40 percent claim to worry more about presentation than they did five years ago.

In this chapter I want to think about some of the reasons for the rise of the food photograph and also offer a number of different conceptual frames for understanding a phenomenon that cannot be understood as purely an offshoot of digital or online technologies and practices and that is likewise not easily reduced to a single group of practices (Lobinger 2015). Food photography today is shaped by a range of different albeit overlapping communities of practices and taste (from food bloggers to microbloggers, from Weibo and Yelp to Facebook and Instagram users) making it difficult to make universal statements about photographic trends. Another key element that is important to highlight is the changing nature—beyond questions of taste and aesthetics—of what we might understand as the function and meaning of a photograph in an increasingly automated, digitally connected context. While I am using the term *photography* in this chapter, arguably some of the practices I will discuss have transformed the photograph into something other than how we usually conceive of them, i.e., as a realist representational or symbolic form. Furthermore, the act of capturing and sharing images with one's smartphone has taken photography into still new territories and produced different and often evolving sets of practices— communicative, conversational, transactional, ritualistic, and habitual.

The chapter is structured as follows: first I discuss the ways in which food photography can be understood as emerging from a larger culture of lifestyle media—from glossy food magazines to celebrity chefs and reality cooking shows. The chapter then turns to thinking about the role of "lifestyled" social media users in a contemporary culture in which people are increasingly expected to shape their own everyday lifestyle practices, linking today's online "creators" and "curators" of food photography to earlier forms of craft consumption. The following section discusses the considerable labor involved in producing food photographs for public consumption, drawing on notions of serious leisure and creative labor to start to map the shift to post-professional practices in online culinary spaces. This leads into questions around the role of online foodies as new "cultural intermediaries" and Instagram in particular as a space where a certain kind of aspirational "hipster" food culture is promoted via glossy high-end photography and savvy food influencers, from celebrity chefs to entrepreneurial homemakers. The final two sections of the chapter take us in a somewhat different direction. Here I start to think about food photography using a non-media-centric approach, understanding the posting of food pictures on Facebook for instance as a connective social practice. Drawing on work discussing the role of photographic imagery as integral to new forms of online conversational and phatic communication, this part of the chapter paves the way for understanding photos as non-representational, non-symbolic devices. The last section takes this argument further examining the ways in which digital photographs today increasingly function not as signs or carriers of meaning but as carriers of "data" or as "interfaces" or points of translation into data systems (Gómez Cruz 2016). The use of food images as sources of nutritional information, the emergence of Twitter photo food mining, photo-based food diaries, and food images as interfaces on new smart kitchen appliances (such as smart fridges) suggests the ways in which food images function as devices or actors within a larger network of social and technical practices, supporting Gómez Cruz's "call to think more about photography as a sociotechnical practice and less about photography as images, representations and depictions" (2016: 240)

Food photos as an extension of lifestyle culture

The very popularity of television programmes that feature food and cooking or the redesign and redecoration of household interiors or gardens, together with the many associated magazines and books, supports the suggestion that there exists a large population of consumers who want to be successful in creating their own aesthetically significant end products.

Colin Campbell (2005: 33)

In tackling a book on food and digital media, it becomes evident that the present digital moment is in certain ways unique, representing a significant break with our previous everyday relationships with food, media, and communicative technologies. Take one key example. While ten years ago, many of us would have turned to restaurant reviews written by professional food critics in the lifestyle section of broadsheet newspapers (with text dominating the review and often accompanied by, rather than centered on, food imagery), today many of us now rely on a combination of star and point ratings, brief review comments and images of food and décor provided by our peers and shared via online review platforms such as Yelp and TripAdvisor. The digital affordances provided by these easy-to-use, GPS-enabled "local" review sites have thus literally revolutionized how we talk about and rank restaurants, in turn having a major impact on chefs and on the restaurant trade (Gander 2017).

At the same time, we cannot understand the rise of food photography on the internet and its current centrality as something purely specific to and produced by the digital realm. Instead the rise of digital food photography (as in the case of food and cookery "shows" on YouTube, the topic of the next chapter) emerges out of and links to earlier media forms and shifts in food culture, i.e., we can understand digital food practices as de- and reterritorializing both earlier and concurrent spaces of food media and forms of consumption. In particular, I argue that the huge popularity of food images on a range of social media platforms, and the growing number of food videos circulating the internet, can be linked to a broader shift in lifestyle, media, and consumer culture over the past couple of decades.

When I started doing research on reality TV in Australia back in the early 2000s I was repeatedly told at the time by producers and TV executives that food television wouldn't make it on primetime TV as "cookery shows" were only of interest to daytime viewers, i.e., housewives and retirees (this was despite the early success of Japan's *Iron Chef* in the 1990s and its cult impact in the United States and Australia, and the widespread appeal of the breakthrough show *The Naked Chef* on BBC 2, 1999–2001). The rise of Jamie Oliver to international stardom, the stadium-ization of food TV via *Iron Chef*, and the international popularity of the *MasterChef* franchise—to name some key moments in culinary media culture—has since seen food TV and food media more broadly become a global cultural phenomenon. From China and India to the United Kingdom,

Figure 1.1 *MasterChef* contestant congratulated by the show's host [Credit: Flickr/ Pedro Lorena].

the United States and of course Australia, where the home-grown version of *MasterChef* has been a huge success, we have seen audiences (across class, gender, and ethnicity) embracing food culture and celebrity chefs as part of a broader "lifestyling" of everyday life and a growing interest in food as a site of leisure, creativity, pleasure, and aesthetics (rather than domestic drudgery and housewifery).

So how did people (young people and the "man in the street" in particular) go from being relatively uninterested in the intricacies of culinary culture in the late twentieth century to being obsessed with food in the twenty-first (as reflected in the rise of the term "food porn"—perhaps one of the most overused phrases in media and food commentary)? How do we explain a situation where food, once the domain of gourmands and chefs and female "homemakers," is now the second most popular type of image on China's major social media Weibo, with pictures of food ranking as twice as appealing as "good looking people" (Danqi 2014).

As I am suggesting, one key way of understanding this phenomenon is to locate the rise of food photos within the broader lifestyle and consumer culture of late capitalist modernity. But what am I meaning by the term lifestyle culture here? Over the past couple of decades, we have witnessed some significant shifts in the nature of consumer and media cultures around how we live and manage our everyday domestic and personal lives, from what we eat, to how we dress, exercise, decorate our homes, manage our pets and children, and govern our existential and psychological selves. Ten years ago, writing about popular primetime lifestyle advice shows such as *Queer Eye for the Straight Guy* and *The Naked Chef*, I noted the trend toward discussing food, diet, grooming, and personal relationships as markers of "lifestyle."

> Used today as a descriptor for everything from New Age religious choices to sports drinks, lifestyle is a term that has become so ubiquitous in contemporary consumer culture it is increasingly hard to pin down. At the same time, its very ubiquity attests to the way it has now become a form of everyday, "commonsense." Representing far more than just a convenient new way for the industry to re-label popular advice media, lifestyle instead has become one of the dominant frameworks through which we understand and organize contemporary everyday life (Lewis 2008a).

If the generation of people we now refer to as baby boomers and their seniors once lived in a world where options around how to live were relatively limited and structured around tradition, particularly for woman and working-class or regular middle-class families, in the contemporary Global North it seems we have many more opportunities to make "choices" around how we conduct and manage our daily lives, at least at the level of consumer and commodity culture. Linked to a shift to late liberal models of politics and governance and the growing privatization of the spheres of health, education, and social support more broadly, over the past two to three decades, then, we have seen this idea of a choice-based notion of lifestyle become key to our lives both in the Global North and more recently parts of the South. Accompanying this ideological focus on the lifestyle consumer as an agent capable of making significant personal change through "informed" choices around diet, health and well-being, family life and parenting, career focus and fulfilment, etc., we have witnessed the rise and mainstreaming of lifestyle advice and lifestyle media, with a wide range of lifestyle gurus and social influencers from celebrity chefs to health and well-being experts like Jamie Oliver seeking to offer people new blueprints for living in a so-called "post-traditional" world.

Overall, the rise of lifestyle culture can be seen to emerge out of a complex conjuncture of social, cultural, and economic factors. Linked to the growing push toward modes of reflexive, consumer-based individualism, the contemporary focus on creativity, lifestyle, and aesthetics is also seen to be increasingly articulated to a neo-liberal culture of self-governance and self-surveillance in which social structural issues, such as the issue of obesity, are increasingly privatized. As Rose puts it (1989: 264), "the well-being of all [...] has increasingly come to be seen as a consequence of the responsible self-government of each." In targeting individuals as sites of relentless self-improvement, the lifestyle expert and lifestyle culture can be seen to play a crucial role in both legitimating and providing the tools and techniques for what French philosopher Michel Foucault would see as a "responsibilised," self-governing model of selfhood. Despite claims that the self-governing consumer-citizen now exists in a *post*-traditional realm marked by the growing irrelevance of social categories like class, as we will see, the ideals and norms held up by lifestyle experts and influencers are often underpinned by class-based (particularly middle class and lower middle class or "aspirational") models of taste and lifestyle. As I argue throughout the book, citizens within the digital food economy continued to be highly constrained by their gender, race, class, and to some extent sexuality. Nevertheless, the realm of food and social media is dominated by broader cultural and political myths concerning the limitless economic and cultural potential of the creative enterprising self. It is also important to note that the flourishing cultural realm of digital food is not just reducible to pure economics even as digital culture is thoroughly entwined with commercial capitalism. That is, there is a large community of people contributing creatively to the digital culinary realm whose contributions cannot and should not be seen solely in terms of enterprise culture or "free" consumer labor. In this chapter then I attempt to discuss the growing democratization of digital food culture via food photographs in ways that speak to the complex tensions between capitalist and communitarian forms of exchange and value in online space.

From craft consumers to creators, curators, and artisans

Given this critique, how might we understand the role of everyday food photographic practices within this turn to lifestyle in late capitalism? As noted, a key element of lifestyle culture over the past two to three decades has been a growing focus on style and aesthetics or an "art of everyday life" (Hollows 2003: 243), with representations of food and cookery being central to this shift. A key actor in lifestyle culture conventionally has not so much been the practitioner or "user" of social media but rather the lifestyle *consumer*. Back in the early 1990s, British sociologist Mike Featherstone spoke of the rise of lifestyle consumers as the "new heroes of consumer culture" (Featherstone 1991: 86). What he was suggesting was that, in an era of what was then termed "postmodernism," consumers were no longer just mindlessly shopping for shopping's sake but were becoming savvy interpreters and users of the signs and symbols (rather than just the material commodities) of consumer culture. For these new heroes, building an optimal and tasteful lifestyle was no trivial matter but involved spending considerable time, energy, and effort in curating, crafting, and projecting a particular image of oneself. This increasingly aesthetically and creatively inclined figure I would argue in certain ways preempts or paves the way for the specific forms of labor-intensive, productive consumerism (or consumerist productivity) we see in the spaces of food and social media today.

A useful text here for understanding the link between the aesthetically savvy lifestyle consumer and contemporary users of Instagram and Facebook is Colin Campbell's *The Romantic Ethic and the Spirit of Modern Consumerism* (1987). Rather than viewing modern consumer capitalism purely as a site of disenchantment and alienation, Campbell argues that romanticism has historically been and continues to be a central force within consumer culture. According to this argument, the romantic emphasis on developing one's moral character through creative hedonism and aestheticism continues to function in the contemporary consumer world with its emphasis on imaginative desires, beauty, and endless novelty. Such romantic concerns one could argue are evident in the world of digital food imagery today where we see the protestant work ethic of consumer culture—digital users driven to capture images of their food practices and to expend significant time and energy on engaging with social media—intertwined with a focus on re-enchanting contemporary life through creative processes and practices. Central to this romantic ethos is a particular kind of creative consumer, one that is a far cry from the passive, feminized dupe of earlier models of consumption or indeed the rational calculative consumer assumed in certain brands of behaviorist economic theory. Instead we see productive and creative consumption combined with a kind of entrepreneurial spirit, and fitting in seamlessly with a neoliberal imagining of self-managing citizens whose creative and emotional labor can potentially be exploited and monetized.

Furthermore, while the ordinary consumer of lifestyle media has conventionally taken advice from popular commercial figures of expertise—health and lifestyle gurus, TV chefs, and the like—increasingly the creative consumer is developing and sharing their own brand of expertise in the art and aesthetics of everyday life, i.e., they are becoming *producers* of and contributors to a highly aspirational and enterprising lifestyle culture. In the digital food realm, this is particularly evident in spaces like Instagram where photographs of food are increasingly expected to aspire to the high-end aesthetics of commercial photography. As a piece in *Macworld*, "Photographing Food? It's as Easy as Pie" suggests, the casual snapshot no longer cuts it in the publicly scrutinized world of social media with the article enjoining readers to "create" stylized masterpieces.

> It seems everyone these days is taking photos of their food and uploading them to Twitter before they've taken their first bite. While some of these photos offer mouthwatering results, most are a mess, poorly lit and unappetizing. (Crabbe 2012)

The article goes on to advise readers about how to use their camera setting, lighting, composition, editing, suggesting the use of apps such as *Snapdish* (www. snapdish), an app designed for enhancing food images, and even recommending "styling" one's food shoot: "Try shooting a fork playfully stabbing pasta rather than a half-eaten plate of ravioli" (2012). It seems the exacting standards of contemporary social media grants no space for the joys of amateur photography and shaky DIY camera work; instead readers are urged to take on the mantle of professionalism and invest a considerable amount of labor in taking everyday photos of their own food.

Figure 1.2 Food-themed photo sharing app *Snapdish* [Credit: *Snapdish*].

Here the social media user is also positioned as a creator and aesthetician assisted by technologies and practices of curation and sharing. Campbell's work on what he terms the craft consumer (2005) particularly resonates with this practice of "creating" within a pre determined design frame, in this case oriented toward the production and consumption of glossy, high-end images, overlapping with wider commercial practices of marketing and advertising. While consumption has been conventionally seen as a process alienated from production, Campbell, extending on Daniel Miller's anthropological work on material culture, offers a much more celebratory account of consumption, arguing:

> Much of the consumption that individuals undertake in contemporary western societies should be conceived of as craft activity; that is, as activity in which individuals not merely exercise control over the consumption process, but also bring skill, knowledge, judgement, love and passion to their consuming in much the same way that it has always been assumed that traditional craftsmen and craftswomen approach their work (2005: 27).

If the opposition between handicraft and machinic factory labor is, as Campbell argues in many ways a specious one, then the craft consumer likewise can be seen as both a consumer and producer. But crucially this aesthetically savvy reflexive consumer is someone who works *with* the material world of commodity culture, designing, crafting, and creating (and presumably has the time and economic capacity to invest in such activities). Campbell thus contends:

> One of the intriguing features of modern consumer society is the way in which machines have become reappropriated by the craft tradition, aiding and abetting craft consumers rather than robbing them of their traditional autonomy. Thus, the power tool has become the crucial aid of all DIY enthusiasts, the electric mixer of amateur chefs and the electric hedgetrimmer and lawnmower of enthusiastic gardeners (2005: 28).

One might extend this argument to the digital realm and note that the online "machinic" world of platforms and apps has likewise "aided and abetted" the craft of an array of digital foodies—from food bloggers through to Instagram "influencers." Which brings us to another key dimension of Campbell's argument that speaks to today's digital food user, i.e., the role of *collection* as a form of craft consumption or bringing together objects into an ensemble.

In 2013, noting the growth of photo and video sharing online, researchers at the US Pew Internet Life Study describe the "54% of adult internet users [who] post original photos or videos online that they themselves created" as *creators* while referring to the "47% of adult internet users [who] take photos or videos that they have found online and repost them on sites designed for sharing images with many people" as *curators* (Duggan 2013). Here the suggestion is that curators are not merely passive transmitters of images and messages but like creators are skilled knowledge producers. As Campbell similarly argues about collecting:

> It is also clear that this process not only requires skill and knowledge, but is essentially creative in nature. For collectors actively recontextualize individual products, situating them in a larger creation called 'the collection' and thereby giving them a new meaning and significance (2005: 34).

Pinterest is a classic case in point with people "pinning" photos into collections (boards) while the labor of hashtagging similarly involves a form of categorization and collection, facilitating the searchability and discoverability of certain topics, words, and phrases.[1] Villi (2012: 651) uses the concept of "social curation" to think about the ways in which consumer communities online contribute to "the networked distribution of media content by adding qualitative judgement and imbuing the content with personal and social significance," a labor again which often provides value to commercial marketers trawling the internet for trends.

Productive leisure and the lifestyling of labor

In the realm of social media and food photography, creators and consumers then are centrally involved, often unwittingly, in forms of production. If we think about the number of hours spent by online users taking and styling food images and in many cases buying the ingredients for and preparing the food being photographed, one of the often-unspoken themes in discussions of top ten food Instagram accounts and food influencers is the sheer amount of behind-the-scenes work involved. While old school cookery shows (and competitive reality shows like *MasterChef* and *Iron Chef*) might dwell on processes of food preparation, digital food photography is overwhelmingly concerned with the stylized finished product, i.e., the dish once it has been "plated up" to use the cooking show phrase. Skill and expertise are implied in the high-end culinary creations found on Instagram, but there is less interest on this particular platform in offering how-to accounts or depicting the steps that one took to creating one's culinary artwork. As I discuss in subsequent chapters, many Instagrammers also have YouTube channels and blogs where they offer recipes and step-by-step instructions on how to make specific dishes.

So how might we understand the notion of "work" in the context of the digital culinary economy, one in which much of the labor that shores up platforms such as Facebook and Instagram (as well as review sites) is consumer labor and is therefore unpaid. In an article for *The Guardian* on "how Instagram is changing the way we eat," food Instagrammer Ruby Tandoh writes:

> Most of us who document our meals online are amateurs, but there exists a sizeable, and hugely profitable, industry of professional food bloggers and Instagrammers, whose pristine food styling sets the tone for a whole aesthetic movement (2016).

While she makes a seemingly easy distinction between amateurs and professionals, the reality is in the world of online food it is often difficult to make such clear delineations. As we will see in the discussion on YouTube, there is a fair bit of slippage between who counts as an amateur foodie versus a cook or chef in the world of online videos, with uncredentialled food personalities (who might be considered amateurs) gaining fame on YouTube and releasing popular cookbooks. And as the discussion of craft consumption has suggested, there is also the question of how meaningful terms like this continue to be in a contemporary context where labor is increasingly occurring in a domestic rather than a professional setting. In her work on craft and the creative economy, Susan Luckman argues that, given this feminized, domestic turn, home-based "craft" and other forms of creative labor might be seen as existing in a "post-professional" context (Luckman 2015: 155).

In Chapter 4 I discuss the question of labor, the rise of the sharing economy and the monetization of practices around digital food in detail. Here though, particularly in relation to food and Instagram, I am interested in the way practices around the preparation and representation of food does a different kind of creative work—one tied to the shaping of a particular kind of disciplined lifestyled selfhood and set in the context of an aesthetic community of peers (or a whole aesthetic movement as Tandoh puts it).

In her book *Food and the Self* (2013), which includes ethnographic research on food bloggers, Isabelle de Solier draws on Robert Stebbins work on "serious leisure" and its role in people's working lives to understand the particular mode of highly engaged food commentary in which amateur food bloggers engage. She argues that while "foodies" blog about their home cooking in part to share their culinary expertise and know-how with the world, blogging also offers a high level of creative fulfillment (with the potential for significant public acknowledgment) for those whose day jobs may be less than inspiring. As she argues "blogging spills over skills from paid work, yet it is also reflexively pursued and experienced as a form of compensatory leisure that makes up for the lack of creative production on the job" (de Solier 2013: 280).

The more conventional long-form food blogging that was the focus of de Solier's research has in some ways been pushed into the background by the rise and sheer popularity of the microblogging community which communicates with a flurry of images and denotative micro-texts rather than in the slower contemplative text-heavy mode of the food blogger (although, as noted, popular cooks and foodies on Instagram and YouTube often do maintain a blog alongside their social media offerings where they may provide written recipes and/or extended commentaries). The serious leisure at play in high-end online food spaces—where we are shown a plethora of images of people's food creations juxtaposed with images of styled up homes, clean and happy children, travel, and dining out—for the most part represents a "lifestyling" of leisure, extending on the lifestyle turn evidenced on earlier forms of food TV where we saw Jamie Oliver roaming around London on his Vespa possibly as much as we saw him actually cooking. Similarly, eschewing images of unwashed dishes, tedious shopping trips, and chaotic post-cook up kitchens, glossy Instagrammed snapshots of domestic life tend to be romanticized and aestheticized, offering an optimal presentation of the public self to foodie peers and followers. Another key aspirational feature of food Instagraming is the focus on food tourism, with many Instagram account blogging about food from exotic locales. Arguably much of the food mobility experienced on Instagram has little to do with actual travel but rather is about aspirational and vicarious experiences of food and cultural difference/otherness as much as anything else (McGuire 2015).

The "lifestyled" food Instagrammer however is not necessarily the "average" social media user, whatever that might mean. As the Waitrose report discussed above indicates (Smithers 2016), different social groups tend to have quite distinct social media practices with online platforms attracting a range of different socio-demographics. Platforms like Instagram tend to be dominated by younger users—statistics suggest that over 70 percent of users worldwide are under thirty-five years of age[2]—and we see this reflected in the food preferences and aesthetics. While members of a younger (18–24-year-old) demographic may be more interested in sharing Instagram's emoji slider to poll their friends on their latest food likes than crafting, capturing, and curating food imagery, it seems the thirty-something foodie may be leading the charge in terms of shaping food taste and aesthetics. As Tandoh describes Instagram's lifestyled food imagery:

Here, you will find beautifully shot, intricately staged photographs of the food and, crucially, the lifestyles of successful, creative thirtysomethings. These are wishful odes to how serene and perfect your life could be, if only you had the money, the £50 ceramic platters and the time. Perhaps in keeping with the broader asymmetry between the numbers of social media users in different generations, there's a lot less to be seen of older people, or past food fashions, in this smart, moneyed, and overwhelmingly young world (Tandoh 2016).

The rise of the online food hipster: Instagram influencers as cultural intermediaries

While photography is a denigrated practice, seen as outside of the realm of art, it is ironically strongly tied to aesthetic, social codes.
Pierre Bourdieu, *Photography: A Middle-Brow Art* (1990: 7).

In reality many of the lifestyled microbloggers on Instagram probably sit at the more aspirational rather than "moneyed" end of the spectrum—lists of Instagram influencers often feature "homemakers" and people employed in various precarious home-based craft industries as much as they include celebrity chefs, food stylists, and restauranteurs. What gets counted as "young" in this world, particularly in the realm of influencers, is also probably somewhat contested given the enormous popularity of 40 and 50 plus-year-old figures like Jamie Oliver and Gordon Ramsay on Instagram. Nevertheless, the aesthetics, style, and food preferences of Tandoh's "creative thirtysomethings" (2016) do suggest a relatively distinct and influential echelon of taste shapers and makers on Instagram, figures who we might think of as the "hipsters" of the food photography world, noting the slippery-ness of this much used and often denigratory term (LeBesco and Peter Naccarato, forthcoming).

An example of public (generationally inflected) contestation over this kind of hipster food culture has been played out in Australia in recent years. A minor media kerfuffle occurred over that often-Instagrammed breakfast meal, "smashed" avocado with crumbled feta. As part of a broader rant against the evils of hipster cafes, self-proclaimed "middle aged moralist," cultural commentator, and (very wealthy it should be noted) trend guru Bernard Salt implied that one of the reasons why young Australians might not be able to afford to buy a home is they are spending too much money on hipster food.

Do you know why hipster cafes have milk crates for seating? To keep baby boomers at bay. They know they can't officially ban us, so what do they do? They rig the seating so that tight baby-boomer hamstrings recoil at the prospect of positioning the buttocks below the latitude of the knees. Sitting is fine. Getting up is problematic. And doesn't the sub-40 set know it. They don't want we over-50s despoiling the authentic grooviness of their cafes (Is groovy still a word?) (Salt 2016).

Rallying against hipsters' preferences for menus with tiny font, toilet doors with non-specific genders, and music-filled cafes with polished concrete floors, the article is a self-reflexive, half amusing dig at the cultural proclivities of "young people today." LeBesco and Peter Naccarato (forthcoming) argue that the mediatized figure of the hipster is often used by figures like Salt to stand in for their own projected anxieties and sense of "culpability for things like rising food costs, cultural appropriation, gentrification, and other consequences of a shifting economic and social landscape."

While framed in terms of a generational divide, the article is also about aesthetics and taste. In particular the growing gap between a middle-aged middle class and the new and emergent global hipster middle class who are aiming, it seems, to redefine the boundaries of good food, decor, and good taste.[3] As Le Grande (2018) has suggested, the figure of the hipster is a source of considerable cultural anxiety and contestation, something he connects to middle-class generational battles over authentic culture. As he argues, "Such contestations are reflected by the increasing legitimacy of emerging forms of cultural capital rooted in popular culture and embraced by young people, and the waning symbolic power of traditional highbrow culture associated with an older generation of middle-class people" (Le Grand 2018). Halawa and Parasecoli for instance, discuss hipster food culture in terms of the rise of a global aesthetic that they term "Global Brooklyn" (Halawa and Parasecoli 2019). In relation to this globalizing taste culture there has been less discussion of the role of the hipster aesthetic and habitus in online space. While focusing primarily on the everyday materiality, designed spaces, discourses, and social practices of hipster food cafe culture around the world, however, Halawa and Parasecoli also point to the key role of social media in "the transmission and adoption of this cultural formation, unfolding in digitally augmented spaces within deterritorialized networked communities of practice, which share and learn from each other online and create new criteria of value."

Can we see platforms such as Instagram, at least in part, as new spaces for a kind of global cultural and aesthetic gentrification? If we can, how might we understand and conceptualize the role and status of the foodie turned microblogger and influencer?

One of the French philosopher Pierre Bourdieu's most famous works is *Distinction* (1984), a masterful account of the relations between social distinction, taste, and class and a work I will return to frequently in this book as it offers a particularly useful framework for understanding the role of creative online consumer/producers as taste markers today, or "cultural intermediaries" as Bourdieu put it at the time. Based on a survey of the everyday tastes and cultural mores of more than 1,200 people in France in the 1960s, *Distinction* mapped, among other developments, the rise of a professional class of symbolic workers or "cultural intermediaries" who acted as mediators between bourgeois culture and a growing petit-bourgeoisie (i.e., an aspirational lower middle class).

In an analysis that, despite its cultural specificity and its age maintains much of its relevance today, Bourdieu described the emergence around this class of an aspirational culture of self-expression. Along with a concern with continual self-improvement, he noted the rise of a "domestic ethics" (369), marked by a preoccupation with a rule-driven approach to daily living. Central to this emphasis on a set of competencies for living was the rise of a new group of cultural professionals "offering (or selling) [their] own art of living as an example to others" (370). As Bourdieu comments, while these "ethical prophets" often peddle fantasies of social mobility, presenting themselves as somehow free of class distinctions, the life competencies or forms of "cultural capital" they promote all "speak of classification" (370).

In *Smart Living* (Lewis 2008a), writing about the "lifestyle experts" proliferating on broadcast and digital media—from celebrity chefs, supernannies, and health advisors to home décor gurus and personal makeover experts—I argued that they could be thought of as "the direct descendants of Bourdieu's new class of cultural workers" (9). At the time of writing though these figures (including Martha Stewart, Jamie Oliver, and the celebrity chefs of *MasterChef*) were primarily associated with broadcast media, though they all had a web presence. The hipster-foodies and "influencers" of today's social media, however, are arguably also close relatives of Bourdieu's cultural professionals, guiding people once again through a morass of lifestyle choices though they also represent something of a shift in the culture of lifestyle media and advice.

In the present context as I have pointed out, the distinction between the cultural professionals of Bourdieu's time and amateurs, "influencers," and "followers" becomes a moot point in a social media space where influencers can be famous chefs, teachers engaging in creative activities on the side, and/ or entrepreneurial stay-at-home mums and dads. Furthermore, where cultural intermediaries in the past have tended to be employed in advertising or traditional media spaces, using cultural technologies of marketing, print and broadcast media to communicate with audiences, the widespread accessibility

Figure 1.3 Image from Instagram account drlexicooks [Credit: Alexia Kannas].

and utility of social media platforms and the central role of networked photography in these spaces make for a rather different set of spaces for media circulation and influence. Advice culture, while highly commercialized (often in subtle hidden ways online) is also, in certain ways, less hierarchical and more participatory, shaped by logics of sharing, networks, and connection, something I discuss in more detail in the next chapter on YouTube and the rise and role of amateur food videos. Nevertheless, class and cultural capital are still strongly at work in online culinary culture and constitute a recurrent theme throughout this book. As Peter Naccarato and Kathleen LeBesco show in their book *Culinary Capital* (2012), while online culinary culture offers up a promise of the democratization of taste and participation, in many ways it shores up and shapes new hierarchies of taste and value. Relatedly Josée Johnston and Shyon Baumann (2010) in their book on foodies note the ways in which the implicit distinctions and forms of cultural capital that underpin foodie culture tend to reproduce social inequalities. As I have discussed, aesthetically crafted food photos on Instagram can be read as performances of personal "culinary capital," i.e., food-inflected cultural knowledge associated with social status (Naccarato and LeBesco 2012).

Facebook and food photography as social practice

Daniel Miller, (Miller et al. 2016), who (as discussed earlier) has recently headed up a large global team of researchers investigating "Why we post" (https://www.ucl.ac.uk/why-we-post) argues that much of what we post image wise is not so much about the self as it is about our relationship with others (see also, for example, Miller 2011; Ito and Okabe 2005; Sarvas and Frohlich 2011; Van House 2009; Van House et al. 2005; Villi and Stocchetti 2011). If we frame digital image sharing as essentially social, the images of baked birthday cakes, lovingly prepared evening meals, and brunches at a local café with friends that form our daily news updates in social media feeds can be read as performing relations of care and love toward others as much as they reflect self-identity and performances of taste. For Miller and colleagues (2016), rather than purely enacting a form of social distinction, the images that others post to your social media page and/or share with you by and large construct a shared sociality, though of course they can do both of these things at the same time.

But what do we mean by sociality and the social in the context of shared images on social media? Another work that came out of Bourdieu's interests in the taste and practices of ordinary people is the collectively authored book entitled *Photography: A Middle-Brow Art* (Bourdieu et al. 1990). Based again on research conducted with French people in the 1960s, the book is concerned with understanding photography as a sociological practice which tells us about people's broader beliefs and values as well as their everyday social practices. As Bourdieu shows us, aside from the odd aesthetically aspirational amateur photographer, ordinary people's photographic practices had a central social or "family function," with the bulk of photography tied to family occasions and rituals—from pictures of birthday parties and newborn babies to standardized snapshots of family travel and key family events such as weddings. Rather than seeing ordinary photographers as artistic or creative, Bourdieu described them largely as "seasonal conformists" dutifully taking stock photos at family or social gatherings or on holiday.

While Bourdieu's study of photographic practices in a pre-camera phone, analogue era might strike us as an anachronistic account, his argument that the *social functions* of photography are the reasons why it is such a widespread practice even though the majority of us have never had training or "institutionalized incentive" (39) continues to hold resonance today. But while Bourdieu's discussion of the social is largely about the links between photography and the intimate private sphere, and in particular photography's role in legitimating and celebrating the family, today photography has become articulated to a much wider range of social practices and arguably has become much more central to everyday forms of sociality.

If we think about food photography, for instance, digital photos have become increasingly tied to social rituals and practices. For instance, for many people taking a photo of one's food is now an essential part of the experience of dining out (Lee 2017; Murphy 2010), even if that image is not shared via social media, while mobile phones themselves, for better or for worse, have become frequent table companions. If it might have once seemed rude to have one's mobile at the table when dining out, in many countries mobile phones are now almost part of the tableware. While some restaurants are developing their menu with an eye to how the food will look on Instagram (Petter 2017), at the other end of the spectrum some restauranteurs have taken a stand against mobiles and have banned their use (Harding 2018; Sedacca 2017). Both photos and phones themselves have become social actors in a sense tied to a broader array of practices around engagements with food. Cashing in on this trend, Samsung Galaxy S8 now features a food mode on its phone.

Similarly, in an article entitled "The Conversational Image: New Uses of Digital Photography," Andre Gunthert (2014) extending on Bourdieu's argument that amateur photography has an essentially social function, points out that while Flickr had been around since 2004 what has made Facebook such a success is its socially connective affordances, i.e., its capacity to act as a broad platform for social interaction. Within the new social media realm, photography has therefore become subsumed by a broader communicative ecology of digital practices. Taking this line of argument further and borrowing from Jean-Samuel Beuscart and his colleagues' (2009) contention (in their study of Flickr) that the image has become integrated into an economy of communicative exchange, Gunthert contends that "conversation online is no longer about photos but *with* photos."

In this context, questions of taste and aesthetics become less relevant that understanding images in terms of their communicative or conversational role. Here he points to Snapchat as being exemplary of a new communicative ecology of images where the pictures people send are ephemeral, purely there to capture a moment or mood, reducing them to their use as conversational devices (though one could argue that aesthetic concerns are still at work on Snapchat but, in contrast to an airbrushed Instagram, it offers up a somewhat different kind of aesthetics and practice, focusing on capturing "the moment," which may include blurred, lo fi pics and less than flattering close ups, or creating playful selfies with Snapchat's many filters).

What this points to is the need to understand photos not only purely in terms of symbolic meaning and realism but also to engage with what has been termed a non-media-centric or non-representational approach to digital media and digital imagery in which photography is located within the context of broader assemblages of practices. As Lehmuskallio and Gomez Cruz argue in the introduction to their edited collection *Digital Photography and Everyday Life* (2016):

> We want to emphasize the usefulness of taking a practice-based approach to studying digital photography in everyday life. We are particularly interested in both the visuality and materiality of photographic practices, maintaining that this approach, in its broadest sense, is helpful for understanding digital photography and the various roles it takes. We suggest that photography is tied to both ways of seeing and representing, as well as to ways of acting and performing (4).

A social practice-based approach treats digital photography not as having a static and pre-given set of meanings or functions but instead views the photographer and photograph as an actor or agent in a large array of potential practices. In the context of a dietary regime, a food photo might act as an inducement to health eating, in a Yelp review it might serve as a promotion device for a restaurant, on a lifestyle microblog it may function as part of a larger array of aesthetic and lifestyle images while a photo of a plated dish taken at the start of a meal might purely act as a ritualistic marker in time and space ("here I am having lunch"); the food photograph, not unlike the mobile phone caller on public transport who announces to their interlocutor and to the world that they are on public transport, becomes in a sense the equivalent of phatic communication.

Vincent Miller (2008) in an article on social media and new forms of sociality extends this argument to suggest that communicative culture online has largely become a "phatic culture" marked by increasingly image-dominated modes of communication. Opening his article appropriately with a tweet from Happywaffle ("eating a peanut butter-filled corny dog dipped in queso. mmmmmmm breakfast"), Miller argues that communicative practice in today's world of networked sociality has transitioned from conversations with content to merely connecting for the sake of connecting—for reaffirming one's personal networks (which may consist of intimates, friends, friends of friends, as well as unknown members of the public). For Miller, one can see the content-less nature of social media communication played out on platforms where text becomes secondary to taxonomies of "friendship" networks and photographs.

Drawing on a larger critique by Wittel of networked sociality, Miller suggests, that "where once social bonds were deep and narrative driven [...] social relations [have] become primarily 'informational'" (2008: 390), i.e., constituted by ephemeral exchanges of data rather than mutually meaningful communication. Along the spectrum from registering likes to sharing gifs and videos, photographs in this setting become purely devices for forging an atmosphere of connection and sociality. For Miller, the microblogging of Twitter where the "births of babies are announced alongside random musings and lunch menus" (396) is the peak of this kind of low-maintenance conversational practice or "phatic communion," as he terms it, borrowing from Malinowski.

Smart kitchens? Food photos, interfaces, and datafication

Miller's account is underpinned by a strong moral and normative critique that at times can feel a little overdrawn. Nevertheless, his article offers a useful way of thinking through another recent development in the function of the digital photograph or image, its role not as a sign or carrier of meaning but as a form of data, as an object in itself and/or as a kind of interface. As I have suggested, "digital photography" is not a singular thing but instead constitutes a range of different practices occurring in different contexts involving distinct groups of "actors," from the lifestyled imagery of food microbloggers on Instagram to the more phatic, conversational use of photographs in spaces like Snapchat and Facebook.

Increasingly, photographs also function not as communicative devices but as ways of linking into and with information systems and databases (Gómez Cruz 2016), with online food affordances colonizing new spaces such as the kitchen and the supermarket. Using QR codes as a case study of new practices around photography, Edgar Gómez Cruz argues that "vernacular uses of photo-technologies are incorporating practices that move away, not only from traditional uses of photography, but even from representational realms. Photography is increasingly being used as an interface, without even involving an image" (2016: 229). One common basic example, for instance, would be the way in which hyperlinked food images in food reviews or advertisements can transport us to a restaurant booking site or purchasing portal via a single click.

The shift from food images as symbols to devices or interfaces chime in with Vincent Miller's charge that online sociality does not just involve the "disembedding of the self" from narrative-based social and communicative ecologies but also the increasing centrality of objects as relational mediators. As he suggests, "Human relationships become increasingly dependent on, and even displaced by, objects" (2008: 394). As Gómez Cruz (2016) points out, the new database-centric assemblages of practices and actors here involve in some cases largely non-human networks of data connectivity rather than being grounded in symbolic modes of communication.

> The bottom-line for these new visual interfaces is that the output resulting from a "click" is, increasingly, not just an image but a connection as well—a connection that can be traced, measured and become part of data-bases. These connections are sometimes visual and between people (as the social studies of camera phones demonstrated), but also through codes, sensors and connections (239).

In this context, the food photograph sheds its symbolic or conversational qualities and shifts us into post-human networks, an internet of things where the "communicative" interlocutors are devices and objects, software connected to appliances, for example, so that you can tell your smart fridge what recipe you want to prepare so that it can communicate the correct cooking settings to your (hopefully equally smart) oven. Meanwhile at the supermarket many of us have already experienced automated systems that allow us to self-checkout food items. While this currently involves the use of information embedded in barcodes; the brave new world of the internet of things involves scanners that can identity fruit without a barcode and cost them accordingly (Cooper 2012).

One perhaps unlikely space in which this digitization of our relations to food (and the use of photographic interfaces in relation to food) has occurred is in the area of ethical or political consumption where concerned consumers can access information about products using their mobile phone as a bar code scanner. Apps such as Treehugger "turn[…] your produce barcode into an extended label" (Markham 2013), while the GoodGuide (one of the most developed online ethical shopping guides) mobile phone app allows you to use bar code technology to get just-in-time information about the environmental, health, and social impact of companies and products (www.goodguide.com).

In Chapter 5 I discuss in further detail these forms of "connected consumption" in relation to what has been termed "apptivism" and the rise of a growing range of mobile phone apps and online plugins in the ethical consumption space. Here though I am primarily interested in the shifting relations of food and photography enacted in these spaces and in particular the focus on informational systems and data. While the commercial world has embraced this "data-fication" of food, there is also a growing interest by researchers in data mining food photographs, for instance using food images on social media to capture people's dietary and nutritional habits. In a highly quantitative vein, researchers have claimed for instance to be able to detect calorific content in social media platforms such as Instagram with 89 percent accuracy (Sharma and Choudhury 2015). While Abbar and colleagues (2015) examine the capacity to use Twitter to access data on US-wide dietary choices by linking people's tweeted dining experiences to their interests, demographics, and social networks. Clearly there are many limitations to this kind of quantitative, data-driven approach to food online (something I discuss later in the book in relation to dataveillance, traceability, and the limits of notions of "transparency" within the context of digital food data) not least the reductive conception of food posting as somehow reflective of an empirical "reality" (captured in Abbar and colleagues' title "You Tweet What You Eat").

On the other hand, the idea of online food photography as data also points to the potentially more interesting question of the role of people in diarizing and "researching" their own lives. As Salazar notes (2012), we have seen anthropologists and qualitative researchers more broadly developing a growing interest in photographs as data as food images become networked and often public, and research participants have the capacity to capture their own dietary habits and map their food journeys through everyday geospatial technologies (Middha 2018). The converse then to state-based dataveillance is people's capacity to map and capture the intricacies of their own daily lives and social, material, and symbolic practices around food, though as I noted earlier, one can also see this as an extension of a neoliberal culture of self-governance and self-monitoring.

As Cynara Geissler argues, today "the impulse to digitally diarize is powerfully present in many (if not the majority) of our social interactions" (Geissler 2010). The often-daily documenting of food practices captured on platforms such as Weibo, Facebook, and Instagram bears some similarly to much earlier "citizen-led" research initiatives such as the Mass Observation movement in the UK where volunteers observed and kept diaries on the everyday lives of ordinary Britons from the 1930s to the 1950s (see website: www.massobs.org.uk). While many view this initiative in positive terms, arguing it involved a recognition of the validity of working-class culture as an "object" of study, the criticism of the Mass Observation movement—around the invasion of privacy and surveillance of others—has resonances with today's critiques and concerns around the ethics and politics of online data collection, in relation to commercial, state, and "independent" research entities (Harrison 2014). Indeed, US scholar Shoshana

Zuboff argues that our digital practices are becoming increasingly shaped by what she terms "surveillance capitalism," with capital increasingly investing in "behavioural futures markets" in which businesses buy and sell data about our everyday lifestyle practices (Zuboff 2019). As I discuss throughout this book, the concern for Zuboff and many other critics is that the "work" that we do mapping our own daily habits, ways of living, and relationships through social media has become primary economic fodder for the immensely powerful digital corporate players that now dominate the internet.

Post-script: Food images after food photos

The rise of amateur, everyday food photography in the context of online networks and social media platforms finds us engaging with a range of new "practices with photo-technologies" (Gómez Cruz 2016: 240) in the contemporary space. Just a couple of decades ago not only food photography but food media more broadly tended to be the purview of specific audiences. Certainly, young people and male audiences were not for the most part watching day time cookery shows in the late 1990s, never mind regularly taking pictures of restaurant food or of their own culinary creations. Today we have seen a huge broadening out of the scope and scale of food photography, with growing numbers of younger social media users and men engaging in food-related practices. Within this context, aesthetically based photographic practices can still be seen to play a role in cultural formations of taste and distinction. However, "the artistic attitude, the permanent and generalized disposition to promote any object to the status of a work of art" (Bourdieu et al. 1990: 39) held by Bourdieu's aspirational, often male, lower middle-class amateur photographer in 1960s France has been passed to a new group of millennial cultural intermediaries who are often women and who are linked to new modes of creative labor and leisure associated with the creative economy.

As we've seen, the aesthetic realm is only one facet of a highly complex image-based socio-economy. The ubiquity of images produced by ordinary people and their networked nature has seen photography tied to non-aesthetic logics of phatic and connective modes of communication in which food images and text become placed in new communicative relationships. "Will Words Soon Be Replaced by GIFs? A Debate in Words and GIFs," a reflexive article on whether gifs might replace words, which uses gifs and text in a complex interplay, is a good example of the new combinations of visual and textual lexicons that are emerging within online communicative ecologies (Hess and Waldman 2015). In these communicative spaces, images of cakes and breakfast foods for instance become a short hand for say celebratory events and temporal markers.

Some two decades back Lev Manovich in a highly prescient article entitled "Database as a Genre of New Media" (2000) traced the evolving language of new media arguing for a shift from a focus on narrative toward a new cultural logic based on databases and algorithms. As I have argued in the latter part of this chapter, the realm of food photography has also become incorporated in part into an informational, database logic though the ways in which this has occurred are plural and complex. Tied to a range of different forms of social practice, from the use of food photos by ethical consumers as interfaces to critical consumer information on produce origin to the rise of everyday forms of photo documentation, again these forms of digital engagement, creative work and "serious leisure" have a problematic association with the digital hegemonic practices of surveillance capitalism.

In the next chapter I discuss another largely consumer-driven popular phenomenon, the world of amateur online food and cooking videos, focusing in particular on YouTube. Again, like Instagram, food videos represent a "genre" that exemplifies digital media engagement as a labor-intensive, creative, often community-oriented practice. As I discuss, they also highlight the growing monetization of video sharing platforms, in particular through the rise of professionalized cookery channels, branded cooks, and product placement with the trafficking of consumer-related data and "behavioural trends" associated with such sites is also being a key source of revenue.

Notes

1   My thanks to Edgar Gomez Cruz for these points.

2   See https://blog.hootsuite.com/instagram-statistics/for a range of Instagram statistics.

3   Tellingly though there is little discussion of the actual structural reasons why young people can't get a foot on the property ladder in countries like Australia where baby boomers like Salt have historically benefited from tax systems that have enabled them to buy investment properties thus driving up the price of "family homes" for everyone else.

2

Eating and Cooking Online: Cultural Economies of Video Sharing from YouTube to Youku

In a series of what might be classified as "how-to" videos on YouTube presented under the banner of "KDeb cooking," a boy of perhaps ten sits crouched under a tree cooking over a fire. With no musical accompaniment, voiceover, or explanatory text on screen, KDeb shows viewers how he makes a range of dishes from "Chicken Feet Cooking with Palm Sugar" to "Mix Vegetable Stir Fried with Pig Ears." While we know very little about KDeb—the blurb on his video channel merely states "Welcome to KDeb Cooking Channel. I am here to show all of you about my daily food in village. Thank you for watching and supporting my videos."—his no-frills cooking show has attracted a sizable audience and he is featured in the "creators on the rise" section of YouTube.

At the other end of the spectrum in terms of production values, we find another popular "amateur" cookery channel called Day Day Cook this time on the Chinese video sharing platform Youku Tudou. Hosted by Hong Kong-based cook Norma Chu, Day Day Cook is a standard "how-to" cookery show based in a very modern kitchen, with glossy aesthetics and English subtitles. While Day Day Cook may seem like a fairly generic if high-end amateur cooking show, Chu's show stands out in the online video crowd. An amateur cook who started blogging about her weekend cook-ups a few years ago, Day Day Cook regularly gets between 200 to 250 million views per month in China while, as of 2017, the channel's associated app has been downloaded around 1.6 million times (Kim 2017). Producing "branded content" in collaboration with a range of leading food and beverages companies, including Kraft, San Remo, and Kellogg's, Chu's "weekend passion project" has now become a substantial online food business with two branches, one in Shanghai, with seventy-two employees, and one in Hong Kong, with around twenty employees. Day Day Cook and e-entrepreneur Norma Chu thus epitomize the increasingly monetized landscape of online video platforms.

A third example of a popular amateur food video channel is American YouTuber Rosanna Pansino's cooking series Nerdy Nummies, a channel that regularly pops up in the top ten YouTube food channels and has over 11 million subscribers. Each video shows viewers how to make a dessert inspired by a pop culture phenomenon. For instance, a popular episode features the wholesome, cute, and perky Pansino showing the audience "How to make a Frozen princess cake" (essentially a cake made around a Frozen doll) alongside her equally cute and perky sister. As the episode description goes: "Today I made Anna and Elsa princess cakes with my sister! I really enjoy making nerdy themed goodies and decorating them. I'm not a pro, but I love baking as a hobby. Please let me know what kind of treat you would like me to make next" (Pansino 2014). While 33-year-old Pansino (see Figure 2.1)—an attractive, chirpy, and very likeable video host—describes herself as "not a pro" and shoots her cooking videos in her home kitchen, according to Forbes the "digital star" is one of the highest earning women on YouTube, due primarily to advertising revenue and marketing partnerships while she also has a range of Rosanna Pansino baking utensils produced by kitchen brand Wilton.[1]

Figure 2.1 Rosanna Pansino discusses *Baking All Year Round* at Build Studio on October 25, 2018 in New York City [Credit: Getty Images/Roy Rochlin].

These three key examples of popular cookery videos, while a drop in the video sharing ocean, provide a sense of the wide range of "DIY" offerings available on platforms like YouTube. As Andrew Strangelove comments in relation to YouTube, the world's leading video hosting and sharing platform, "Randomly exploring YouTube is like channel surfing through 100 million lives" (Strangelove 2010: 10). Around the world, making and watching videos, increasingly via mobile phones, has become a common part of many people's lives, with online video being described as early as 2013 as "the prototypical experience of the internet" (Dowling 2017). Indeed, the rapidity and enthusiasm with which people around the world have embraced video sharing culture is nothing short of astounding. While YouTube for instance only started out in 2005, by 2017 daily consumption on the platform reached 1 billion hours, with internet consumers now using more video data than all other kinds of online data (Dowling 2017). As Stuart Cunningham and David Craig argue in their book *Social Media Entertainment: The New Intersection of Hollywood and Silicon Valley* (2019) the "global reach" of YouTube is largely due to the fact that the platform acts as an enabling conduit for creators to make and share online content in contrast to traditional media's hold over content production, ownership, and distribution (Cunningham and Craig 2019).

The truly global nature of the video sharing phenomenon is reflected in data from Digital TV Research (DTR) that the global online TV and video market will reach nearly $65 billion in 2021. Though the United States will remain the dominant territory for online TV and video revenues, China will move into second place while DTR estimates that Latin American revenues will nearly triple, with even greater growth expected in Eastern Europe and the Middle East and Africa.[2] Meanwhile the leading users of YouTube in 2016 were the United States, India, Japan, Russia, and Brazil.[3] In China where censorship of "foreign" platforms means that the video market is dominated by a number of local players such as Youku Tudou (often referred to as "China's YouTube"), they nevertheless have 2.5 times the number of online video users than the United States. As of December 2017 for instance 579 million internet users in China watched online videos (Zhuge 2018). Cunningham and Craig nicely characterize the extraordinary international mobility of the content of sharing platforms like YouTube as a "near-frictionless globality."

While the online video sharing market also includes video streaming sites modeled along the lines of Netflix (the big video sharing platforms like Youku in China are increasingly entering into licensing agreements with the likes of NBC and Sony for instance), my interest in this chapter is in the realm of *amateur* DIY video making and sharing. Of course, I make this point with the caveat that the very notion of amateurism is being challenged in a digital context in which "users" have become "content creators" (Burgess and Green 2018). In particular, this chapter discusses the diverse and highly popular area of food videos which as the examples I opened with suggest range from very lo-fi, how-to cookery videos to glossy culinary clips with relatively high-end production values. Food videos are a major contributor to the online video ecology with advice videos related to cooking, for instance, being "one of the top ten most popular how-to searches on YouTube" (Cooper 2015), with people watching them on their computers, TV screens, and increasingly on their mobile phones. Another highly popular subgenre is food reviews, with YouTubers rating everything from the latest fast food offerings, to restaurants, food trucks, and markets. As we will see, the food video "genre" also includes a broad array of often unlikely practices, including people livestreaming themselves eating their own meals, and using food and eating videos with heightened sound as a form of relaxation.

Speaking to the broad array of formats and practices encountered in the video sharing culinary space, this chapter is structured around three broad and related areas: in the first section I examine online food videos and popular food hosts in terms of the rise of "ordinary expertise" (Lewis 2008a), or the valuing and mainstreaming of domestic skills and knowledge in contemporary culture and lifestyle media over the past couple of decades; in the second section I discuss the ordinary expertise shared in food videos as an example of the participatory "cultural economy" of platforms such as YouTube, which started out life as user-driven spaces of DIY content production, collaboration, and sharing. The third section discusses the growing monetization of the culinary communities on video sharing platforms through the rise of professionalized cookery shows and branded cooks, a process increasingly managed by commercial intermediaries (Lobato 2016). In the fourth section I shift gear a little and consider the related issue of genre and content. In this section, and in the conclusion, I debate whether the video sharing world is merely becoming more like mainstream commercial media, arguing that in key cases the interactive and participatory worlds of food videos suggest new genres and practices that require thinking beyond the space of media production and reception. Resonating with the argument made in Chapter 1 about food images as post-representational, I conclude by examining how we might understand elements of the food advice practices in video platforms in terms of non-media-centric understandings of everyday life practices.

Food advice videos: The rise of ordinary expertise online

In a recent piece on Star Media's Malaysian site, online journalist Abirami Durai profiles three ordinary home cooks, who thanks to Facebook, Instagram, and YouTube, have become "online cooking superstars." One of the cooks profiled—fifty-something Haziah Jaya, known as Azie, is a bank manager. Azie uses online platforms to share the Kelantanese (food from the rural state of Kelantan, in Malaysia) and more broadly Malay meals that she cooks on a daily basis for her family with the broader online culinary community. As Durai notes, "Azie posts recipes nearly every day and uses her phone to take videos for YouTube and a camera to take pictures of the food for her blog" (Durai 2018). Her popularity has enabled her to make money from both her blog (www.aziekitchen.com) and her YouTube channel of the same name.

Durai's two other examples (31-year-old admin assistant Sheena Haikal who uses her phone to take pictures and video to share Indian-Malay recipes, and middle-aged real estate agent and dad Lim Boon Ping, who has a YouTube channel called "Cooking Ah Pa") are also amateur home cooks with a solid base of online followers. While these three figures are hobbyists with no training in cooking or media presentation, as Durai puts it, their "recipes and tutorials are eagerly-anticipated and emulated by today's time-strapped generation who look to them as realistic models of what can be achieved in home kitchens" (2018).

Just as amateur online cooks have become highly popular sources of culinary advice in Malaysia, YouTube's research in the United States has found that nearly half of all American adults watch food videos on YouTube, with millennials (users between the ages of eighteen and thirty-four) "powering a 280% growth in food channel subscriptions over the past year" (Delgado et al. 2014). As the YouTube "Insights Team" put it:

> You're having friends over for a Fourth of July barbecue, and you need to plan a menu. Or you want to recreate an amazing dessert you tried at a restaurant last week. Maybe the kids need something other than spaghetti for dinner, again. Come to think of it, so do you. Where do you turn? Increasingly, the answer is YouTube (Delgado et al. 2014).

Food videos are also hugely popular on China's various video streaming platforms. While YouKu is increasingly dominated by TV shows and films it also has user-generated content including decidedly lo-fi videos such as the tongue-in-cheek "house wife burns leeks" (where we see a Chinese woman highly competently preparing a basic evening meal in her kitchen shakily videoed with a smartphone by her husband). Anime, youth-oriented video platform Bilibili also has a significant amount of lifestyle content, and a growing interest in food videos reflecting broader Chinese millennial tastes with channels like Make Food/Eat Food (www.bilibili.com/video/av9765196) offering basic instructional videos showing how to make simple dishes such as chicken curry.

Around the world, then, we see a large amateur advice culture with many internet users turning to online video platforms for information and inspirational how-to videos for managing their daily lives. One way to think about the rise of this distinctly amateur food video culture is in terms of the concept of "ordinary expertise," a concept I found useful in *Smart Living* (Lewis 2008a) for understanding developments in mainstream commercial lifestyle media in the late 1990s and early 2000s. Published a decade ago, *Smart Living* mapped what was then a relatively new development; the rise of a whole range of gurus on primetime television telling us what to wear (and what *not* to wear as the eponymous show put it), what to eat, and how to "makeover" our houses, gardens, and in some cases lives. What was interesting about this development at the time was the way in which every day domestic skills and advice once relegated to the realm of women's magazines were "becoming valued as forms of expertise in their own right" (2). As I argued at the time:

> In contemporary popular media—particularly those forms oriented towards lifestyle advice, such as makeover television and lifestyle supplements in newspapers—"domestic goddesses" and "style gurus" (figures associated with these more "ordinary" modes of knowledge and skills) increasingly find themselves placed in the same discursive category as other "experts," such as doctors, psychologists, and dieticians (3).

The focus of *Smart Living* was largely on examining this phenomenon on reality and lifestyle television which, in the first decade of the twenty-first century, was one of the main and most visible spaces in which DIY skills and knowledge around diet and weight loss, cooking, home décor, parenting skills, etc. were being aired (highly popular TV "advice" shows at the time included the revamped primetime version of *MasterChef, Changing Rooms, Extreme Makeover: Home Edition, Supernanny, Iron Chef, The Biggest Loser,* and *Queer Eye for the Straight Guy*).

There are some interesting links between mainstream media's growing interest in the 1990s and 2000s in forms of ordinary expertise and life skills and subsequent trends toward the "democratisation" of expertise within online video culture. While, as I discuss below, the range and diversity of food practices in video sharing spaces today is large and is marked by a variety of forms that bear little resemblance to conventional media and its concerns, the present-day popularity of food cookery videos and host-personalities online clearly can be linked genealogically to the earlier mainstreaming of interest in food and cookery on TV and in commercial media (such as the burgeoning lifestyle sections of broadsheet newspapers).

On primetime TV in the 2000s the embrace of everyday domestic skills saw chefs become a bit more "ordinary" with figures like "domestic goddess" Nigella Lawson and Jamie Oliver's "naked chef" positioned as "friendly guides" rather than authorities. Meanwhile TV shows like *MasterChef* took this democratization of expertise still further, embracing and validating the amateur foodie skills of accomplished home cooks, most of whom had never previously appeared on television. Ex-lawyers with hidden culinary skills, Italian nonnas drawing on family cooking traditions and recipes, and foodie husbands/fathers were branded as the new hot property in the culinary world, in the process blurring "the boundaries between media celebrity and ordinariness" (Lewis 2008a: 15). These shifts on primetime TV in the 2000s—including the rise of food TV— heralded (and intersected with) an emergent and burgeoning amateur advice online, aided and abetted by increasingly affordable, easy-to-use mobile video technology and the rise of accessible DIY online sharing platforms such as YouTube from the mid-2000s onwards.

Online culinary advice culture today—from bloggers and food hackers to DIY restaurant reviewers—in many ways represents the ultimate triumph of ordinary expertise. Many food videos are produced by and feature ordinary people whose popularity may often trump that of celebrity chefs. For instance, the *Boston Globe* noted in October 2014 that OpenSlate, a New York-based video analytics company, had ranked Laura Vitale of "Laura in the Kitchen" as the current number one YouTube chef ahead of UK celebrity chef Jamie Oliver and his professionally backed and produced channel "Jamie Oliver's Food Tube," which was ranked at number five. Italian born Vitale, who had learned to cook in her father's restaurant, became a YouTube superstar after her husband Joe filmed and uploaded a nine-minute video of her making bruschetta in their basement kitchen.

Major YouTube successes like Vitale in some ways represent extensions of the world of lifestyle TV and celebrity gurus, and in Laura Vitale's case she literally embodies this link. Following on from her huge popularity on the platform she was picked up by the major US cable channel the Cooking Channel who launched the "Simply Laura!" series which continues to air today. While Vitale's case is an unusual one, it foregrounds the fact that it is increasingly difficult to draw a clear line between the professionalized realm of commercial media institutions such as broadcast TV and that of video sharing platforms. Tolson, in his scholarship on YouTube make-up tutorials points out that, while operating in part under a different set of discursive conventions from commercial television, how-to videos made by ordinary people on YouTube are, at the same time, "another example of a cultural activity that, as a commercialised creative practice, is at best profoundly ambivalent and contradictory" (2010: 286).

In the next two sections I want to discuss how we might understand the food and cooking practices of online video platforms in the light of, on the one hand the proliferation of very ordinary and amateur forms of food advice and expertise and the associated rise of cultures and economies of sharing and participation in online space, and on the other hand the monetization of user-generated culinary content and the rise of YouTube food stars. What is the relationship between the various food cultures and communities on sites like YouTube and the realm of commercial lifestyle media? What might be distinct about the spaces of culinary sharing and engagement offered via user-generated video content online? What do the evolving forms and practices on food video sharing platforms tell us about the broader emerging online media and cultural ecology and economy and its increasing articulation into every aspect of people's daily life? As Stuart Cunningham and David Craig suggest, in their book on social media entertainment, the rise of this new media ecology requires us to rethink how we map out and categorize the relationship between DIY and professional, monetized online media practices, especially given that the sharing, participatory ethos of YouTube—with its emphasis on "authenticity" and "community"—is also central to the logics of the entrepreneurial practices enabled by and through the platform (2019).

Share plates: Cultural economies of participation

A key way in which the video sharing practices of home-grown chefs and amateur foodies on YouTube has hitherto been understood is as a form of sharing—or what Henry Jenkins termed back in 2006 "participatory culture"—a culture where "fans and other consumers are invited to actively participate in the creation and circulation of new content" (Jenkins 2006: 290). In their important early contribution to video sharing scholarship *YouTube: Online Video, and Participatory Culture* (2009), Jean Burgess and Josh Green critically engaged with and complicated Jenkins's concept. Originally published in 2009 (they have recently published an updated version in 2018)—the first edition of the book includes a chapter by Jenkins as well as one by the media and cultural studies theorist John Hartley—they argued that online media engagement is no longer about consumers and producers, professionals and amateurs, non-commercial versus commercial players but instead needs to be understood in terms of "a continuum of cultural participation" (2009: 57).

Enabled by the affordances of web 2.0 and by video conversion and sharing technology, websites like YouTube heralded what was a dramatic shift from the digital consumer as passive downloader—streaming food videos and reading online food articles—to an upload culture of creativity and prosumerism. In the latter space of participation and exchange, ordinary people produce and share pictures and videos of themselves eating and cooking often in their own homes, contributing to a wider online "public" culinary community in which experts in ordinariness and domesticity reign supreme. Or as Andrew Keen puts it rather less flatteringly in his 2008 book *The Cult of the Amateur*—a diatribe against sharing platforms like YouTube—"Amateur hour has arrived, and the audience is now running the show." Speaking to one of the many "garage entrepreneur" origin "myths" of YouTube (Burgess and Green 2009), Keen contends the platform originally started out as an unsuccessful dating site with the rather lame name "Tune in-Hook up." YouTube's developers claimed however that once they enabled the capacity for users to upload videos to their own websites "YouTube began to take on a life of its own, conducted by the users themselves" (Keen: 15), with people uploading a wide range of clips unrelated to dating. The rapid success of the platform—the *Washington Post* noted its "DIY popularity, fuelled by word of mouth" (Keen: 20)—saw YouTube being bought by Google in October 2006 while in the same year *Time* named YouTube "Invention of the year" and "you," i.e., users, as "person of the year."

While Keen's book offers a jeremiad against YouTube's culture of amateur free spin offs which he sees as undermining "traditional" (read professionalized, monetized, and copyrighted) American cultural institutions such as newspapers, music, and movies, Andrew Strangelove's 2010 book *Watching YouTube: Extraordinary Videos by Ordinary People* is by contrast a celebration of the *un*professionalism, ordinariness, and amateurism of YouTube. Obviously we are now a decade down the track and the YouTube Strangelove engaged with is a somewhat different animal today (as we discuss below). Nevertheless, his key arguments—that YouTube content is largely user generated and (relatively) non-monetized, that the platform represents an amateur space that breaks with traditional media institutions and their logics and conventions, and that

YouTube continues to represent a space of DIY, domestic culture—still have some relevance. In their preface to the second edition of their book on YouTube, Burgess and Green contend that more than ever participatory culture is "core business" for the platform (2018). As they put it:

> The cultural logics of community, openness, and authenticity are embedded in the YouTube platform and brand at all scales of commerciality, from everyday documentation through to those star YouTubers with six-figure incomes, billions of views and millions of subscribers (Burgess and Green 2018).

For Burgess and Green, while commercial and participatory cultures on YouTube have become intertwined at the same time they argue that "the two YouTubes (the corporate media business and the open platform for vernacular culture) are still in dynamic tension" (2019). Emphasizing these tensions, Strangelove foregrounds this largely non-monetized, vernacular realm of online video culture. Contending that online content is largely produced by individuals rather than corporations, a somewhat difficult distinction given the role of corporate branding and product placement in the success of many monetized food influencers and YouTube food celebrities, Strangelove has a broader point to make however about the realm of amateur DIY culture online (2010: 17). He suggests that, while YouTube creators (as per much online engagement) may unwittingly provide free labor for commercial culture, the content they produce more often than not has little or no commercial value. And he points out more broadly "much amateur cultural production takes place outside the economic system" (182), suggesting that the logics of exchange and value operating in much of YouTube are tied more strongly to an ethos of gift giving and sharing rather than entrepreneurialism, though clearly for many YouTube creators this is not necessarily an either/or scenario.

Strangelove's argument that amateur online video culture has little to do with the economic sphere is tied to an argument about domestic realism and ordinariness. YouTube, he claims, "is the world's living room" (2010: 62–63). Everyday life is central to YouTube, with most user-generated content being made in a domestic context and capturing some aspect of people's daily existence. The low cost and easy-to-use nature of phone video cameras which can shoot in poor light at a moment's notice means that domestically shot videos are often lo-fi and unedited—the ultimate actuality footage. Not surprisingly children and adolescents are thus among the most active contributors to YouTube (53).

While Strangelove was writing about YouTube nearly a decade ago, a 2018 article by Chris Crowley on the website of *Saveur*—a high-end food, wine, and travel magazine that specializes in essays about various world cuisines—similarly celebrates YouTube's participatory ethos, though in a global culinary context. Crowley argues that while much has been made of the impact of food blogs and social media on "democratizing" food knowledge and expertise, surprisingly little attention has been paid "to the expansive digital cookbook flourishing under most of our noses: YouTube." This is despite the platform becoming a huge repository of food knowledge via video "tutorials on everything from Southern fried turkey necks to homemade Korean condiments, with hosts from India, Ghana, Vietnam, and other countries well outside the usual hubs of Western media attention" (Crowley 2018). Crowley's enthusiasm for the participatory, sharing capacities of the platform (at least in the food space) makes him go so far to suggest that "collectively, they [YouTube tutorials] form the greatest compendium of cooking knowledge the world has ever seen" (Crowley 2018).

Like Strangelove, Crowley applauds YouTube cooking videos for their amateurism, and anti-commercialism:

> They're often adorably lo-fi—sometimes you can hear the shooter's kid in the background—and while YouTube's ad revenue is certainly part of the appeal, most programs are hardly what you would call commercial.

Similarly, he also reads YouTube's community of "lo-fi" advisors as authentic social actors concerned with sharing knowledge rather than accruing fame. YouTube's "home cook" we are told is "a world away from the cheese-pulling hands over bowls chasing viral Facebook success without a lick of genuine advice" (Crowley 2018). Further, just as Strangelove's living room videographers capture slices of mundane, everyday life, much global culinary culture on YouTube for Crowley has a quality of anthropological realism:

> Compared to the studied performance of the perfect Instagram dinner snapshot, YouTube's collection of recipes function as a community cookbook for the modern age, an anthropological log of how people *really eat* [my emphasis].

As a case in point, Crowley introduces us to "a granny" based in India called Mastanamma (see Figure 2.2), whose watermelon chicken video has been watched over 10 million times and who calls herself the "world's oldest YouTuber" (she was 107 years old as of 2018). Mastanamma is held up as the real deal, a traditional cook whose approach is not modified for a broader audience. Quoting Tejal Rao, a food reporter at the *New York Times*, on the raw authenticity of the "genre" of "rural cooks shooting with their phones, in places like India," we are told that in most cases "they are making their own cooking shows without the editing and production and substitutions and caveats and apologies that American food media might offer if they were filtering their cooking. They tell their stories however they like" (Crowley 2018).

Putting aside the rather suspect colonial politics of critics from the Global North reading YouTube cooks from sites "other" than the United States as "authentic" and "traditional," the way in which the affordances of video sharing platforms have enabled a diverse range of people to potential link globally around the topic of food is clearly a remarkable development. As the Indian newspaper *The Week* notes regarding Mastanamma becoming "a YouTube sensation" (Iyer 2017) what is even more remarkable is that she lives in a small hut in a village in Andhra Pradesh (in southeast India) and until 2016 was living "hand to mouth" working in the fields earning Rs. 300 (around US$4). Mastanamma's journey to success however was not perhaps the rough and ready, lo-fi experience conveyed by *Saveur*. *The Week*'s account of her rise to fame points out:

> All credit for her new-found stardom goes to her grandson Karre Laxman, a graphic designer who has worked with a couple of television channels. "She had made a brinjal curry for me and my friends, when we came home one day. It was appreciated so well that I decided to put a video on YouTube and it went viral. This was in August 2016," recalls Laxman. Laxman's friend Srinath Reddy adds: "It was a block buster and just that single dish had 75 lakh (lakh=100,000)

Figure 2.2 YouTube star Mastanamma cooking in her village [Credit: Country Foods YouTube Channel].

viewers. I would say it was a bigger hit than *Baahubali* (a hugely popular South Indian-produced film)." Realising the power of the internet and social media, Laxman and Srinath launched the YouTube channel Country Foods, which has 4 crore [million] followers and still counting (Crowley 2018).

Cashing in on cooking?

The case of Mastanamma's success on YouTube—the cultural traditionalism and authenticity of her videos and her YouTube identity relying on a team of "producers" including people who subtitle her videos for a global audience—highlights nicely Burgess and Green's conception of spaces such as YouTube as "a continuum of cultural participation" (2009: 57) where binary conceptions of professionals versus amateurs, authentic versus produced, non-commercial versus commercial make little sense. The YouTube food space thus represents a complex digital cultural economy in which a wide array of actors, communities, and institutions operate, and in which ordinary expertise bears a range of types of exchange value: social, informational, communitarian, and monetary.

While YouTube has enabled anyone with adequate internet access, skills and resources to participate in the distribution and sharing of ordinary, amateur expertise, as has been well publicized, Google has also become increasingly concerned with both managing and attempting to partially regulate some of the practices and content on the platform, concerns primarily linked to commercial logics. Social media and collaborative platforms more broadly have of course becoming increasingly monetized, with spaces like YouTube known these days as much for personal branding, entrepreneurialism, and micro-celebrity (Marwick 2015) as for advice and information. Stuart Cunningham and David Craig (2019) use the term "social media entertainment" (SME) to encapsulate the new industrial practices that have been born out of the broader world of popular online screen culture played out on YouTube and increasingly on platforms like Instagram and Facebook. As they put it:

> We see SME as an emerging proto-industry fuelled by professionalizing, previously amateur content creators using new entertainment and communicative formats, including vlogging, gameplay and do-it-yourself (DIY), to develop potentially sustainable businesses based on significant followings that can extend across multiple platforms (Cunningham and Craig 2019).

These same new media platforms have of course afforded foodies with little interest in the business potential of social media significant capacity to create and share content with their various communities. Nevertheless, the flipside of digital engagement, whether through the act of demonstrating one's dining preferences through apps or through producing food videos for YouTube, is that it provides lifestyle data and "free labour" (Terranova 2000) to commercial players. As van Dijck argues, while social media initially emerged out of a participatory, community-based ethos of creativity and exchange: "Connectivity quickly evolved into a *resource* [my emphasis] as engineers found ways to code information into algorithms that helped brand a particular form of online sociality and make it profitable in online markets" (van Dijck 2013: 4).

YouTube is no exception to this drive to monetize user-generated participation and interactivity. Indeed, Google has been very public about its efforts to attempt to make more profit from the video sharing platform, revising its governance processes and structures in response to pressure from advertisers concerned with potentially offensive content, and launching YouTube TV, a subscription-based service streaming more than seventy live networks, in 2017 (Burgess and Green 2018). As Lobato argues that, while YouTube started out with "the promise of direct, DIY communication with a global audience" (2016: 348) a decade down the track (after it was bought out by Google) it has evolved into "a more structurally complex, managed ecosystem designed to monetize both amateur and professional content" (348).

A good case study of the way in which elements of YouTube's communitarian video culture have become professionalized and increasingly tied to a commercial ethos is the evolution of YouTube's popular cookery channel SORTEDfood. Starting life in a local pub in the UK where a group of cooking-challenged men decided to start making amateur food videos for their circle of friends, the overwhelmingly positive response the founders received saw the venture soon developing into a fully fledged, professional cookery channel as suggested by the marketing speak of the following statement on Microsoft's website to access SORTEDfood.

> [A] global movement of over a million people who share a passion for food, friends and laughter. From absolute cooking beginners to kitchen pros, SORTEDfood is the place to learn how to cook your way, share inspiration around recipes and have a laugh with friends all around the world.[4]

While the SORTEDfood "mission statement" still attempts to capture the impetus of that early moment of "food, friends and laughter," as one of YouTube's top cooking channel offerings (Mediakix 2017), SORTEDfood is now supported primarily through advertising revenue, and sponsorship. The channel thus illustrates Banet-Weisner's argument in her book *Authentic™ the Politics of Ambivalence in a Brand Culture* concerning the paradoxically generative nature of brand culture (Banet-Weisner 2012). The SORTEDfood team of ordinary punters-turned-professionals at once enables the building of a culture of community and sharing around food practices, drawing on the rhetoric, aesthetics, and practices of friendship and participation through zany "amateur" media antics like "fridge cam" TV and food-related music video parodies. At the same time, it inscribes such practices within a normative, neoliberal logic of entrepreneurialism. Indeed, it is the "keeping it real," foodie-buddy culture performed on SORTEDfood that arguably has enabled it to be so effectively monetized. SORTEDfood's branding of its laddish food videos as a space of sharing and sociability troubles Strangelove and Crowley's tendency to reify the amateur online video community as a site of authenticity and realism in opposition to an increasingly inauthentic, monetized, and professionalized social media realm. As Cunningham and Craig suggest, building upon Banet-Weisner's argument, rather than understanding authenticity and monetization in oppositional terms, "the relations are trilateral among the 'authentic' creator, the fan community, which validates all such claims to authenticity, and the brand which is seeking to buy into, and leverage, that primary relationship" (Cunningham and Craig 2017).

A relatively under-discussed aspect of YouTube's drive to professionalize and monetize user-generated content has been the rise (and, in many cases, rapid decline) of multichannel networks or MCNs (Cunningham and Craig 2019; Lobato 2016). As Lobato explains:

> MCNs are intermediary firms that operate in and around YouTube's advertising infrastructure. A common business model is for MCNs to sign up a large number of popular channels to their network, then, using YouTube's content management system, to sell advertising and cross-promote their affiliated channels across this network, while also working with popular YouTube celebrities to develop them into fully fledged video brands (Lobato 2016: 351).

While Cunningham and Craig have pointed out that MCNs, like creators, have faced a large degree of precarity (2019), one successful MCN operating in the foodspace is Tastemade, an LA-based start-up that produces online food videos with high production values including documentary-style programming such as *Sourced* (focusing on the origins of famous foods) and *Tiny Kitchen*, a somewhat bizarre show where Tastemade staff made tiny dishes in a set complete with miniature furniture. Its bread and butter so to speak, however, stems from trawling the digital culinary universe (from Instagram to YouTube) for talent, and supporting "creators" to produce glossy content with high production values in its internationally based production studios (in Los Angeles, Sao Paolo, and more recently London). One example for instance is British blogger-baker turned vlogger Matt Atlard (one of the first UK "talents" to be recruited by Tastemade). Tastemade is managing Matt's "brand" as digital personality-star the "Topless Baker"—Matt combines working out with baking and presents his baking videos while wearing an apron that reveals his muscled upper torso—helping him produce quality content (Matt presents on Tastemade's video channel, his own YouTube channel, and also livestreams via Facebook) and enabling him to break into new markets through using data analytics to understand audience preferences. As Tastemade's head of programming, Oren Katzeff comments, "Since day one of launching in the UK, we've looked very closely at the data. Specifically what UK talent performs well in the US" (Rath 2017).

Such partnerships between home-grown digital culinary personalities and branding/production agencies or intermediaries like Tastemade again highlight the complex ecology of and relationship between "authentic" online cooks and their followers, and processes and practices of commercialization in the digital culinary space. For instance, one of Tastemade's founder's Steven Kydd is at pains to emphasize the grassroots nature of the culinary hosts that Tastemade has recruited around the world. The company has talent scouts in a range of countries looking for hosts—on for instance Instagram—with screen potential who already have a local following that Tastemade can boost and who have also an "understanding of local style," referring to their roster of hosts as "tastemakers." As Kydd explains:

> We don't call them talent or stars because their job isn't to jump up and down in front of the camera and be loud. Their job is to have taste and find something and curate the best and then deliver that to the audience (Rath 2017).

Kydd's comments here resonate with the discussion in Chapter 1 on food photography and Instagram and the role of foodies on Instagram as culinary cultural intermediaries in the culinary space, setting the bar for taste and style for aspirational foodies both off- and online. The case of Matt Atlard also foregrounds a development we have been seeing in cookery media since the rise of reality TV shows like *MasterChef*—that is the attempt by homegrown cooks to move from the space of "amateurism" into professional, money-making ventures whether as food entrepreneurs or as branded-food personalities

(Lewis 2011; Lewis and Phillipov 2015). With the growth of intermediaries like Tastemade, and a host of other measures to enable creators to monetize their content (such as channel memberships and merchandising options), platforms such as YouTube are structuring the entrepreneurial logics of reality TV into the very fabric of the online community. Popular YouTube figures like Rosanna Pansino (mentioned at the start of this chapter) are a classic case in point. Having had a number of brief forays into acting and featured in the reality show *Scream Queens*, Pansino segued into YouTube as a space where she might leverage her acting career but of course ended up having monetary success as a cooking star rather than an actor.

As I noted earlier, a key part of her business success (like other successful YouTubers) has come from marketing partnerships, with product placement being central to this. In a recent video she makes a "princess cake" but instead of basing it around the princess from Frozen, Captain Marvel is the center piece. Aside from her own baking utensils produced with Wilton (which we see in the background and next to Pansino while she is cooking), during the video Pansino is also surrounded by Marvel-related products, with the Marvel Legends action figures perched in boxes next to her on the kitchen bench while at one point she pointedly introduces the audience to the latest Lego Captain Marvel set. Product placement is a common way of monetizing videos on YouTube; for instance, in the next chapter on food masculinities online we discuss ChefSteps, an online cooking enterprise which includes a YouTube channel and which centers around promoting *sous vide* (or under vacuum)-based cooking and in particular promoting ChefSteps Joule cooking devices and related *sous vide* cooking paraphernalia. Like Pansino, however, a number of the online culinary "dads" we discuss in the next chapter take product placement a step further and bring the latest pop culture and media phenomena into their cooking, overtly featuring branded products in their videos and blogs while making food creations that, like Pansino's Marvel Princess cake, are also branded (for instance, Harry Potter and Nintendo-themed birthday offerings).

Given the increasing role of monetization in the YouTube universe what are the financial realities for DIY video makers? Despite increasing competition from players like Instagram, YouTube claims that "the number of creators earning five figures on the platform is up 35 percent, and the number of creators earning six figures is up 40 percent" (Rath 2017). Cunningham and Craig note that despite the industry only being ten years old an impressive number of YouTube creators (2.5 million globally) now receive some kind of payment while "more than 2000 YouTube professionalising-amateur channels [have] at least a million subscribers" (2019). As Cunningham and Craig contend such statistics reflect what it is in many ways a new media industry paradigm, with the YouTube of today being a far cry from the rough and ready community it was in its early days. Nevertheless, the platform largely continues to function and flourish as a space for sharing mundane everyday content, albeit within this broader context of data management and monetization. Much of the decidedly unprofessional "content" provided by the food community, for example, would be of little interest to professional intermediaries like Tastemade and has clearly not been produced and uploaded with fame and fortune in mind.

Furthermore, for those who *are* seeking to "brand" their culinary content, a 2018 piece by Todd Frankel for the *Washington Post* entitled "Why Almost No One Is Making a Living on YouTube" which discusses a university study of YouTube, suggests that claims about the monetization of YouTube may be overstated. As Frankel points out, while stardom can potentially occur for anyone on the platform, "the odds of striking it rich on YouTube—or even making a modest living—are small" (Gesenhues 2018). For instance, as the university study (the first to research YouTube's data from the point of view of creators) points out, even the top 3.5 percent of YouTube's most-viewed channels (i.e., those content creators who get at least 1 million video views a month) only bring in about US$12,000 to $16,000 a year in advertising revenue. High-earning YouTube stars like Rosanna Pansino it seems are very much the exception rather than the rule.

YouTube, then, is indeed a hybrid and "complex ecosystem" as Lobato terms it, in which both professional and amateur production coexist and at times feed into each other as part of Burgess and Green's continuum of participation. However much of this content continues to exist not so much outside of YouTube's professionalizing and economic logics but rather on the fringes of "mainstream" lifestyled forms of culinary content as I discuss below.

It's cookery programming but not as we know it: From online video genres to everyday digital practices

Alongside and linked to the discourses and debates framing YouTube as a site of monetization and professionalization versus a DIY culture of amateurism and participation are questions of media content and genre. As Lobato points out, part of the push to support "creators" to produce glossy content with high production values can be seen to be linked to "Google's drive to make YouTube more like TV" (2016: 357). In the culinary space this involves an assumption that food video content on YouTube largely emulates and is essentially an extension of televisual cookery programming. Certainly, many food videos featuring hosts in kitchen settings providing "tutorials" on how to cook a dish can be read as doing just that. As a story in *The Japan Times* "YouTube: Picking up Where TV Cooking Shows Left Off" by O'Donoghue puts it: "YouTube, like its precursor, television, is a haven for cooking shows" (Frankel 2018). As I have argued here, the world of food videos inevitably draws upon and remediates elements of a broader global food culture which in recent years has been strongly televisual. Indeed, the fact that Google *can* make a platform like YouTube for instance "more like TV" is, in part, because its participants are so familiar and able to play with the conventions not just of television but (and this is particularly the case of "millennial" and younger creators) of a range of media forms and practices. Strangelove, for instance, speaks of "generation YouTube," a whole cohort of online creators and participants who are "schooled in the art of blogging and video production" (2010: 187). For these digital users, "transmedia" modes of storytelling, across a range of digital platforms and reworking and inventing new genres, have become "conventional" in many ways. The remediation and re-articulation of televisual-like genres such as cooking shows via YouTube, then, needs to be understood in this broader context.

What then are some of key genres, forms, and practices that have emerged in food videos online? As the examples I have chosen to open this chapter with suggest, one popular strain of amateur food video is the cookery tutorial, which no matter how "lo fi," will often incorporate and rework some element of conventional televisual cooking shows. Essentially these videos feature a presenter talking the audience through the preparation of a dish—though in the case of "KDeb cooking," there is no music accompaniment, voiceover, or subtitles, while our erstwhile host cooks and prepares dishes outside over a fire rather than in the generic modern kitchen of the instructional cookery show genre.

As we speak, however, there are many thousands of online cooks around the world posting videos of themselves cooking in their domestic kitchens and sharing their favorite recipes and tips, often with unwanted pets and children popping up in the background. In some ways we can see this as a return to earlier modes of cooking advice TV except of course without the celebrity chef or well-known cook at the helm. But where reality television has increasingly moved away from the kind of old school instructional cookery shows that Generation X and older viewers associate with "traditional" food TV to a focus on spectacle, YouTube's home cooks take us out of the competitive spaces of the kitchen stadiums featured on *Masterchef* and *Iron Chef* and back to the how-to moment of cookery TV.

Niki Strange (1998) in her now classic structuralist account of the cookery TV genre refers to this subgenre of cooking show as the "cookery-educative" category, discussing British 1970s TV icon, English cook Delia Smith as the ultimate embodiment of cooking as "a practical and social skill" (1998: 310). While homegrown cookery tutorials in many ways follow the form of the "cookery-educative" category, offering a step-by-step demonstration of how to replicate a recipe, instead of the pseudo domestic settings of daytime TV studio sets, on YouTube we see *actual* householders in their own kitchens laboring over food.

The domestic location of online cookery tutorials has also enabled another distinctive development in digital culinary culture, that is the phenomenon of children "hosting" food videos (the development of *MasterChef* for children arguably set a precedence for this development), and the growing involvement of pets on screen (from the hugely popular Japanese show *Cooking with Dog*— the pet in question is unfortunately deceased—to *Jun's Kitchen*, which features Jun's two cats and often includes recipes *for* cats).

These somewhat idiosyncratic developments mark the ways homemade food videos tend to be highly intimate and tied to the rhythms and rituals of individual households. If day time food cookery on TV attempts to represent an extension of domestic space (the pseudo-domestic décor of magazine shows being a classic case in point) and of the intimate mode of the address of the friendly advisor, on video food tutorials this sense of the intimacy with the host and with video space (where there is less of a sense of a fourth wall) is greatly heightened particularly in videos that involve family members—often heard and sometimes seen in the background shakily filming the "action" with their smartphones. Of course, as Ahmed points out in her research on YouTube Cooking Videos, cookery channels such as the popular ShowMetheCurry, which attempt to marry professional production values with traditional Indian cooking, offer up rather more polished, edited productions "without all the background chaos that one might expect in amateur videos" (Ahmed 2014: 114). So that while the videos on ShowMetheCurry represent "short clips of the lives and work of [home cooks] Anuja and Hetal," the everydayness depicted is one that has been "crafted to look performed and perfected" (114). As Ahmed suggests, such food videos are "positioned somewhere between the professionally produced cooking shows on mainstream TV and other amateur videos on YouTube that celebrate disorganization and chaos" (114).

In contrast to ShowMetheCurry, whose content is not far off what one might find on a cable cookery channel, much of the online food video world, however, continues to be decidedly lo-fi and oriented toward more just-in-time forms of everyday advice. Nowhere is this more evident than the popular food-hack genre—where commonly unseen interlocuters show the viewer various innovative ways to optimize food preparation—often with a kind of science experiment edge—from how to remove strawberry stems with a straw and how to melt chocolate with a hairdryer to the potentially hazardous practice of cooking eggs in a microwave. While the term "hack" has become rather overused on the internet, in the food space it suggests finding an ingenious, simple way to make everyday food preparation and cookery quicker and more efficient. As I discuss in Chapter 3 not surprisingly the food hack is a genre embraced by men while according to a *Think with Google* article (2015) "forty-one percent of the millennials we surveyed are interested in them," with a large percentage of millennial mums and dads claiming to search how-to videos while cooking (Cooper 2015). While the food hack genre also sometimes features "personalities" (YouTube's CrazyRussianHacker, a master of the genre, has a very sizable subscriber base while Jamie Oliver also offers Kitchen Hacks on his FoodTube channel[5]) an overwhelming amount of the how-to content in the food space consists of videos with subtitles purely demonstrating how to prepare a particular dish.

Aside from occasional background music, these videos (which can be user generated or part of a professionally produced food channel) score low on entertainment value and seem largely concerned with instruction. As such they represent the "how-to" cookery tutorial in its most stripped back form. As I discuss at the end of this chapter, this kind of searchable "just in time" short form video content is highly attuned to the pragmatic needs and everyday habits and practices of households. In some ways, these varied genres of food videos speak to Hartley's essay in the first edition of Burgess and Green's book on YouTube (on the wider realm of digital literacy and storytelling) and Strangelove's point about the new modes of storytelling that have evolved on YouTube. But in other ways, they move us beyond narrative to a focus on embodied practices, something I want to explore further by discussing some of the more novel though highly popular online food practices associated with short-form online video, *mukbang* and ASMR, two related variants of food-based livestreaming.

Originating in South Korea around 2010, the practice of *mukbang* (a portmanteau of the Korean words for "eating" and "broadcast") involves live broadcasts of people eating food often accompanied by a focus on the auditory dimensions of the experience. Highly popular in South Korea where *mukbang* is associated in particular with AfreecaTV, a peer-to-peer video streaming service, *mukbang* "broadcast jockeys" or BJs can earn a solid salary eating dinner on a nightly basis with a live audience paying through sending their BJ digital tokens to watch (and listen to) them eat. The "genre" if we can call it that is a highly unique one, emerging (according to general wisdom) out of the South Korean tradition of food and sociability. In a nation with a growing echelon of young, live-alone singles, sharing one's meal with a BJ and their watching audience "may provide a way of alleviating the loneliness some experience by eating alone each night" (de Solier 2018: 54). In this sense, *mukbang* is arguably related to and extends upon earlier kinds of co-present practices first enabled by webcam. In their 2014 book on *Webcam*, for instance, Miller and Sinanan note that, as internet connections became more reliable, it became possible for people to leave their webcams on in the home 24/7 while going on with their everyday practices such as cleaning and cooking, sharing their lives with distant loved ones in a form of intimacy that assumes "the co-presence of the other" and is "analogous to the experience of two people merely living together in the same place" (2014: 55). As they note in their research on webcam use in Trinidad "with older informants, the most common activity mentioned as occupying always-on time was cooking" (57). They point out that this largely occurred in the context of an intimate living overseas rather than being conducted with a person who is living in the same country.

Aside from its enabling co-present eating, the practice of *mukbang* is also often associated with *over*eating and there are clearly pleasures for certain audiences in watching often slim, young *mukbang*-ers, many of them women, bingeing on excessive amounts of greasy, calorific food, challenging normative conceptions of Asian feminine food propriety. It is perhaps no surprise that US YouTubers, hailing from the home of overconsumption, have more recently also embraced *mukbang*, though in the United States eating online tends to be framed in terms of competition rather than as a social event per se though the divide between these forms of *mukbang* of course is not always necessarily clear cut. As Donnar argues, in the post financial crisis setting of a Korea wanting to celebrate its new-found prosperity, *mukbang* can similarly be seen as a performative embrace of excessive consumption for consumption's sake (Donnar 2017).

Another rather more perverse pleasure associated with *mukbang* but representing an online video trend in its own right is the Autonomous Sensory Meridian Response-based or ASMR phenomenon. In lay person's terms ASMR refers to the sensory buzz that one can get from listening to and experiencing the highly stimulating auditory and visual stimuli associated with, in the case of food ASMRs, people cooking, handling, and eating certain kinds of sensual, noisy foods, from crispy deep-fried prawns to an abundance of thick sauce-laden noodles. While for some *mukbangers*, the ASMR effect is part of the overall *mukbang* experience, ASMR videos are a whole world unto themselves with a wide range of variants, from professional ASMR whisperers to ice-crunchers while "ASMRtists" will often use packaging—"crinkling wrappers" and "cracking open cans"—rather than food itself to stimulate the senses of their audience.

As a *ThinkWithGoogle* article entitled "ASMR Is the Biggest Trend You've Never Heard Of," points out, while ASMR might sound like a fringe activity, at the time the article was written (2016) there was more "search interest" on YouTube for ASMR than for "chocolate" (Mooney and Klein 2016). A further marker of its (under-the-radar) popularity is the fact that KFC has made an advert featuring George Hamilton dressed as Col. Sanders whispering softly about pocket squares and noisily devouring a bucketful of fried chicken. KFC hopes that its alternative advertising will expand customer product knowledge. According to Kevin Hochman, KFC's chief marketing officer, "Most customers don't know that we actually have a second type of fried chicken—extra crispy [...] It makes a loud sound when you bite into it, versus our original recipe. It appeals to a very different customer" (Gibson 2016). The popularity of ASMR videos such as ice-eating in China has led to the government, suspicious of the erotic dimensions of ASMR, banning the phenomenon from major video streaming sites such as Youku, Bilibili, and Douyu (Abraham 2018). Such suspicions are perhaps not completely surprising given, as Anderson points out, that ASMR tends to be highly gendered, extending feminized, domestically located forms of sensual caring and intimacy into a space of "distant intimacy" via YouTube (Anderson 2015).

While ASMR is represented as a new online trend, just as Henry Jenkins places YouTube in the historical context of a range of other DIY media productions, from garage cinema to fanzines (Burgess and Green 2009), one can link ASMR and its therapeutic associations to a longer history of what Paul Roquet (2016) terms "ambient media." Examining a range of media—from music to video art—as tools of atmospheric design in contemporary Japan, Roquet argues that these media can be understood as a resource for personal mood regulation and as part of broader techniques for self-management in challenging social times. ASMR similarly is often represented as a boon to stressed individuals and rather than being used for erotic ends is most commonly associated with rather more mundane, daily practices such as relaxation and sleep techniques. As Mark Gallagher's (2016) analysis of ASMR video culture suggests, the largely practical, sensory concerns of the ASMR world places into question the relevance of conventional media and aesthetic paradigms for understanding this video sharing phenomenon. As Gallagher puts it:

> Less concerned with symbols, narratives or ideas than it is logging and cultivating a propensity towards a certain kind of involuntary response, ASMR culture provides support for those critics who claim that hermeneutics' "stalwart interpretive techniques" are of little help when it comes to contemporary media cultures more concerned with feeling than sense (Gallagher 2016).

Conclusion: From media genres to life practices

As we have discussed in this chapter, what we are seeing in the burgeoning food video space are a range of new and evolving practices, some of which extend upon traditional cookery TV, offering home cooks and celebrity chefs alike diverse and potentially global markets and audiences. While others challenge the ways in which we have conventionally understood the role and status of media and technologies in the home. ASMR food videos are aids to sleep in the bedroom or relax in a stressful workplace. Livestreamed eating videos offer co-present companionship to singles living alone. Smartphones and laptops are increasingly invading kitchens and can be seen in a way as new kitchen tools.

These varied examples of food-related practices shared around the world through video platforms point to the diversity that defines these spaces, where a large range of communities, uses, and co-evolved commercial and collaborative publics of a sort have emerged (Burgess and Green 2009).

As discussed in Chapter 1, like food photography, the lifestyle concerns and taste cultures of some of these food communities have roots in and continue to have strong links to broader developments in lifestyle and food media and in particular television. However, when it comes to genre and food videos online, as we have seen, it is not just a simple question of "TV on the Internet." Much of the popular food video universe such as live eating videos and food hacks bear little resemblance to conventional food media. As Cunningham and Craig argue, the formats emerging from YouTube are very different from those of traditional media and are shaped by what they see as the "intrinsically interactive audience-centricity and appeals to authenticity and community in a commercialising space" that they see as characterizing "social media entertainment" (2019). Further, while practices like *mukbang* have successfully entered into the world of social media entertainment (Cunningham and Craig 2019), the food content on digital platforms functions via systems of perceived exchange that are not always primarily driven by non-monetary concerns, even as Google attempts to code and embed monetary logics into the fabric of the platform. One example is the common practice of users subtitling favorite food videos for free and sharing them with other foodies. While other users speak of a primary drive to attract a community of foodies rather than necessarily to make money from subscribers.

These caveats suggest it might be useful to supplement our thinking about user generated food content on video sharing platforms with models that go beyond media institutions and genres, instead understanding people's growing production of and use of food videos in the home in terms of a non-media centric or practice-based approach. Nick Couldry, in a key essay entitled "Theorising Media as Practice" calls for a new approach that "sees media not as text or production economy, but first and foremost as practice" (2004: 115). David Morley, similarly has argued for a "non-mediacentric media studies" (Morley 2009) in order "to better understand the ways in which media processes and everyday life are interwoven with each other" (200). This is not to bypass a political economy approach but to suggest that digital engagements (increasingly a complex hybrid of the cultural and economic) often do not fit neatly into traditional understandings of media practices and institutions.

In an ethnographic study media anthropologist Jo Tacchi and I conducted with colleagues over a three-year period (Lewis et al. 2017) on everyday household digital media in Australia, one of the things we were struck by was the way the digital has become profoundly ordinary and in many ways invisible—tied to the repetitive habits, rituals, and rhythms of daily life. Over the period of the study, one shift in people's everyday practices we witnessed was the growing colonization of kitchens by smartphones, laptops, and tablets, with people using the internet to access recipes and videos of cooking demonstrations. For instance, Martha, a retired professional in our study, had gotten a special wrought iron stand custom made for her iPad so she could use it when cooking, while Matthew, a thirty-something social worker uses his blender base as a laptop stand so he can access how-to videos while cooking.

As O'Donoghue notes in "YouTube: Picking up where TV cooking shows left off"

> In many ways it is an even better medium, as smartphones and tablets allow us to disconnect from the TV and bring the cooking show into the kitchen. For many home cooks, the smartphone is as essential as a good knife, a chopping board and the holy trinity of soy sauce, *mirin* and sake. (2018)

In the context of food videos in the home, these examples all illustrate the need to shift from media studies' usual focus on meaning making, audiences and institutions to thinking about the ways in which people use technologies (such as laptops and smartphones) and content (such as "how-to" videos on YouTube) in their daily lives and how this intersects with a range of other practices (i.e., using online food advice to cook a quick meal while looking after the kids after a long day at work). Or, as Couldry puts it, "What, quite simply, are people *doing* in relation to media across a whole range of situations and contexts" (Couldry 2004: 119).

Chapter 6 of the book examines some of the political, economic, and governance implications of these mediated everyday practices. Focusing on the mixed social and monetary economies of domestic digital food, it examines, for instance, the way food corporations are seeking to channel, control, and above all monetize the everyday connective practices of digital users. The next chapter continues to discuss the world of YouTube, focusing in particular on gender, and the way in which digital platforms have afforded new spaces for a range of performances of domestic culinary masculinity.

Notes

1   See Forbes's profile of Pansino: www.forbes.com/profile/rosanna-pansino/#1331c0bd22b7, accessed May 1, 2019.

2   https://www.digitaltvresearch.com/ugc/Global%20OTT%202016%20sample_sample_149.pdf

3   https://www.globalmediainsight.com/blog/youtube-users-statistics/

4   https://www.microsoft.com/en-np/p/sortedfood/9nblggh4mg56?activetab=pivot:overviewtab

5   see https://www.youtube.com/watch?v=YEDP-2ZJDoA

From Naked Chefs to Epic Bros: The Rise of Food Masculinities Online

In a web article entitled "millennials Eat Up YouTube Food Videos," the Google Insights Team asks "Who's hungry for food content on YouTube?" (Delgado et al. 2014). Unsurprisingly the researchers find that millennials (the generation born in the early 1980s to the early–mid 1990s) are key participants in YouTube's "foodie fan culture."[1] Perhaps a little more unexpected is the central role here of "millennial dads" and "millennial men" not only as food fans but as home cooks (at least as framed by their findings). While, around the world, women continue to be the main cooks in the home kitchen, beyond the millennial marketing buzz of Google "insights" there is some evidence of shifts occurring in the gendering of cooking in the home and in housework more broadly. Associated particularly with middle-class households and more marked in certain national and cultural contexts, the rise of men cooking at home has gone hand in hand with a growing number of men showcasing their cooking skills online.

For men with culinary leanings, online food culture is no longer just a spectator sport. Trawling food blogs, YouTube cookery videos, and Instagram food profiles we find spaces heavily populated by men cooking and providing food-related advice. Indeed, a striking finding when one searches for the top ten YouTube cooking channels or cooks online is the number of men on these lists. While one could say the same for TV chefs and personalities, where top ten lists often feature professional chefs such as Gordon Ramsay, Jamie Oliver, and Bobby Flay ahead of "domestic goddesses" like Nigella Lawson and Martha Stewart, what is interesting about the rise of male cooks online is the growing number of more ordinary, non-celebrity figures in the mix. Meanwhile the emergence of a new breed of millennial food players online—from EPIC Food Time's cooking "bros" to what I term "meatrosexuals" and "dadpreneurs" to an array of male and female food "hackers" and chef-scientists providing "how-to" food advice online—suggests some degree of re-gendering of expertise in online food culture and the blossoming of a range of male food masculinities online.

This chapter examines food and culinary masculinities online, looking at Instagram and YouTube as two sites where men are increasingly engaging with food culture. In order to set the scene for this discussion, the first part of the chapter maps some of the complex and shifting terrain around men's cooking practices in the home in recent decades. The chapter then turns to a discussion of the shifting role of men in the kitchen on television from the 1990s onward, followed by an examination of dominant representations of culinary masculinity in food media more broadly. As we will see, while the world of online food masculinity is in many ways a very different and much more diverse space it has strong historical (and ongoing) links to food television and the figure of the celebrity chef. What kinds of food masculinities are we seeing emerging in this online space and how does this relate to shifts in the gendering of home cooking? What are some of cultural politics at play in masculine representations and practices around food and cooking online?

Who is wielding the spatula?

Around the world, food culture has traditionally been highly gendered, with the public world of the chef historically seen as a masculine realm while domestic duties around food shopping, preparation, and cooking for the family associated with women's work, and with an element of drudgery and monotony (Kelly 2015). Where women *have* been involved in paid food work it has tended to be in "caring" public service settings, such as in schools and hospitals while men have worked in the more glamourous, high-status realm of the restaurant industry (Neuman et al. 2017). Indeed gourmet restaurants have been characterized as stridently masculinist spaces that actively nurture "nostalgic and conservative masculinities" (Hermelin et al. 2017) distancing themselves from caring feminized modes of cookery. A profession overwhelmingly dominated by men—the UK national ratio in 2011 was 80 percent male to 20 percent female chefs—commercial kitchens are often portrayed through "metaphors of hell, the engine room and the cauldron of fire," imagery that has worked to exclude women from this "adrenalin driven," highly competitive world.

In his doctoral research on "The chef as an emotional and aesthetic labourer," David Graham quotes Gordon Ramsay discussing Harveys, a top-end restaurant where he worked as a young aspirational chef:

> It was the toughest place to work that you could imagine. You had to push yourself to the limit every day and every night. You had to learn to take a lot of shit and to bite your lip and work even harder when it happened. A lot of the boys couldn't take the pace. They fell by the wayside. When that happened, you felt that you had been able to survive what they hadn't (Ramsay quoted in Graham 2015: 40).

The owner of Harveys, British chef Marco Pierre White, describes his own role in "breaking" Ramsay, reducing him to tears on his last night working at the restaurant.

> He had been a protégé at Harveys and he was always a hard worker and showed tremendous resilience when it came to my bollockings. He never cracked. Or rather, he never cracked until his final night at Harveys (Alleyne 2006).

Working in a high-end restaurant setting is constructed here as a kind of a homosocial boot camp, where senior male chefs drive their junior counterparts to the edge. Hearing these descriptions, one could easily forget that the prime activity engaged in these professional kitchens is the preparation and serving of food for the enjoyment of others. But arguably this is the very point of these narratives and practices, which aim to delineate and enact certain kinds of sharp-edged culinary masculinities within an arena whose practices and concerns constantly threaten to bleed into feminine practices and duties. Such enactments foreground Judith Butler's classic argument regarding the instability of gendered identities and the role of performative acts in terms of attempting to shore up and naturalize gendered social roles. That is, on the stage of the competitive kitchen we see a certain kind of anxious but nevertheless hegemonic or dominant culinary masculinity "instituted through a stylized repetition of acts" (1988: 519).

In the home kitchen, cooking practices stand in stark contrast with those of the restaurant world. Long associated with feminized qualities of nurturing, domestic food preparation has been conventionally seen as a key part of women's unpaid labor in the home. In conventional patriarchal family structures—structures which persist in many parts of the world despite large shifts in the gendering of the paid workforce— men have purely cooked in the home as a "special occasion" activity or when voluntarily assisting the wife/mother as central home cook (Neuman et al. 2017). Research on gender and cooking at home has shown that when men do engage in the occasional home cookery, they also tend to conceive of the practice rather differently from women. As a choice-based activity rather than a duty, men have often seen cooking as a form of leisure or as a hobby with Szabo noting that "male home cooks take their lead from the masculine-dominated professional culinary world. In other words, they frame their cooking as culinary art or performance" (Szabo 2014). For women on the other hand cooking is for the most part understood in terms of caring for and pleasing others while also taking responsibility for the health and well-being of the family, a set of responsibilities that comes with satisfactions but also significant anxiety and pressure (Szabo 2014).

However, in recent years, studies have suggested shifts are occurring in the scope and scale of men's cooking practices in the home, particularly in Nordic countries where, alongside a progressive cultural discourse of gender equity, a suite of policies have sought to support structural changes in gender roles in families and to promote gender equity. Altintas and Sullivan's large-scale study of housework and gender, which draws upon time use data across nineteen countries (primarily European but also including Israel, Australia, Canada, the United States and the United Kingdom) over a fifty-year period (1961–2011) suggests that, despite major differences across national settings and a persistent significant gap between men and women, "there appears to have been a general movement in the direction of gender convergence in housework" (2016: 466). In a fascinating study of shifts in US home cooking, nutritionist Lindsay Taillie (2018)—using data from the American Time Use Survey—points to the growing role of men cooking in the home in America, particularly men with higher levels of education. Building on trends from an earlier time use study, the percentage of men who cooked increased from 29 percent in 1965 to 46 percent in 2016. While women continue to do the majority of food work in the home, the percentage of women who cooked decreased from 92 percent in 1965 to 70 percent in 2016.

In contrast to these two fairly positive accounts, Kan and colleagues, drawing on similar Multinational Time Use data as Altintas and Sullivan complicate accounts of this decreased labor gap. While they acknowledge "the overall evidence for slow gender convergence over time" (Kan 2011: 238), they point out that there continues to be marked gender differences around the types of work that men and women do in the home (238). In short, women still do the majority of the routine domestic work—cleaning, cooking, and laundry—while men engage in the arguably less routinized activities such as DIY and shopping (238). While the gender gap in labor is narrowing they point out that this is only in part due to an increase in men's activities but is mainly the result of a large reduction in women's routine housework time over the past few decades (240). In summary, Kan and colleagues contend:

The continuing gender segregation among these categories of domestic work points to the ongoing significance of gender ideologies and the interactional aspects of gender ("doing gender") in the performance of domestic work (238).

While there is evidence for some increased male labor in the home kitchen—particularly in Nordic countries where there has been significant long-term policy support for encouraging gender equity in the home and workforce—such statistics tell us little about how such shifts might be experienced at an everyday level in terms of changing family dynamics and gendered social roles and relationships. The next section examines some of the recent qualitative research emerging on practices and conceptions of masculinity in the context of a growing engagement with domestic cookery.

"Coming out" as a home cook and as a "new man": Shifting conceptions of domestic masculinity

For the past 40 years, women have been coming out as workers [...] Now men have to come out in public, in our workplaces, as dads.
Dr. Michael Kimmel, Speaker at the fourth annual Dad 2.0
Summit (Steinmetz 2015).

According to a 2015 article in *Time* magazine, given that more young fathers are now involved in child care and are doing more housework than ever, these shifting roles in gender require a shift in conceptions of masculinity (Steinmetz 2015). But what might it mean to have men increasingly participating in the mundane, everyday practices of meal planning, food preparation, serving (and feeding in some cases), and cleaning up? How might men engaging in care and fatherhood understand and enact their relationship to home-based work such as cooking?

As Canadian sociologist Michelle Szabo (2014) has pointed out, while studies in the past have indicated that men cooking at home more often than not see themselves as culinary artists bringing the restaurant into the home kitchen, this research has not engaged with that subset of men who actually do regularly cook in the home and who do so as a responsibility rather than as a choice-based leisure activity. Szabo's research with thirty men from Toronto deliberately sought to focus on men whose daily lives involve "significant domestic cooking responsibilities" (2014: 18) with her in-depth study not just relying on men's self-perceptions through interviews but also engaging with ethnographic observations of cooking and the collection of meal diaries to capture actual practices in the home.

Examining the ways in which men doing half or more of the cooking at home understand, negotiate, and legitimate their experiences and subject positions, Szabo's findings paint a complex and variegated picture, with men drawing on both "traditional culinary masculinities" (21) and also often identifying with feminine positionings as a caring, nurturing (and anxious and at times bored) home cook. On the one hand, while many of the men were the primary cooks in the household, over two-thirds still framed their cooking in traditional masculine terms, i.e., "as an aesthetic or artistic enterprise" or "as a kind of relaxation or entertainment" (24).

On the other hand, Szabo found that "a significant number of men, including those who drew on traditional culinary masculinities, *also* spoke about their cooking in terms of traditional culinary femininities" (25). Half of the men in the study spoke of cooking in terms of caring and looking after others, with participants speaking of "nurturing" through food, food as "an expression of love," as providing "comfort," and of developing intimacy with others through cooking.

Confirming a conception of gender as a socially produced construct shaped through everyday practices and performances, Szabo's research found that the men who were the main cooks "drew to an even greater extent on traditional culinary femininities. These participants talked about sacrificing their own needs for those of others, and about how feeding others influenced their subjectivities." For Szabo's participants, having responsibility for provisioning and cooking for family involved a complex negotiated identity straddling notions of leisure and labor, personal pleasure, and care.

Nevertheless, Szabo argues that approaches to cooking continue to be framed by hierarchies around gender, class, and cultural identity. For instance, women from poorer, racialized groups tend to see cooking as an oppressive duty, while men have a different "emotional association" with the labor of food and a relative freedom in the kitchen (Szabo 2013). For instance, her male participants sought to make cookery experiences largely enjoyable through "symbolically demarcate[ing] their cooking time and space as leisurely" (Szabo 2013: 631). As she notes, the men "combined cooking with music or alcohol, fused the domestic and the social worlds by cooking with loved ones or friends, and slowed their cooking down to enjoy its sensual and meditative aspects" (Szabo 2013: 635).

While men may be more present in the home kitchen than ever before, it appears they are not necessarily replicating feminine forms of housework or purely acting as chef-like professionals but instead may be attempting to forge new ways of doing home cooking. In recent years, lifestyle television shows featuring men as experts in the home have arguably been a key influence in relation to new domestic practices and identities (Attwood 2005; Lewis 2008a; Meah and Jackson 2013; Rezeanu 2015). This next section examines the so-called "malestreaming" of food media, drawing on the work of scholars Joanne Hollows, Josée Johnston and colleagues, and Jonatan Leer, and their mapping out of key categories of shifting and emergent modes of (masculine) chef-dom, before moving on to discuss the food masculinities enacted via the realm of food videos and Instagram.

Naked chefs in the kitchen: Domestic masculinity and the lifestyle turn on cookery television post the 1990s

Domestic topics such as cooking and gardening were once only seen on day time television and were largely associated with "women's issues." The late 1990s however saw the rise of primetime reality and lifestyle shows focused on the home (television producers often hold up the UK show *Changing Rooms* as a breakthrough moment). Speaking to a large "malestreamed" audience with what Feona Attwood (2005: 90) has called "a mixed gender address," these shows also increasingly featured men as hosts, experts, and participants while modeling a range of forms of masculinity—including gay and/or relatively feminized or "metrosexual" men.

In the culinary space, *The Naked Chef* on UK primetime television (followed soon after by a US version called *Oliver's Twist*) first aired in 1999, was pivotal in reframing cooking as a lifestyle interest rather than a women's issue (Hollows 2003). As Joanne Hollows (2003) argued in an early, influential piece on Oliver's negotiation of domestic masculinity on the show, if daytime cooking shows were once fairly stolid "here's one I prepared earlier" affairs, Jamie Oliver's performance as both a highly personable "new lad" and as a laid-back cosmopolitan, proto-hipster gave a once-feminized and marginal genre itself a makeover, turning the cooking show format into an edgy, fast-paced format complete with MTV-style editing.

What was groundbreaking about *The Naked Chef* at the time was its particular representation of a man engaging in the "womanly labour of home cooked food" (2003: 238). Exploiting Oliver's playful "laddish image" and performative persona, domestic cooking was reframed as a special event with the kitchen figured as Oliver's stage. As Hollows puts it, "In this way, domestic masculinity in *The Naked Chef* draws on some of the dispositions associated with feminine domestic cookery while keeping its mundane and repetitive aspects at a distance" (239).

Along with figures like Emeril Lagasse in the United States (*Emeril Live*, 1997–2010) and Australia's Curtis Stone (*Take Home Chef* 2006–8), Oliver helped to turn the televisual kitchen from a space of feminine labor into a stage for performing and celebrating the creative and artisanal dimensions of cooking. Meanwhile, shows like Gordon Ramsay's *Hell's Kitchen* (2005) in the UK—which promoted aggression and culinary competitiveness—and Japan's *Iron Chef*—one of the first formats to turn high-end cooking into a spectator sport (as reflected in its construction of a "kitchen stadium") and an influential precursor to the revamped version of *MasterChef*, similarly changed the face of food television. Indicative as Rachel Moseley stated with much prescience back in 2000, "of more general cultural shifts around gendered expertise" (2000: 309), the popularity of Ramsey's culinary hypermasculinity and Oliver's foodie metrosexuality ushered in a new era for men and cooking on television in (and out of) the kitchen.

So, what has happened in the space of men and food media since this "lifestyle turn"? In their study of "food personalities" with cross-platform media presences, food sociologist Josée Johnston and her colleagues (2014) set out to "question whether we are witnessing a new area of culinary (and cultural) democracy in which the stereotypical white male French-trained chef no longer dominates, and new voices (e.g., fans of streetfood) gain culinary authority in the field" (2014: 2). Focusing in particular on the ways in which celebrity chefs are packaged by their media and marketing machines as "personas" or public identities, Johnston et al.'s systematic analysis identified seven distinct types of culinary persona, namely, the homebody, home stylist, pin-up, chef-artisan, maverick, gastrosexual, and self-made man.

While noting that *Forbes* magazine's 2012 list of top-earning chefs included a range of types of identities, including "two self-trained white women" (Johnston et al. 2014: 2), Johnston and colleagues' broader analysis of representations of female personas indicates the ongoing marginalization of female cooks within culinary culture, with women's skills presented in terms of "practicality and necessity (homebodies), food esthetics (home stylists), and food's potential to provide self-gratification and pleasure (pin-ups)" (9).

By contrast they argue that the diverse personas offered to the male chef— the chef artisan, the maverick, the gastrosexual, and the self-made man—link their knowledge and authority to occupational and artisanal roles; even if they have no formal training the male chef tends by default to be associated with a professional world of culinary skill and/or "artistic genius" rather than with domestic expertise (Johnston et al. 2014: 13). Represented by figures like Gordon Ramsay and Marco Pierre White, the "chef artisan" represents an arena of culinary expertise that blends both artistic mystique and creative genius with an emphasis on craftmanship and "tough-skinned masculine perseverance" (15). The "culinary maverick" is likewise often associated with hegemonic modes of masculinity and includes figures whose claims to culinary expertise have little to do with professional cheffery or domestic cooking but rather draw from science (with male experimental "cooks" often clad in white coats) or adventure narratives. The "gastrosexual" is not surprisingly the category in which they place figures like Jamie Oliver and Bill Granger. Attractive, metrosexual types who embrace the home kitchen as a space of culinary exploration and expertise, "the gastrosexual persona can be seen as displaying elements of the feminine cooking personas discussed above (such as caring for others by feeding them)" (16) while working to link home cooking to professional knowledge and expertise. Lastly, the self-made man (a similarly recurrent figure in online narratives) is fairly self-explanatory but again offers the male cook a way of distancing themselves from cooking as a feminized domestic skill through a focus on enterprising selfhood and personal and professional self-improvement.

Overall, then, while Johnston et al.'s study indicates some increase in cultural and class diversity in the food and media space, gender roles seem remarkably fixed within the world of celebrity chefs. As they put it, "Even in a time of cultural openness and shifting gender norms our study of celebrity chef cookbooks and culinary personas uncovers surprisingly stereotypical gender patterns" (2012: 18).

In his research on European cooking shows, Danish food scholar Jonatan Leer similarly sees the range of culinary food masculinities on offer as less than encouraging. Highlighting the important role of Jamie Oliver and *The Naked Chef* in representing a relatively progressive break with conservative media images of male chefs, his research examines what has happened on European food television since then, focusing on ten popular shows in France, the UK, and Denmark from 2005 to 2012 that featured high-profile male presenters. Revisiting the arguments offered by Hollows and other scholars regarding Oliver—in particular his role as a kind of marker of a "post-traditional," negotiated identity—Leer argues that a key aspect of Oliver's persona was his deliberate distancing from traditional French models of chef-dom and from "patriarchal masculinity," reflecting a broader shift during 1990s food media toward what Leer terms "de-chefisation." Despite this momentary liberation of culinary masculinity, Leer contends that the cookery show post-*The Naked Chef* has seen a return to conventional constructions of masculinity, outlining four "tendencies" on European television: rechefisation; the TV chef as a "moral entrepreneur" (Hollows and Jones 2010); the TV chef and the revitalization of the national myth; and cooking as masculine escapism. These categories in part overlap with those of Johnston and colleagues's personae, with the aggressive almost cartoonish modes of masculinity embodied in figures like Gordon Ramsay on shows such as *Hell's Kitchen* (2004) and *The F Word* (2005) speaking to the "rechefisation" of the televisual cooking arena and the rise of the "chef-artisan" and "self-made man" as heroic masculinist archetypes. Likewise, as Peter Naccarato and Kathleen LeBesco argue, cooking shows like *Iron Chef* similarly integrate men seamlessly into the world of culinary capital via tropes of sports and competition (Naccarato and LeBesco 2012).

The role of TV chefs such as Jamie Oliver as what Hollows and Jones nicely term a "moral entrepreneur" (2010) (i.e., as moral or ethical gurus and lifestyle activists) has been discussed extensively (Hollows and Jones 2010; Lewis 2008a, 2014) but here Leer also points to the growing role of male chefs in teaching women—particularly working-class women who have fallen by the wayside—how to cook for their families. The linking of male chefs to nationalism and in particular to "authentic" masculinities as well as the turn to masculine forms of escapism through food are two further tropes highlighted by Leer, which I will discuss in more detail in the next sections of this chapter in relation to online culinary masculinities, first through the sphere of Instagram and then via a discussion of YouTube.

Men and food online: The Instagrammers

Spoon Fork Bacon, Food Minimalist, Food 52, The Feed Feed, Modern Honey, Joy the Baker, Half Baked Harvest, Diane Morrisey, Vegetarian Ventures, and ChefSteps. These are the account names of *Esquire*'s "10 Instagram Accounts That Will Make You a Better Chef."

One of many such lists, these countdowns of the top food Instagrammers are marked by considerable diversity in terms of gender and ethnicity (and food ethics) and indeed, as these account names suggest, the identity of account holders is not necessarily immediately obvious since images of food rather than selfies are often given primacy on these accounts. Nevertheless, compared with top ten lists of celebrity chefs in food media, where men dominate, Instagram is notable for the number of women featured. Given its relative diversity as a site, I am interested in discussing Instagraming as a productive point of comparison and contrast to the forms of culinary masculinity emerging on YouTube.

Instagram, as discussed before, is a quite specific online cultural space, dominated by users in the 18–30 age bracket and women (68 percent of users) (Omnicore Agency 2019). Given Instagram's focus on visuality, not surprisingly it tends to feature high-end photography and design, erring toward cosmopolitan middle-class taste, lifestyles, and aesthetics. While most of the female foodies on Instagram tend to be far from the simple "homebodies", "home stylists," and "pin-ups" of traditional food media they do often emphasize food aesthetics and everyday style as do the lion's share of male foodies on Instagram. For men and women, domesticity often tends to be positioned on Instagram as a post-traditional enabling space of creative living, or, as British sociologist Anthony Giddens puts it, as a reflexive "project" entailing "the strategic adoption of lifestyle options" (1991: 243).

As part of their "lifestyle options," the lion's share of food Instagrammers also tend to focus on high-end healthy eating—images of kale, quinoa, and acai abound; however, Instagram lists invariably feature at least one account (such as ChefSteps on *Esquire*'s top ten list) that challenges feminized modes of healthism and nutrition emphasizing instead copious amounts of meat and high-fat food. Such accounts are often fronted by figures who I term "meatrosexuals," i.e., softly masculine foodies who pedal meat in a non-aggressive, non-confrontational style via such hipsterisms as "street food," "authentic eats," and "comfort food." As *Esquire* (2018) comments in typically tongue-in-cheek fashion about popular Instagram account (and YouTube channel) ChefSteps, "While we'd never utter a phrase as hideously outdated as 'man food', ChefSteps' greasy delicious treats such as fried chicken sandwiches and melted nacho cheese is a haven far away from health food." As we'll see, this meaty but savvily post-traditional mode of "dude food" is alive and well on YouTube, tapping in part into the mode of male foodie escapism noted by Leer.

Equally however there is a distinct strain of masculine healthism and ethical eating evident on Instagram via figures like Gaz Oakley (@avantgardevegan), a Welsh ex-Rugby-playing Vegan personality and creator of the cruelty-free Kentucky fried chick'n burger,[2] and Russ Crandall, whose food blog "The Domestic Man" is popular among the Paleo, gluten-free and whole foods communities. Both figures exhibit elements of the self-improving and enterprising "self-made man" as foodie with their "food stories" involving journeys of recovery from what one might read as forms of unproductive, "toxic" meat-eating masculinity; Oakley from being a heavy-set body building type to becoming a born again vegan, and Crandall, who had a stroke in his twenties, turning to Paleo eating and transforming his life in the process. Key to their depictions of their life journeys as successful is the fact that both Oakley and Crandall have branded and monetized their new modes of culinary masculinity with regular media appearances, speaking tours, and spin off cookbooks (*Avant Garde Vegan* and *Vegan Christmas*, and *Paleo Takeout* and *The Ancestral Table* respectively) as well as, of course, presences of various online platforms.

Another successful "ordinary guy" turned celebrity food Instagrammer and influencer is Canadian Dennis Prescott, whose food "story" is again tied to a life transformation, this time from a struggling musician who cooked for his bandmates to a cook turned food photographer and eventual Insta star, boosted by Nigella Lawson reposting an image of his on Instagram in 2015 and *Food and Wine* signing him up to write a column called Stacked. Key to his narrative is the role of Jamie Oliver in inspiring him to follow a food path, despite being completely self-taught. While at aged thirty-seven, he is only six years younger than Oliver, in terms of food career and culinary masculinity he exemplifies a new online generation of food influencers whose claim to authority come from an ability to style and visually present their food and themselves (Prescott is a certified pork pie hat-wearing and tattooed hipster-bro) rather than from any particular culinary credentials. As Publishers Weekly put it on the website for his 2017 cookbook *Eat Delicious: 125 Recipes for Your Daily Dose of Awesome*, "Prescott, a Jamie Oliver-inspired self-taught Canadian cook and photographer, practically epitomizes contemporary food media, which runs as much on visuals as it does on recipes."[3]

Prescott in many ways carries on the "gastrosexual" legacy of Oliver but as I suggest he offers a more millennial updated take on food masculinity, blending elements of all Johnston and colleagues's male chef persona traits, including the chef artisan, the maverick, the gastrosexual, and the self-made man as well as representing what I am calling a "meatrosexual." While not presenting his brand of cuisine as "man food" per se Stacked, his column for *Wine and Food*, offers up recipes and images of dishes quite literally stacked with layers of meat and laden with calories, with a strong emphasis on creative versions of burgers. While presented as "globally-influenced comfort food dishes," with recipes like "Fried Chicken and Biscuit Burger with Country Sausage Gravy," "Latke Poutine with Smoked Salmon & Sour Cream Gravy" and "Bacon-Wrapped Onion Ring

Cheeseburgers" (Food and Wine 2018), this is meatrosexualism par excellence, i.e., food targeting an audience of creative hipster foodies and millennial males unashamedly wanting to cook and eat meat.

As Leer has noted in relation to links between male chefs on European television and a revitalized masculinist nationalism, there's also a trend in male online food toward rediscovering "authentic" food tied to place tradition (the US South figures heavily here via fried chicken as does Quebecois cuisine such as poutine), a trend that also often attempts to link food to authentic modes of located, working-class masculinity. Prescott who hails from Moncton, a former shipbuilding central of Canada, for instance emphasizes his link with the maritime in his cooking. His cuisine (depicted as global comfort food) is also quietly cosmopolitan, introducing readers to ingredients like gochujang and featuring culturally hybridized dishes like "Fried Chicken Ramen," "Loaded Greek Fries with Halloumi, Spiced Lamb, and Tzatziki," and "Chicken Shawarma Sandwiches with Garlic Sauce."[4] Rather than being depicted as "exotic" cuisine, these dishes are all positioned as forms of authentic, street food. Just as Oliver managed to negotiate both the class-marked world of Italian cuisine and the feminine space of the home kitchen via his performative persona as both a "new lad" and in later years as a "new man," Prescott presents his cooking as ordinary (disavowing any semblance of classed or culinary capital) and male-friendly via a creative but grounded, hipster-bro identity.

If Instagram's focus on visuality and photography has enabled a large number of non-culinary professionals such as Prescott to enter the ranks of food influencer, it has also created a space for the emergence of relatively non-traditional culinary identities, at least within the commercial parameters of lifestyle and consumption. In offline food media, the culinary world tends to be represented in heteronormative terms and is often dominated by white male chefs. As Johnston and colleagues point out (2014), while their analysis of representations of top celebrity chefs in mainstream media indicated some degree of cultural diversity, black chefs (along with working-class whites) tended to all fall into the persona of "self-made man." As Johnston et al. suggest, race, gender, and class (and I would add sexuality) hamper one's capacity to occupy a range of media roles whereas as they point out "not only do white male chefs have a greater number of legitimated personas to occupy, but male culinary personalities appear to have much more 'mobility' across persona types" (2014: 19).

By contrast, in the online culinary world there is relatively more diversity, both in terms of the range of identities on show and the ways in which people present themselves online, though of course that varies significantly depending on the media outlet and/or platform. For instance, while Instagram "identities" are dominated by white middle-class foodies often hailing from North America there are a significant proportion of popular food Instagrammers from non-Anglo backgrounds, in particular South East Asian food influencers and YouTube chefs such as Nik Sharma, Kenji, and Ryoya Takashima, who all represent quite different and distinct food personalities. The diversity of representations of sexuality in online culinary culture is harder to assess especially on Instagram but researching some of the key popular influencers a number of queer cooks both male and female regularly make appearances on Instagram lists such as popular food Instagrammer Jake Cohen. While Cohen is playfully sexualized in some of his Instagram images and text, it should be noted much of his self-branding online via his blog for instance is not overtly queer. On his blog "Wake and Jake" for instance he purely describes himself as "a nice Jewish boy who loves food. I love food so much that my entire existence, personal and professional, is pretty much centered around cooking and consuming it." Summarizing his extensive food experience and training he sums up "now, freelance is my game. Need a recipe conceived/tested/developed/styled? I'm your guy."[5]

A gay man hailing originally from India, identity politics are more central to the food identity of US-based Instagrammer Abrowntable, aka Nik Sharma, though again this varies depending on the media outlet and context. A regular figure on food influencer lists, Sharma's blog has won several major nominations and awards, including International Association of Culinary Professionals' Best Food Photo Based Culinary Blog 2015, while his growing online following led to him writing a food column for *The San Francisco Chronicle* since 2016. As narrated in an article in the *New York Times*, starting his blog in 2011 Sharma was shocked by the racist comments he received about his skin color, briefly going offline in response. However, he resumed his food writing and posting, keeping his brown hands central to his Instagram images and to the pared back photographs he features in his cookbook.

As per many celebrity chefs, Sharma's identity is integral to his particular culinary style and personal "brand" but there is a particularly subtle performativity about Abrowntable and its emphasis on skin color that points to the complex role of the politics of visibility in the culinary sphere and more broadly. Sharma's pictures of his own brown male hands preparing and arranging food offer one small attempt to represent other culinary male identities within an otherwise largely white-dominated culinary landscape.

Like Jake Cohen however, Sharma's queer identity is much less apparent online, though in an interview with queer food magazine *Jarry* (Sharma was the "cover guy" for the second print issue) he argues tha online "our community is much more visible than before. With the barriers to free speech and accessibility removed through blogs and social media platforms, the gay community has found a voice without any limits" (Byrnes and Sharma 2016). However, Sharma's identity politics, in terms of queerness at least, are not necessarily evident on his blog or Instagram profile—Buzz Feed's 18 Foodie Instagram Accounts Every Serious Cook Should Follow lists Sharma as number 7 due to his "beautiful (and moody) food photos" (Szewczyk 2017). The "about" blurb on his blog speaks passionately about his love of food and his cultural background but there is no mention of his queerness, while his Instagram feed is dominated by images of his dishes and pictures of articles headlining Sharma's culinary talent, with only the odd intimate domestic photo of him and his husband. His food column for *The San Francisco Chronicle*, however, narrates cooking and recipes through stories of identity, featuring articles such as "An Upside-Down Fig Cake to Celebrate Gay Rights in India" (Sharma 2018) while in his first cookbook *Season* he breaks the (rising) celebrity chef mold by confiding in the reader "mine is the story of a gay immigrant, told through food" (Sen 2018). Sharma's raced identity is a much easier one to accommodate and indeed brand in a culinary world than that of the queer foodie or cook, and while, as I discuss below, the YouTube space is a particularly diverse one, queerness does not get much of a look in in top ten YouTube video lists.

Dads 2.0: Food and fatherhood online

Compared with traditional food media where, as Johnston et al.'s and Leer's work suggest, largely hegemonic modes of masculinity continue to prevail, Instagram's foodie world appears to be a space of relative, albeit middle class, progressiveness—featuring professionally educated post-traditional males negotiating complex raced and gendered (if not sexual) identities that are a far cry from the aggressive culinary machismo of Gordon Ramsey (though it should be noted—as of January 2019—that Ramsey does have 5.6m followers on Instagram, just short of Jamie Oliver's 6.9m).

One particularly complicated figure here in terms of new domestic masculinities is the emergence of the "foodie father" on Instagram. Most top food influencer lists figure a dad-cook or dad-chef in the mix, such as recurrent favorite, Californian journalism graduate and father of two boys @ dad_beets—"one passionate and overly meticulous modern-day dad expressing himself through home-cooked meals and food adventures"—who despite working full time for Yahoo was the SAVEUR Blog Awards Winner for best food Instagram in 2016.

As I noted in the introduction to this chapter, Google's research (Delgado et al. 2014) suggests that among women and men, with and without children, millennial dads—"proud of their role as the family cook"— are the "most engaged" of the four groups when it comes to YouTube food videos. Moving from engaged viewers to online food identities, the rise of the foodie father on Instagram is part of a broader trend toward mediatized dads. For instance, the popular weekly podcast *The Life of Dad Show* represents itself as "the world's largest network for fathers." Featuring stories on relatively ordinary dads (including food dads on Instagram), *The Life of Dad* also airs a Facebook Live show featuring life advice and parental strategies from celebrity dads such as basketball player Shaquille O'Neal and Star Wars' Mark Hamill.

The celebrity dad goes hand in hand with the rise of food dads as "influencers"; as we will see below one of the food dads discussed here was a participant in the Dad 2.0 summit, an event that promotes itself as a space for connecting "with today's most influential dads, media and marketers" and as "an open conversation about the commercial power of dads online."[6] Where does this new figure of the enterprising online foodie father come from and why has he emerged now? As I have suggested in this chapter, a key context for understanding food and men online today is the shifting nature of gendered labor and domesticity under late capitalist conditions. American philosopher and feminist theorist Nancy Fraser has recently framed this (in a brilliantly incisive essay in 2016 for the *New Left Review*) as a "crisis of care" in financialized capitalist societies. As she argues, while capitalist societies have always required large amounts of social reproductive labor to be performed in the home—unpaid (and often historically undervalued) labor that nevertheless forms the bedrock of society and the economy—it has never really adequately accounted for and supported that labor (Fraser 2016: 108–112).

In the present economic paradigm of the "two-earner family" where women now largely inhabit the paid workforce, the growing gap between the labor required to maintain families and communities and the inequities of a financial capitalism that has largely removed welfare support structures, devolving and privatizing "carework" in the process, means the crisis of care has become more intense than ever (Fraser 2016: 112–113). Neoliberal disinvestment in "rights" like childcare, for instance, sees the emergence of "a new, dualized organization of social reproduction, commodified for those who can pay for it and privatized for those who cannot, as some in the second category provide carework in return for (low) wages for those in the first" (112), such as the lowly paid, racially marked care workers I discuss in Chapter 4 on the meal sharing economy. The rise of the professionalized foodie father on Instagram, then, can be read as a symptom or a response to this crisis. As we see with the three dads I briefly discuss below, they have all to varied degrees marketized their role as family cook, though they represent their food dad roles in quite different ways.

With 31.9K followers, all-American food Instagrammer @dadwithapan aka Derek Campanile represents the more traditional end of culinary masculinity online. An IT professional, he frames his online food identity in terms of food and caring while also emphasizing his masculinity.

He introduces himself on his blog, for instance, as "a dad, food blogger and fixer of broken toys," placing himself in the can-do handyman space of domestic masculinity while on his Instagram account he frames himself as a "Family man," "Recipe maker," and "Hockey junkie" rather than as a home cook per se. Cooking for the family is figured then as a kind of "hobby" and indeed, as his "food story" on his blog suggests, he sees himself in the masculine tradition of "occasional" cook:

> Growing up we always gathered at the dinner table and ate dinner almost every night, enjoying Mom's cooking, or Dad's barbecue. Now that I'm a father I see the importance of having that same routine and I want to instill that in my kids by not making it a chore, but something they look forward too by giving them great food to eat! My mission for this site is to get dads who may or may not know how to cook, to give mom a night off in the kitchen, and make it fun to come back to the table by enjoying great food! [...] I challenge you to get in the kitchen, become the Dad With A Pan in your family and get the family back to the table for dinner![7]

Dad number two—a frequenter of best dad "influencer" lists—Matt Robinson's @RealFoodByDad's Instagram account features highly styled and lovingly photographed images of his daily cooking for his family along with pictures of himself exercising (he is a fit, muscled hipster-ish dad) and posing with his kids (see Figure 3.1). While, like many dad-cooks, his Instagram and blog focus less on domestic drudgery than on his role as "explorer" and "maker of things" along with his "kitchen adventures," in contrast with @dadwithapan, Robinson stands out as a dad foodie who does in fact do the majority of the cooking at home (though he frames this in terms of cheffery rather than merely domestic

Figure 3.1 Images from @RealFoodByDad's Instagram page [Credit: Matt Robinson].

cooking). As he tells it, he sees being a parent as a key life role, albeit one he has framed (along with his very stylish and highly photogenic partner, popular food Instagrammer @bakersroyale_naomi) as a kind of urbane and lifestyled enterprise.

In an interview with Yahoo Food, for instance, Robinson references the somewhat heroic and caring capacities of his own mother who raised nine children, keeping them "well-fed with a steady stream of hearty casseroles and pot roasts. Now a father and chef to three young boys himself, the blogger behind Real Food by Dad has new appreciation for her labor of love. 'As I get older, I don't know how she did it'" (Paley 2015).

Robinson's own embrace of the function of the chief family "chef" speaks to the re-gendering of domestic roles discussed earlier in this chapter, but in particular in the context of both the crisis of care (in this case how to be a parent and spend time at home while also surviving economically) and the rise of the gig economy, in this case the monetization and professionalization of food blogging and Instagraming more broadly in recent years. While he didn't cook much in the past, Robinson became the chief family cook when his wife left her job to focus full time on her food blog Bakers Royale, with Robinson also subsequently quitting his job in finance to become a full-time food blogger.

The duo is an exemplar, then, of the new realm of domestically based creative labor enabled by digital devices and platforms. Their ability to segue into such roles from previously full-time high-earning jobs, however, places them in a rather different position from the majority of independently "employed" digital workers. With little emphasis on the daily labor of child care and food preparation, or discussion of the time pressures of juggling parenthood and work, such blogs can tend to present what Susan Luckman describes as an "unrealistic image of seemingly blissful hipster domestic perfection" (Luckman quoted in Littler 2018: 191) common to many aspirational lifestyle blogs and Instagram accounts. Indeed, much of the world of Instagram food influencers is arguably fairly escapist—one of airbrushed, aspirational lifestyle fantasies with relatively little focus on cooking as a daily duty of domestic care and provisioning.

Finally, a figure standing at the more mainstream end of the online foodie father spectrum is Beau Coffron aka @lunchboxdad whose culinary specialty is creating pop culture inspired "food art" with children's lunch boxes (see Figure 3.2). In contrast to the focus on high-end design aesthetics evident in Matt Robinson's domestic cuisine, Coffron is more of an ordinary dad figure. While not dissimilar in some ways from Derek Camparile's @dadwithapan's mode of what we might call "hobby" cooking, Beau Coffron is much more overtly entrepreneurial in his approach. As part of the @lunchboxdad brand, Coffron has styled himself as a lifestyle and parental expert, appearing on day time TV shows such as *Good Morning America*, blogging for *The Huffington Post* and www.lifeofdad.com and speaking at conferences such as the Dad 2.0 Summit and Social Media on the Sand, a social media conference hosted by a beach resort company. Like famous YouTubers Feast of Fiction and Binging with Babish, his food creations are similarly influenced by the latest popular media phenomenon whether Netflix series like *Arcadia* or video games such as Super Smash Bros. A successful food dad who has overtly monetized his personal culinary brand, many of his posts (such as "How to Throw an Amazing Nintendo Themed Birthday Party" and "Harry Potter Birthday Party Ideas on a Budget") are sponsored, while his blog often includes advertorials for products like Water Wipes or product reviews with embedded shopping links.

Coffron's @lunchboxdad has openly embraced the possibilities of the "social media industry" and beyond, bringing domestic concerns of care and social reproduction as well as children—his daughter sometimes participates in his media appearances—directly into the market sphere. At first glance, Insta-dads @dadwithapan and @RealFoodByDad seem somewhat more circumspect.

Figure 3.2　Image from @lunchboxdad's blog [Credit: Beau Coffron].

Nevertheless, they have also thoroughly monetized their foodie father brands; @dadwithapan for instance has a section on his blog called Kitchen Essentials where he promotes particular products (such as a particular brand of skillet, stock pot, and rice cooker) as key to optimally completing certain cooking tasks (Dad with a Pan 2019). Meanwhile, @RealFoodByDad's blog is highly commercial, employing extensive product placement while he also features sponsored posts, such as one of his "family adventures" with Volvo's new XC90.[8]

These enterprising dads resonate with Jo Littler's work on the "mumpreneur," a term that "has been regularly used over the past decade to signify a mother who establishes her own business from the kitchen table whilst her children crawl beneath it" (Littler 2018: 179). As she argues, the figure of the mumpreneur is a product of a precarious gig economy of often underemployed but over worked home-based laborers, with the enterprising parent pitched in "the array of mumpreneur articles, how-to guides and memoirs […] as a solution to the problems of combining work and childcare" (2018: 180–181). As Littler contends, the growing phenomenon of enterprising mothers online has seen the space of social reproduction not only become monetized but parental identity and the caring role itself becomes a site of investment in a "creative" and resourceful self (199). While the fatherpreneur or dadpreneur I am focusing on here is clearly an exception rather than a rule, the rise of the branded foodie dad online similarly offers a kind of enterprising (and self-improving) capitalist solution to the problem of domestic care under neoliberalism. Further, the dadpreneur enables men to embrace domestic carework but to reframe it in lifestyle terms, as a form of outward-facing, public and highly visible form of professional labor, while also effectively monetizing, branding, and professionalizing domestic culinary masculinity.

Cooking with men: Online food videos and food masculinities

In an episode of YouTube's notoriously macho Canadian cooking show *Epic Meal Time* (2010–), a show known for creating extremely high-calorie meals, generally out of meat products and including alcohol, we find Jamie Oliver trapped in a fridge and gagged with bacon. As he is forced to listen to hefty, bearded cook Harley Morenstein and his crew of "bros" create a giant fish and chips sandwich consisting of 59,144 calories and 2,840 grams of fat, Oliver calls out in apparent desperation, "Who put you up to this? Gordon Ramsay?" In this moment of *Jackass* style meta irony, the Epic boys signal the passing of the cooking baton from the British icon of metrosexuality and healthy family eating, once a symbol of new masculinity in the kitchen to a new generation of (apparently tongue in cheek) hypermasculine kitchen adventurers, figures who could be the offspring of that other figure of cartoonish machismo Gordon Ramsay, except that they are food amateurs with no culinary training or credentials whatsoever.

While *Epic Meal Time* is in many ways more food satire, with at times a kind of Rabelaisian carnivalesque edge, than "how-to" cooking show—episodes have featured Arnold Schwarzenegger frying ostrich eggs on an M47 Patton tank— the show's huge popularity speaks to some of the major trends in manly cooking occurring in the YouTube cooking space and beyond. In this next section I want to examine YouTube food videos as an important cultural arena today in which men and food come together, including increasingly targeting a male, millennial audience as per *Epic Meal Time*. In many ways, we can see YouTube as an extension of the forms of masculinity at play on Instagram. Compared to the relative restraint and politely middle-class aesthetic of much of Instagram's food space however, YouTube, represents a space for a range of explorations of food and masculinity. These range from the "extreme" (Hesse 2011) cooking of the Vegan Death Metal Chef (complete with kitchen dungeon), and Regular Ordinary Swedish Meal Time ("how-to" cooking meets angry Swedish men),

Figure 3.3 Brian Manowitz on his popular YouTube cooking show Vegan Black Metal Chef [Credit: Getty Images/*The Washington Post*].

to outdoor BBQing (BBQ Pit Boys) and Bushcraft and Hunting (Deer Meat for Dinner)—with the latter "genre" concerned with rediscovering masculinity and "hunter gatherer" skills in and through food and meat animals, usually in the outdoors and most often emphasizing survival skills and the art of self-sufficiency in the mode of *Man vs Wild*. Lest we see this as a fringe interest, Gordon Ramsay's 2016 YouTube video of him "Hunting, Butchering and Cooking Wild Boar" has received over 18 million views.

The platform is also an extremely culturally diverse arena featuring food videos from around the world and representing male foodies of all ages. For instance, one popular YouTube channel that regularly appears in "best of" lists but that is by no means millennial in content or intended audience is "Food Wishes," instructional food videos made by Chef John. An ordinary, mild-mannered American man in his mid-fifties, Chef John is an ex-instructor for chef training (and now a full-time online food vlogger whose brand has been purchased by allrecipes.com) who stays out of shot during his videos, which only feature his hands and (very pleasant and rather soothing) voiceover.

The majority of YouTube channels featuring male cooks on Anglo-American "top ten" food YouTube lists, however, are oriented toward millennials. As Google's research (Delgado et al. 2014) pointed out, millennial men are "confident cooks" and are "most likely to watch YouTube food videos to be entertained by food personalities, such as Jamie Oliver, or popular food shows such as 'Epic Meal Time.'" Examining the recurrent male figures and most popular male-oriented channels cited in media coverage on cooking and YouTube, I have mapped out the following (often overlapping) areas of interest and figures, with some of these categories replicating and/or extending upon those found in other forms of food media, namely, "gastrosexuals," "beards and tattoos," "chef-scientists," and "food hackers."

Gastrosexuals

Despite being a Generation X cook in his forties—and having transitioned some time ago from *The Naked Chef* status into the none-too-glamourous realm of family cooking—Jamie Oliver continues to feature heavily on YouTube's most popular lists. He is also often cited as an influence and/or cultural reference point (a la *Epic Meal Time*) by younger male cooks. The figure of the gastrosexual, likewise, continues to have a major presence on cooking shows from South East Asia to Australia. On YouTube's most popular lists Oliver has been joined by a growing number of thirty-something male cooks, who combine attractive looks and big personalities with family-friendly cooking, often with an accessible cosmopolitan edge. On his very popular YouTube cooking channel, for instance, ex-boy band singer, Dublin-born, LA-based Donal Skehan blends Oliver's quirky charisma with an Irish accent, offering simple "no-frills" cooking and helpful food tips from his home kitchen. As per Oliver, he has begun forging a multimedia, multi-platform career from his focus on accessible, easy recipes including a number of cookbooks (*Eat, Live, Go* 2016; *Meals in Minutes* 2018) and television shows such as *Follow Donal to Europe*, where he blogs his way around Europe meeting up with fellow online foodies along the way.

Coming out of a very different cultural context, Ryoya Takashima's YouTube channel Peaceful Cuisine offers what we might see as a Japanese take on gastrosexualism. Noting in an interview (James 2014) that he aspires to be "a vegan version of Jamie Oliver," his channel is nevertheless quite distinctive from conventional cookery television. Featuring beautifully shot, aesthetically minimalist videos of Takashima preparing dishes (usually involving just shots of his hands) with no voiceover but just the gentle sounds of food being chopped or flour sifted, the channel represents a combination of healthism, ASMR, and a focus on serious leisure and consumption (the channel also includes travel vlogs, DIY videos of Takashima making pottery and building his own kitchen, and seriously detailed product review and consumer advice videos, such as, what to look for when buying a new suitcase).

Beards and tattoos

> 10 years ago, something happened to food culture. Now, the cool kids with the tattoos want to cook to be cool. That's a huge shift: there is real passion for food culture, but no one is capturing it. That's what our job is (Eddy Moretti, the Chief Creative Officer for Vice Media discussing their online cooking channel Munchies, Dredge 2014)

A key area where culinary masculinity has blossomed on YouTube is in relation to food fare aimed at millennial males. Some of this fare lies at the more serious end of the spectrum, such as boys own cooking shows like *Brothers Green Eats*, in which two highly personable Brooklyn brothers (who have also been picked up by MTV) educate millennial audiences as to how to cook good food on a budget from the comfort of their own student-ish flat. At the more parodic end of the spectrum lie a large range of Jackass-influenced, food entertainment in the vein of *Epic Meal Time*, and low-budget, "how-to" videos such as *You Suck at Cooking*.

Sitting in between and offering serious food shows with a bro-ish edge, one of the biggest success stories in the millennial space has been Viceland's entry into cooking, with its Munchies channel and shows such as *Fuck, That's Delicious* (2016–) featuring rapper and ex-chef Action Bronson, *Bong Appétit* in which chefs create elaborate cannabis-based dinner parties, and *It's Suppertime!* helmed by "rogue" Canadian chef and internet personality Matty Matheson.

Set up in conjunction with Fremantle Media, the content producer and distributor associated with numerous lifestyle shows including Jamie Oliver's new series *Jamie's Quick & Easy Food*, Vice Media's Munchies channel, however, was set up to "disrupt the cosy world of TV cookery shows" which, according to their 2014 promotion video, are "dull, bland and flat-out boring to the group that matters most in food: young people" (Dredge 2014). As the then chief executive of Vice Shane Smith noted at the launch, "There's not a lot of programming for Gen-Y, which is the cohort that goes out and spends the most on food" (Dredge 2014).

Vice Media star, Matty Matheson is in many ways a pin up for a new Gen-Y culinary masculinity that, while embracing cooking in the kitchen, is set up

Figure 3.4 Matty Matheson (L) and Bill Nye at the 2018 Outside Lands Music and Arts Festival in San Francisco, California [Credit: Getty Images/ Film Magic].

as a reactionary counterpoint to gastrosexualism, healthism, and the polite masculinity of much mainstream cooking television. Depicted as a "bad boy chef," Matheson, as one journalist put it, "drops F-bombs the way Jamie Oliver drops 'Pukka tukka!', the way Emeril Lagasse drops 'Bam!'" (Shea 2016). Matheson who features regularly on the Munchies channel has a hard-living image, as an ex-drug user who recovered from a heart attack at twenty-nine. A big man with a large personality to match, his publicity machine includes shirtless selfies in the kitchen featuring his large tattoo-covered torso. If Oliver used a performative laddish persona to masculinize and undercut his domestic cooking role, figures like Matheson turn the kitchen into a kind of boy's own DIY space with a strongly comedic edge. Nevertheless, there's a seriousness to the food cooked here and a strongly educational element to the show—for instance Matheson introduces his audience to a wide range of cuisines, including Carribean, Moroccan, French, and Japanese cooking. This is all offered up with a playfully ironicized denial of cosmopolitanism and culinary literacy along with somewhat knowingly sophomoric quips like "Oh, banh mi! It's a vietnamese sandwich" (Viceland 2018). While reflexively self-knowing, the broader Munchies channel and its audience exhibits a serious interest in food. Vice has broadened its offer of "food-themed" programming following the positive response to Munchies—in its first year the audience for the channel grew by 280 percent (Jarvey 2015) with its most popular video *How to Eat Sushi: You've Been Doing It Wrong* receiving over 14 million views.

Chef-scientists

In an article by rhetoric scholar Casey Kelly entitled "Cooking without Women: The Rhetoric of the New Culinary Male" (Kelly 2015) he examines the rhetoric of contemporary cookbooks. He notes that one way in which cookbooks in recent years have sought to masculinize the space of the culinary is through depicting kitchens as laboratories. YouTube features a large number of channels that seek to distance cooking from the realm of domestic labor and feminized care and focus on food and cooking as a science rather than as a culinary art. ChefSteps is a popular YouTube channel featuring a male cooking team that brings elements of homosocial cooking collectives and millennial foodie-ism together with this shift toward the scientization and technologization of cooking. Regularly featured on best YouTube cooking channel lists and winners of various James Beard awards (often referred to as the Oscars of the culinary world), the ChefSteps team offers a "problem solving," systematic and science-based approach to cooking based on a particular cooking technology and product (e.g., Joule, the *sous vide* cooker).

Co-founded by chef and mustachioed hipster Grant Lee Crilly and Chris Young "famed chef-scientist" (a self-styled food maverick) and co-author of *Modernist Cuisine*, ChefSteps provides a more mainstream, "cross over" take on modernist cuisine's high-tech approach to cooking. As culinary website Tasting Table sums up the YouTube channel's offerings, "Handsomely aproned development chefs break down the science behind making everything from Michelin-worthy desserts to what might scientifically be the world's best corn bread" (Warman 2018). The chefs also combine high-end aesthetics and a focus on creative drive with culinary experimentation. In a cinema-quality clip on their ChefSteps website *Why We Cook: A Film by ChefSteps* we see the team (who look like an advertisement for fashionable male hipsters) on a stony shore of a beautiful misty lake, bonding through foraging for wood and building a fire on the shore to cook seafood. Meanwhile voiceovers of the ChefSteps' co-founders offer philosophical insights—"cooking is what makes us human"—into what drove them to develop ChefSteps: "to bring out our talents together as scientists, as chefs, as photographers, as film makers" and encourage the viewing audience "to feel more confident to push their creative limits."[9]

Another famous chef-scientist James Kenji López-Alt, or Kenji, author of the online column "The Food Lab" seemingly represents a new breed of avant-garde food masculinity. The child of a Japanese mother and white American father (geneticist Frederick Alt) his name comes from a merger of his surname with that of his Colombian wife Adriana Lopez while on his Instagram account he describes himself as "dad," "crypto-husband," and "feminist." At first glance Kenji appears to offer a negotiated potentially post-gendered engagement with food but his focus on bringing science into the kitchen represents in many ways a classic recuperation of a rationalist masculine approach to a once-feminized sphere. This perhaps is not surprising given that Kenji comes from a family of chemists and biologists though while an undergraduate at MIT he switched from biology to architecture. Calling himself "the nerd king of Internet cooking" (Weinstein 2015), Kenji engages in masculinist food experiments which have echoes of the world of food hacking (discussed below) including using a softball pitching machine to throw hamburger patties against a wall at high speed (while wearing safety glasses and a protective helmet) in order to demonstrate how salting ground beef produces a denser, tougher, burger (Duggan 2015). Again, the home kitchen in the world of "The Food Lab" has been transformed into a site of adventure and play. Kenji and his hipster-cool-meets-science-nerd compatriots the ChefSteps men, then, are in many ways the ultimate late capitalist citizens— enterprising, creative, rational, and scientific, with a strong focus on DIY and innovation, but with very little emphasis on labor, domesticity, and care.

Food hackers

As mentioned in the chapter on food videos, the food-hack genre has become a huge hit on YouTube with Google's research suggesting 41 percent of millennials are interested in them (Cooper 2015). Many YouTube food hacks are short clips featuring ingenious tips on how to optimize one's cooking or manage food preparation and storage, i.e., creating a DIY vacuum seal for food with a balloon, often purely featuring a voiceover and demonstration of the hack in question. The food hack places food and cooking in the realm of craft, DIY, and handy work, often using tools that would not normally be seen in a kitchen for preparing or transforming food. Preparing and managing food in the "hack" space is framed as a MacGyver-ish challenge, a space in which technological ingenuity and DIY nouse can be brought together to problem solve, i.e., make a meal.

The modes of food masculinity performed in the food hacking realm, then, tend to straddle those of millennial men (doing zany things in the kitchen) and chef-scientists, who see food and cooking as spaces of experimentation and innovation, with a dose of "culinary maverick" thrown in for good measure. CrazyRussianHacker is a good exemplar of the genre; mixing food hacks alongside a range of general life hacks, US-based Ukrainian-born Taras Kulakov won the Best in DIY Shorty Award in 2016, and, as of January 2018 has nearly 11 million subscribers. Specializing in rather spectacular chemical experiments (such as "What Happens If You Drop 30 lb of Dry Ice in POOL") and a range of rather more useful life hacks, all from his own home, Kulakov turns life (and food) management into a kind of fun form of everyday survivalism. Starting all his food videos with "Welcome back to my laboratory where safety is number one priority,"[10] Taras puts on his safety goggles and proceeds with his video which, along with food hacks, includes tips such as things to do with egg cartons after you have consumed the eggs as well as a range of kitchen gadget reviews. A fairly ordinary looking thirty-something with his thick Ukrainian accent and deadpan mode of address, there is something compelling about Taras's hacks, whether he is testing egg gadgets or showing us how to survive the apocalypse and open cans of food with just our hands and a block of concrete.

Conclusion: Online culinary masculinities

The image accompanying *Toronto Life*'s article "The Ravages of Matty Matheson," an article detailing his past alcoholism and coke addiction and his resurrection post-heart attack, pictures Matheson sitting down to a lavish meal in what looks to be an expensive gourmet restaurant with his baby lying in his arm and his free hand poised with a fork laden with meat in the other. The picture has a classical still life feel to it—Matheson's swathe of tattoos, visible on his arms and neck, stand out strikingly against his white shirt while chiming with the backdrop of the restaurant's ornate high-end wallpaper, while the contemplative baby, one finger in its mouth, brings an almost biblical quality to the image. Meanwhile the meal set before Matheson (his last supper?) features a platter of the "comfort food" Matty and his new generation of millennial chefs are known for—an abundantly overflowing prawn cocktail, a large jacket potato alongside the obligatory steak, a pile of doughnuts, and to top it all off a bottle of coke.

Matheson's image is a nice summation of one strong trend I have delineated in the online food space, that is, a trend toward a playfully ironicized and slickly hipsterized culinary culture, with self-taught male cooks—often represented by heavy-set tattooed "bro" types—offering down-home and none too healthy forms of cuisine. On the other hand, alongside Matheson's performatively masculinized cheffery, an array of relatively feminized slim male cooks from family food-oriented gastrosexuals to comfort-food cooking meatrosexuals have also flourished on YouTube and Instagram. But what do these seemingly contradictory developments tell us about the realm of food and masculinity more broadly?

In this chapter I have sought to examine emergent forms of culinary masculinity online in the broader context of a shift in social reproduction away from conventional models of "housewifery" (Fraser) and associated pressures on men to take more responsibility for labor in the home. As we have seen, food media since the 1990s has been marked by moments that reflect this broader social and cultural shift, with hugely popular global food guru Jamie Oliver in many ways leading the charge to new representations of domestic masculinity. Oliver's *The Naked Chef* of the late 1990s, however, was still a highly glamorized take on domestic cooking, with "the domestic culinary" itself turned into a kind of high-end cuisine and a masculine lifestyle pursuit. Nevertheless, Oliver's mode of softened masculinity and his subsequent embrace of concerns around healthy food and educating children in eating and cooking healthily have marked a significant transformation in representations and practices of celebrity male chefs. While Johnston et al.'s and Leer's work have shown that the world of celebrity chefs continues to be marked by remarkably traditional constructions of gender roles and masculinity, the ongoing popularity and major influence of Oliver's model of relatively domesticated cookery at least suggests some space for a masculine engagement with issues of care.

In the online space of amateur male foodies and chef-personalities, we have seen some complex shifts around how men are depicted in the kitchen. As my discussion of Instagram indicated, in this relatively middle-class arena there is something of a post-traditional trend around food, identity and representation with some engagement with cultural difference and queerness, though domestic masculinity (or domestic femininity for that matter) tends to be represented in commodified and highly stylized terms with little reference to the pressured realities of the two earner households discussed by Nancy Fraser. Meanwhile, the emergence of the online foodie father represents one kind of (again highly commoditized) emergent late capitalist "solution" to Fraser's "crisis of care," whereby provisioning and cooking for family itself becomes public and monetized.

YouTube is a hugely diverse space when it comes to food and masculinity, with a range of highly progressive images of domesticated men set against an array of reactionary images of masculinity. As I have discussed, those channels featuring male cooks that have large audiences and that have become monetized bear some similarly to the realm of celebrity chefs and traditional food media; the cook as artisan, the maverick adventurer, and scientist, the focus on male escapism from healthism and domestic duties, and the celebration of "authentic" place-based masculinities are all tropes we see enacted in online cooking channels and Instagram. There is however arguably much more diversity in the online space so that food masculinities are not necessarily limited to gastrosexuals on the one hand and bros on the other, and there is a lot of intermixing between cooks and chefs online both male and female. In popular collective cooking spaces such as the YouTube cooking channel for Condé Nast's *Bon Appétit*, for example, male and female chefs work side by side, along with the odd drag queen. While it may not yet have a large subscriber base, similarly the innovative and highly watchable YouTube series *Home: A Queer Cooking Series* which tells the stories of queer couples and individuals through food has featured in articles by both *Bon Appétit* (Sparks 2018) and *Food & Wine* (Sherman 2018). Offering a welcome alternative to masculinist YouTube fare, there is a sense of a culinary friendship and community in these spaces that feels very different from the carnivalesque homosocial spaces of *Epic Meal Time*.

Which brings us to one of the major shifts in online culinary culture—the rise of the male hipster foodie and cook. The handing on of the baton from Jamie Oliver to the Epic Meal Timers, while perhaps tongue in cheek, does speak to the power of a new young male audience. Many of the depictions of food males for this audience are I would suggest somewhat limited in that they continue to attempt to distance men from the realm of caring and the nurturing, healthy domestic kitchen (whether through seeing cooking as a science or form of experimentation, turning kitchens into DIY workshops, or framing cooking as a mode of boy's own escapism through excess). On the other hand, we are seeing an array of new millennial males in the kitchen focusing on family and everyday cooking from Donal Skehan to the Brothers Green, figures who hold out hope for the flourishing of domestic masculinities online. Everyday domestic cooking is also valued in online spaces in a way that it has not been in conventional food media, while domestic kitchens, whether featuring female or male cooks or both, are seen as spaces of considerable skill and expertise. It is not a stretch to suggest, then, that online we see much more of a democratized culinary culture than in the realm of traditional food media and one that speaks (relatively) to social and cultural diversity in a way that offline food culture often fails to do.

Notes

1   Based on their own survey research (conducted with a consumer research company) and analysis of YouTube data.
2   See: https://www.avantgardevegan.com/recipes/kentucky-fried-chickn-burger/
3   See: https://www.harpercollins.ca/9781443449885/eat-delicious/
4   See: https://www.foodandwine.com/fwx/food/skip-street-meat-classy-chicken-shawarma-sandwich
5   See: https://www.wakeandjake.com/about/
6   See https://www.dad2summit.com
7   See: https://dadwithapan.com/about/
8   See: https://realfoodbydad.com/part-1-volvo-family-adventures/
9   See: https://www.chefsteps.com/activities/why-we-cook-a-film-by-chefsteps
10 See https://www.youtube.com/user/CrazyRussianHacker

4

Cooking in the Cloud: Domestic and Digital Ecologies of Meal Sharing

Introduction: Meal sharing, creativity and labor

In November 2016, Airbnb introduced a platform for travel services known as Trips, the heart of which is known as Experiences, a new category of bookable excursions with locals. Tourists concerned with authentic modes of travel are now able not only to live in the homes of locals but they can also share various experiences of local culture and everyday life. One of the more popular types of local experiences is not surprisingly food related. While these include the usual range of offerings one might expect, from discovery tours of hard-to-find cafes and bars, to trips to local food markets, a rather more unusual variation is the option of having a meal in a local's home. Airbnb Experience Host Bjorn for instance offers, for $65 per person, a "Taste of Norway in a private home." As he explains:

> You will see one of the oldest houses in Trondheim from the inside. We will sit around the kitchen table and you will taste and learn about lots of local food: Brown cheese, smoked salmon, reindeer sausage, smoked viking ham, kaviar, Norwegian Bacalao, flatbread and more. You will taste a unique dessert. We will drink Norwegian milk, water, local beer (with or without alcohol) and the very Norwegian Aquavit! I am a musician and will entertain you with songs and stories. What else you should know [*sic*]. Don't be afraid that the food is strange, you will find something you like, and you will feel like home. And you will not be hungry when you leave this house.[1]

This offer of a rather intimate food experience in someone's private home—to be shared with the other potential strangers who might book this particular food "experience"—far from being an idiosyncratic option on Airbnb is exemplary of a range of new practices enabled by digital platforms and apps, practices that bring together domesticity, cooking, and experiences of sociality, conviviality, and sharing.

For instance, Homecooked, a "Social dining" app offered in the New Haven area of the United States, provides a platform through which local amateur chefs can invite 6–8 guests into their own kitchen. The app processes payment and allows guests and hosts to connect, to add fellow diners as friends, track mutual interests, and book future food events together. Initially set up to combat social isolation, one of the co-founders refers to the app as "an Airbnb for food, with a Tinder twist." As he points out, the app is about "relationships and community [...] We can define success based on number of active monthly users and revenue, but I'm dreaming of the day when someone picks up the phone and they call me and go, Kev, you won't believe it: I met my wife through Homecooked" (McCormack 2018).

While Homecooked is still a small, local venture, the major body representing the hospitality industry in Europe (Hotrec) have recently produced a detailed report on the rapid rise of what they call the "meal sharing platform economy" (Hotrec 2018). Discussing the growth of "meal-sharing" and home-restaurants over the last six years they note that while these currently represent a drop in the ocean compared with large economic players like Uber and Airbnb, these developments mark an important broader shift in the food and hospitality space.

As they argue, the growth of meal sharing first suggests a transition toward an "experiential paradigm" shaped by "the ubiquitous presence of technology across different sectors of tourism." Secondly, they see it as a product of the broader growth of what's been termed the "collaborative" or sharing economy. While there may still only be a few large international meal sharing and home-restaurant apps at present, as the Hotrec report points out such apps characterize a significant transition in "social" food practices from viewing "home" cooking as purely something familial and intimate to seeing it as a practice that can be shared and experienced with strangers (Hotrec 2018: 8).

This chapter uses the rise of meal sharing apps to discuss some of the key issues raised by, on the one hand, the politics and practices of sharing underpinning this collaborative realm, and on the other hand the increasingly domestic location in which both digital practices—such as setting up profiles on apps and producing associated blogs—and food production and consumption practices—from preparing meals in one's own home as a paid host for a group of strangers to making extra lunches for neighbors in need—occur. While meal sharing extends domestic and community-based practices of collaboration and caring into the digital sphere, at the same time it also sees domestic space become a site of publicity, economics, and value in a range of new and emergent ways. As Kylie Jarrett argues, drawing on the work of Italian digital media theorist and activist, Tiziana Terranova, the digital economy represents "an important area of experimentation" (Terranova quoted in Jarrett 2014: 17), where we see enacted "broader social trends around the reorganisation and re-valuing of forms of work once associated largely with the feminised, domestic sphere i.e. unpaid, voluntary, emotional and symbolic forms of everyday social relations" (2014: 17).

In order to examine some of these emergent and evolving trends, the chapter examines a wide range of empirical examples of meal sharing using digital technology. On the one hand, I examine meal sharing apps and platforms concerned primarily with economic profit, which we might see as part of the "uberisation" of domestic food production and consumption. On the other hand, the chapter discusses the sharing and social end of the meal app spectrum, where the distribution of food and conviviality can be seen as part of a broader post-materialist, pro-community turn that has been in part enabled by social media technologies. In doing so I want to ask a range of key questions about this emerging domestic digital food ecology. What kinds of practices are involved in these collaborative domestically based initiatives? What forms of creativity and labor are involved? Why do people seek to share as hosts and participants and who is involved in this emerging and evolving meal sharing ecology? What do these developments mean for the changing role of the domestic sphere in social and economic life?

Monetizing meal sharing

One of the key ways in which the world of sharing apps (from platforms enabling the sharing of commodities such as cars to apps focused on sharing skills and labor) has been understood is in economic terms. From the realms of business and marketing to journalism and critical Marxist-inspired media theorists, these developments have been largely framed in terms of new models of labor and markets variously described in terms of the collaborative and the sharing economy, the experience paradigm and the gig economy. Indeed, for some the rise to prominence of new global players in the digital realm, such as Airbnb and YouTube's owner Google, heralds nothing less than a new economic system, "a platform economy" (Kenney and Zysman 2016) with Botsman and Rogers (2010) arguing that the shift to collaborative consumption is as important as the Industrial Revolution in terms of changing how we think about ownership.

In the food space, we see aspects of the platform economy and so-called post-ownership models of infrastructure sharing reflected in what has been termed the uberization of food and delivery systems (see Figure 4.1). In a 2017 article on international fresh-produce transportation business IFCO's website on "how the sharing economy is transforming the supply chain for the better," the piece applauds the emergence of a gig economy driven by "contractors" rather than employees, while observing the potential infrastructure savings associated with "restaurants without seats and seats without restaurants" (IFCO 2017). In the online, on demand food delivery market, for instance Deliveroo Australia has been experimenting with restaurants without seats or what's been referred to as "dark kitchens," i.e., commercial kitchens operated by Deliveroo through which restaurant chains can produce orders without having the overheads of a traditional shopfront (Redrup 2013).

Figure 4.1 Advertising billboard for Marley Spoon, a takeaway food app, on Melbourne tramstop [Credit: author photo].

Meanwhile platforms for offering "seats without restaurants," that is, home-based cooking either experienced in another person's home or delivered to other households, mean "the lines between eating at home and eating out are becoming increasingly blurred" (IFCO 2017). An article in the *South China Morning Post*, for instance, discusses the role of Beijing-based company Home Cook app in providing "a sharing economy solution for the kitchen" (Chen 2017). Started in 2014 by former Alibaba manager Tang Wanli, Home Cook now operates in six Chinese cities and has 23,000 registered hosts and around 2 million registered users, who consist primarily of white-collar workers (between 20 and 30 years of age), and other people who want the convenience and time-saving benefits of having home cooked food delivered to their homes. On a smaller scale, in Iran, the MamanPaz app set up by female entrepreneur Tabassom Latifi (under her husband's name since women can not run businesses in Iran) enables households to order traditional home-cooked fare. The food is prepared by Iranian women (the business currently has 50 female cooks) and then delivered by men, as only men are allowed to ride motorbikes in Iran.[2]

In terms of platforms enabling "culinary experiences" in a broader sense, EatWith has become a large international player (www.eatwith.com), with an estimated valuation above €30 million (Hotrec 2018). From "exceptional dining" in London to tasting "the city with locals" in Budapest and enjoying dinner parties in New York "in beautiful homes and spaces," this is high-end cosmopolitan culinary tourism in the strain of Airbnb food experiences. Promising users they can "experience the magic of social dining" around the world, the app's profile has been boosted by major business partnerships such as with Huawei, with the partnership allowing Huawei phone users in China and Europe to download the app in a variety of languages, including Mandarin.

Aside from these large and high-end players, there is a growing "grey" social media economy around domestic food production in low-income communities. For instance, as part of the *Why We Post* project on social media use around the world, Nell Hayne's fifteen-month ethnographic study in a poor city in Northern Chile found that many women make use of Facebook as an opportunity to set up a side business to their usual work, such as selling lunches from their homes, taking orders through Facebook and WhatsApp (Haynes 2016). She found, for instance, that "Home-made sushi delivery businesses at times seem to dominate my Facebook newsfeed" (Haynes 2016), with people advertising ahead of time what they would be offering and then on the day of production preparing large batches of home-made sushi and then sending "a family member for delivery along with the small cups of soy sauce and sweet teriyaki" (130).

These various examples of meal sharing and home-restaurants, while often referred to under the umbrella term of the collaborative or sharing economy clearly represent quite a range of different sets of practices. However, it is important to make a distinction between apps driven by "collaborative" concerns "based on peer-to-peer transactions, generating small-scale financial benefits and with a strong community character" (Hotrec 2018: 9) and services at the Uber end of the business model, with "its focus on growth and profits through unequal relationships between the platforms and the service providers" (Hotrec 2018: 9). As Ticona and colleagues point out in their study of the rise of ride-hailing and domestic care apps, "The dominance of Uber in public understandings of on-demand labour platforms has obscured the different ways technology is being used to reshape other types of services—such as care and cleaning work—in the 'gig' economy" (Ticona et al. 2018: 3). Hayne's work in Chile also points to the importance of understanding the role of cultural context in shaping different kinds of sharing economies (2016). These caveats aside, there are certain common features and concerns raised by the co-articulation of domestic cookery and connective and collaborative forms of digital technology that constitutes the digital meal sharing space.

Digitizing the domestic

As we will discuss, the digital meal sharing economy relies on a range of kinds of work, from the labor of cooking to the so-called immaterial or cognitive labor of the digital consumer. While housework and caring have traditionally been "women's work" who is doing the work in the home in an increasingly digitized domestic realm? As we discussed in the chapter on food and masculinities, men are increasingly entering the (digital) kitchen as bloggers, Instagram influencers, and YouTube chefs. There is also some evidence of gendered shifts in the less public realm of home-based or household labor, i.e., the realm that has been associated with housewifery, with men—at least in middle-class households in the Global North—starting to engage more in the behind-the-scenes labor of home cooking (though data from the Australian 2016 census, for instance, showed that women still do "the lion's share of housework") (Ruppanner 2017).

At the same time, women are stepping out of the kitchen (or at least extending their kitchen practices) into a wide range of digital spaces, from blogging to

Instagram to recipe sharing and YouTube cookery videos. If the public world of TV personalities and TV chefs has tended to be dominated by men (with the exception of domestic goddesses like Nigella Lawson), in the private–public realm of social media the world of food expertise is female dominated. As social media monitoring company Brandwatch found, analyzing the Twitter bios of "self-identifying food bloggers and food vloggers," 76 percent identified as female while 21 percent were male, with words like "Mom" and "Wife" being prominent in many of the bios of these DIY food experts (Joyce 2017).

Clearly there are some complex transitions occurring around gendered labor practices in the food space. However, there continues to be a tendency to associate unpaid, domestic labor, i.e., food purchasing and preparation in the home with "women's work" while the realm of privatized food preparation still tends to be a space of relatively invisible labor. For instance, while the internet is enabling home cooking to gain more visibility, much of the work that goes into buying and preparing food is glossed over. In Instagram feeds and even in the majority of YouTube videos we do not see the actual labor that has gone into producing the food and meals on display in the digital realm where, as on most cookery shows on television, food appears magically in kitchens that get cleaned up, again in a magical fashion. As Kylie Jarrett argues, while women and men's different laboring practices may no longer be easily mapped on to binaries of public/domestic (if they ever were), the term women's work continues to be useful, then, for characterizing "the social, reproductive work typically differentiated from productive economics of the industrial workplace. Such work is often associated with unpaid domestic labor" (Jarrett 2014: 16). Similarly, like food provisioning and preparation, traditionally, much of the caring work associated with the housewife or homemaker more broadly has been largely seen as falling outside of "the market" while being devalued by male culture (Belk 2010: 717). As Ticona and colleagues argue, in their study of ride-hailing and domestic care apps in New York, even paid forms of work in the home such as nannying, cleaning, and baby-sitting have tended to be marginal.

> Domestic work—comprising in-home care and cleaning services—is a paradigmatic example of "invisible" work, typically performed off-the-books with little documentation of work agreements. Historically, domestic workers have faced formal exclusion from many federal workplace protections and have been subject to contingent and informal employment relationships that take place behind the closed doors of clients' homes (Ticona et al. 2018: 5).

In post-industrial economies around the world however we have started to see some complex shifts around the world of work in relation to domestic versus so-called public work places. The formal public world of work, for instance, has become increasingly "feminised"—marked by a focus on flexibility, part time and gig-based forms of labour, as well as an emphasis on emotional work and relationship building (Healy et al. 2017; Hochschild 1983; Rubery 2015). At the same time the home is increasingly becoming a site of paid or partially paid labor—whether via "traditional" employees being increasingly encouraged to work from home (offsetting infrastructure costs) or via the growing home-based labor economy enabled by digital platforms and apps, which includes the kind of very low-paid, informal outsourcing of home cookery (discussed above) being offered by households in Northern Chile (Flanagan 2019; Folmer and Kloosterman 2017; Unni 2001).

The rise of meal sharing and home-restaurants apps, then, exemplifies a broader shift toward forms of "home work" becoming to a certain extent more visible, public, and increasingly monetized (even if not always as part of the mainstream economy). Aside from more traditional masculine areas such as delivery and ride-hailing, much of the outsourced labor offered through these apps extends upon traditionally feminized unpaid domestic practices in the spaces of the home, including child care, cooking and provisioning, cleaning, relationship management, and caring work more broadly. Tellingly, when Chileans' Gonz and his brother Victor started their sushi delivery business they listed it on Facebook as "Ana's sushi," using Gonz's wife's name reflecting (as Hayne's notes) the fact that these home-based food businesses are so closely associated with women's labor (Haynes 2016: 130). Similarly, as Japanese YouTuber Ami Nishimura (aka Ochikeron) puts it (see Figure 4.2): "Japanese home cooking is changing […] For my mom's generation, it was just housework. But now it is something creative and fun to do at home" (O'Donoghue 2018). Nishimura, who shares Japanese recipes on YouTube via her channel Create, Eat, Happy (which has 882,000 subscribers), has also monetized her creative engagements with what used to be counted as "just housework," putting out a Create, Eat, Happy cookery book.

The domestic cookery represented by Gonz and David's Facebook business and Ami Nishimura's YouTube channel points to the somewhat ambiguous status of the "work" represented in the digitized cooking realm, something we see reflected in the broader meal sharing and home-restaurant realm. While on the one hand a significant proportion of these apps are concerned with profit and with (at least partially) monetizing home cooking, on the other hand the

Figure 4.2 Ami Nishimura's Youtube channel "Ochikeron" has over 880,000 subscribers [Credit: Ami Nishimura]

role of cooking as paid labor within this business model is often ambiguous, with cooking framed as a practice of care and creativity as much as work.

Canadian food sharing platform LaPiat—which describes itself as "Everyone's Private Chef: Providing Healthy Gourmet Meals for a Fraction of Restaurant Prices" (www.lapiat.com)—is a classic case in point. In an article on the app (Deschamps 2018), LaPiat's founder explains the thinking behind the app.

> Creator Arber Puci said the app spawned from the idea that everyone has friends and family who are amazing cooks and can use that talent to make some extra money, while consumers will find it cheaper than restaurants, take-out joints or other food delivery services such as Uber Eats. The app targets home cooks like parents who are making lunch for their kids and can easily put together a few more portions to "make some cash on the side," said Puci, who will take a five per cent cut from chefs using the platform.

LaPiat's business model essentially relies on low-paid home-based cooks doing piecework, with no requirement for credentials. By contrast the website addresses its potential workers as "chefs," i.e., as professional food workers while the app's emphasis on "gourmet" meals implies it employs a battalion of high-end cooks. At the same time the LaPiat website suggests that its would-be "chefs" might engage with the app purely for the joy of cookery. As the web page headed "For Chefs" puts it, "If you love cooking and it brings you happiness, now you have a reason to do it more often! If you like the Chef life or just want everyone to try your delicious meals then LaPiat is for you."[3]

Domesticating the digital: From immaterial labor to the experience economy

The LaPiat app exemplifies many aspects of the emerging app-based meal sharing economy. While on the one hand the platform draws on the discourse of creativity and sharing associated with the larger digital foodie community, revaluing and reframing the labor of cooking for others as an act of creative caring ("Make some money doing what you love!"), on the other hand the labor model it encourages is one that also, in many ways, extends upon and reinforces the world of feminized labor and the home cook, a world where "flexibility, precarity, and largely unregulated working conditions have long been the norm" (Ticona et al. 2018: 17). As the "For Chefs" page on the LaPiat website puts it, "Be in control of your own schedule! You are in charge of food preparation and timing. Create your meals in whatever window of time you have available."[4]

As discussed in the introduction, what we are seeing here are some complex transitions (or "experiments" as Terranova puts it) in digital space around the gendered nature of work—marked by not only a reorganization and re-valuing of forms of work once associated largely with the feminized, domestic sphere but also a refiguring of forms of labor around digital practices, practices that have conventionally been associated with the public, masculine world of work. In this next section I want to touch on a range of shifting labor and social relations that are occurring around the digital sphere and that are exemplified by the emergent space of meal sharing apps. First, the revaluing and monetization of the informational, experiential, and emotional labor involved in digital content creation, practices that thoroughly blur the domestic–public divide. Secondly, the growing role of what has been termed "digital housekeeping" practices in the maintenance of the home as a digitally connected space. In this latter space, we are seeing something of a refiguring of the homework-based gender divide with both men and women engaged in the various kinds of (again relatively invisible) labor involved in maintaining the digital home and the digital economy. As we will see, what is particularly interesting is the way that these practices complicate notions of immaterial versus material labor.

While the rise of meal sharing apps enables everyday domestic practices such as cooking family meals to be public-ized and often monetized, the digital sharing economy also requires users (both customers and hosts) to expend a significant amount of time and energy engaging with the apps and platforms themselves. On the majority of these apps chef-hosts are required to take and upload photos of their culinary creations and are often also expected to create appealing personal profiles in order to attract customers. As Ticona and colleagues note about the people using caring apps to obtain work, it is not enough to be a good reliable cleaner or childcarer to do well in this space; job seekers also need to possess a capacity to engage with the tacit cultural dimensions of the digital realm (Ticona et al. 2018). Aside from understanding the technical elements of apps or platforms they also need to know "how to navigate the unspoken cultural norms that shape activity on these platforms. These include transparency about one's private life, the appearance of a compelling employment history, and the ability to simultaneously present to diverse audiences" (Ticona et al. 2018: 26).

These apps also require workers to be constantly "on"—in terms of both technology access but also responsiveness (29). Likewise, customers find themselves unwittingly contributing forms of labor to sharing apps and platforms. For instance, as these apps rely on systems of trust and reputation rather than external modes of credentialism users must expend considerable effort building the preferences, ratings, and reviews processes integral to such apps.

One way of thinking about these developments is through the concept of "immaterial labour," a term developed in the 1990s by Italian sociologist and Marxist Maurizio Lazzarato to capture the ways in which late informational or post-industrialist capitalist economies generate value from people's everyday emotional and cognitive practices. Employed by a range of scholars including post-Marxist philosophers Antonio Negri and Michael Hardt the concept works to foreground the "widespread expansion of the informational and cultural content of commodities alongside a general increase in the informational aspects of production processes. This points to the expanding amount of value being generated from affect, communication, cognition, and the immaterial actions of workers and consumers in contemporary capitalism' (Jarrett 2014: 16).

Drawing on Lazzarato and the work of other Marxists from the Autonomist movement, in the digital space Tiziana Terranova developed the idea of "free labor" (2000) to capture the ways in which our everyday engagements with the digital realm, whether through the act of demonstrating one's dining preferences through apps or through producing food videos for YouTube, can provide a range of forms of value for commercial players.

Aside from the labor that users provide as they interact with and upload data online, another key area where the digital realm has converted user engagement into a resource is through the generation of *data*. As Lupton discusses in relation to digital food, "In the context of the digital data economy, digitised information about food and eating-related habits and practices are now accorded commercial, managerial, research, political and government as well as private value" (2018: 74).

Finally, another useful concept for thinking about the ways in which food-related practices and experiences, both offline and online, can become commodified is through the concept of the "experience economy" (Pine and Gilmore 1999; World Economic Forum 2016), a term used to capture a transition from consumers purely buying goods to a growing focus on participation and engagement. US writers Pine and Gilmore, who first coined the term in 1998, conveniently frame the shift to the experience economy in food terms, in particular using the analogy of the "evolution" of the birthday cake.

> As a vestige of the agrarian economy, mothers made birthday cakes from scratch, mixing farm commodities (flour, sugar, butter, and eggs) that together cost mere dimes. As the goods-based industrial economy advanced, moms paid a dollar or two to Betty Crocker for premixed ingredients. Later, when the service economy took hold, busy parents ordered cakes from the bakery or grocery store, which, at $10 or $15, cost ten times as much as the packaged ingredients. Now, in the time-starved 1990s, parents neither make the birthday cake nor even throw the party. Instead, they spend $100 or more to "outsource" the entire event to Chuck E. Cheese's, the Discovery Zone, the Mining Company, or some other business that stages a memorable event for the kids—and often throws in the cake for free.

Since the 1990s we've seen a further evolution in the experience economy with the rise of social media and app-enabled "experiences." On the one hand the birthday cake could now be cheaply outsourced to and delivered by a home chef who wants to earn some money on the side via a meal sharing app. However, as our opening example of Airbnb host Bjorn providing a "Taste of Norway" in his home, along with traditional song and stories, suggests, the digital realm has enabled a large range of non-professionals to offer various "food experiences." Today's app-enabled birthday party could (hypothetically at least) be hosted by a budding chef in a local park, emphasizing a more intimate and authentic experience than an event at a commercial venue.

Home is where the LAN is: From communications hub to nodes in a digital network

If the digital realm (and the conventionally rational and masculinist public sphere of work) is becoming domesticated and feminized in terms of the growing role of emotional labor, experiences and affect, the home itself has been increasingly colonized by digital labor practices. Despite the central role of "mobile" technologies in particular smartphones in many people's lives—with users engaging in digital practices while at work, commuting, during leisure time, and at home—research at least in the Global North has indicated the home is increasingly becoming "a communication hub." For instance, in the late 2000s Hjorthol and Gripsrud's (2009) data from a nationwide Norwegian sample of 2700 respondents with access to domestic internet indicated that people were conducting many ICT-based activities at home, from shopping online to playing games, to completing work tasks at one's own pace, searching the web for information and socializing via online chat groups (116).

More recent qualitative research at the Digital Ethnography Research Centre, drawing on research conducted over a three-year period with twelve Australian households in rural and urban locations, indicates that Australian households today—from suburban and urban to remote, low to high income, student to elderly—are similarly immersed in digital activities, often across a range of practices and devices (Pink et al. 2016; Lewis et al. 2017).[5] Whereas in the past people might have had a dedicated household desktop computer or laptop for family use, alongside the odd personal device, most households now take for granted the fact that their daily lives and household spaces are filled with a wide range of digital media technologies, often requiring considerable consumer expertise to use and adapt to their personal needs. Electronic devices have entered into every part of the household and now shape a broad range of practices from child care, food shopping and cooking, to news gathering and financial management. For instance, in the food space, many households now routinely use laptops and iPads in the kitchen to access recipes and "how-to" cookery videos, integrating these devices in unique ways into the ecology of the kitchen (see Figure 4.3).

The increasing concentration of information and communication technologies in the home has led to a number of studies looking at the sheer impact of domestic energy consumption as part of our overall energy and data demand. The growing popularity of apps and platforms such as meal sharing and food restaurant apps depends on an array of domestic infrastructural and

Figure 4.3 Digitally connected mobile devices are increasingly used in domestic kitchens [Credit: Andrew Glover].

energy needs, with the home not only functioning as a communications hub but as a significant energy-consuming hub as well, though there is of course a growing movement toward homes producing and storing their own energy (Parag and Sovacool 2016). The addition of a swathe of internet-connected and data processing technologies to UK homes, for instance, has resulted in computing and consumer electronics together consuming around 20 percent of non-heating-related electricity use (Morley et al. 2018: 128).

Households are also considerable users of data with a study by Cisco finding that consumers (including households, university populations, and internet cafes) account for 81 percent of internet traffic (Morley: 129). All of this is underpinned by significant shifts in household expectations around "normal" technology use and access, with home broadband being seen increasingly as a household "necessity" (Morley: 132). As the chapters in this book on the growing role of householders in content provision and information sharing on the internet indicate, beyond the presumption that all households should and will have high-speed continuous connectivity, is a growing set of normalized practices around household engagement with areas once primarily solely associated with the public sphere of broadcast media and news but which have evolved into a complex co-articulation of private–public practices. In this sense homes are moving from communication hubs to being highly productive nodes in a broader network—an ecology as it were—of digitally linked social relations, shared content, and information flows.

Aside from the major energy and ecological implications of what have become normalized expectations for many households, the other hidden dimension of turning homes into digital nodes is the considerable cognitive and material labor involved in maintaining such systems and infrastructure. We started this chapter discussing the ways in which much of the outsourced labor offered through profit-oriented meal sharing apps extend upon traditionally feminized unpaid domestic practices in the spaces of the home, including child care, cooking and provisioning, cleaning, relationship management, and caring work more broadly. The growing integration of digital devices and practices extends upon but also complicates the gendering of household labor.

Past research on the introduction of household technologies and in particular on the introduction of so-called labor-saving devices such as washing machines and vacuum cleaners have emphasized the ways in which these devices often increased women's work in the home. As Jenny Kennedy and colleagues (2017) argue in relation to the work and knowledge required to maintain the "networked" home, "Far from serving to realize the putative end of labour in the home, new technologies often require significant work" (410). Drawing on Tolmie and colleagues' use of the term "digital housekeeping," their study on the impact of high-speed broadband in Australian homes "found that digital housekeeping, like its traditional domestic counterpart, is not evenly distributed across both genders, but unlike traditional housekeeping, is more likely to be performed by men" (419).

In their research on the "smart home," Yolande Strengers and Larissa Nicholls (2017) likewise argue that the narrative of convenience associated with smart home marketing, much like the previous myth of convenience associated with labor-saving devices, "masks and legitimises opportunities to increase household labour and energy demand, through the promotion and circulation of new lifestyle expectations" (87). As they argue:

> Resonating with the industrial revolution of the home which aimed to save women time and labour but actually created "more work for mother", industry professionals in our study already point to the extra education, work and effort required to live in smart homes. Given that much of this labour involves tinkering with, programming or updating technology, it's possible that smart

home labour might be positioned as enjoyable DIY hobbies (possibly particularly for men), rather than typical household chores. However, if smart home devices continue to shift from novelties to necessities, it's also possible that "keeping the home running" will become an everyday chore, similar to washing the dishes or doing the laundry. Software updates, control rooms, product integration and customisation could be viewed as essential household labour if households increasingly rely on smart home technologies to perform everyday practices (92).

In summary, we see that the rise of a meal sharing economy reliant on digital technology speaks to a complex broader set of transitions occurring around the relations between the increasingly networked home, the digital sharing economy, and the digital-public sphere. What is particularly interesting about the space of digital food in relation to home-based labor practices is that we are seeing a set of practices associated symbolically with women's material labor being extended into the digital-economic sphere while, as I have noted, immaterial and material work practices in the digital realm, both in the so-called public sphere and in the home, is also often feminized, i.e., un or underpaid, precarious, and invisible. At the same time, the gendered nature of labor is to some extend being challenged on the ground with men (in some social and cultural contexts) starting to do more food-related labor in the home while, as work on digital housekeeping suggests, men (and women) are also engaging with domestic housework around the setting up and maintenance of digital infrastructures in the home.

However, while men may be increasingly involved in what might be seen as "digital DIY"—extending on earlier forms of domestic masculinity and forms of DIY in the home (Lewis 2008a)—it is important to recognize the key role of women involved in the outsourced home-based digital economy as workers who provide both material goods and services, and who also engage in a range of digital practices and content creation. The e-commerce website Etsy, for instance, is an important case in point as one of the most success online marketplaces for homemade goods including art, photography, furniture, food, and clothing. In a recent interview with seller growth manager at Etsy, Jennie Smith, she notes that Etsy sellers are predominantly female (about 94 percent) while many are parents with children at home (Thompson 2018), a statistic which is likely to reflect the labor force constituting the meal sharing and home-restaurant economy.

More research however is needed on the ways in which digital technological affordances are shaping how people are working in the home and vice versa. For instance, as discussed in chapter two, the YouTube success of Indian grandmother and cook Mastanamma relied in part on the skills and labor of various friends and family members including her grandson Karre Laxman, a graphic designer with a background in television. In Chile, the home-restaurant examples discussed above also involved shared family labor. Meanwhile, work on digital housekeeping is suggesting some interesting shifts around the gendering of elements of home infrastructure maintenance. While there may in part be class and cultural elements to these specific family-based digital domestic practices, they speak to the significant transitions we are seeing within the digital economy in relation to the role of the home and the family.

Meal sharing and the collaborative commons

> Shaking loose of the former wisdom that, "You are what you own" and converting to a new wisdom, "You are what you share," indicates that we just may be entering the postownership economy (Belk 2014: 1599).

While thus far we have discussed the rise of domestic and digital ecologies of meal sharing in terms of economics and labor, as per much of the foodie community on line, a large element of the digital meal sharing world is driven by non-profit concerns of connection, caring, and conviviality. The strain of communitarianism that runs through the digital food sharing economy is nicely summed up by the Hotrec (Europe's key hospitality organization) report on digital meal sharing. As the report puts it, "The platforms in question have managed to plant a familiar notion—food and conviviality—in something unfamiliar—a stranger's house—by using new technologies" (Hotrec 2018: 8). In an article on "the sharing economy as the commons of the 21st century," Karin Bradley and Daniel Pargman (2017) argue that there has been a tendency to conflate a range of phenomena underpinned by very different values under the umbrella of the sharing economy. Seeing this "economy" as a space where people share "under-utilised resources" with others, not necessarily for monetary gain, they suggest viewing these practices through a range of other non-economic lenses "such as sharing, reciprocity, bartering and gift-giving" (232).

In their report documenting the sharing economy in Melbourne, Kennedy and colleagues likewise discuss the significant social and communitarian dimensions of this movement which they describe as:

> an umbrella term used to describe various forms of exchange that range from renting and lending, to swapping, bartering, giving and sharing. It invites individuals, communities and organisations to forgo ownership in favour of access to resources or experiences shared between parties through a variety of

mechanisms. These sorts of exchanges are not new. However, digital media have provided the means to efficiently connect those requiring access to particular shared resources at a distribution and scale that is disrupting numerous sectors, and established patterns of ownership and exchange. Through the sharing economy, people rent rooms in private homes, loan locally available cars, source funds to commence projects, eat food prepared in other people's kitchens, circulate used objects, and learn from others, among other things (2017: 7).

In the digital meal sharing realm there are a growing number of platforms that, while potentially enabling monetary exchange, are also focused on community and relationship building and sharing more broadly. The South African Mapha Food Share app, for instance, represents a mixed set of social, community, and economic concerns. The Mapha Food Share website explains that users can either "post," "sell," "buy," or "share"—"Feeling charitable? Why not make your dish free"—while the "about us" statement emphasizes an ethos of sharing and community building. Similarly, in a media interview, one of the founders, Loyiso Vatsha describes the business model in terms of a mix of social justice and enterprise.

> Due to harsh economic times and increases in unemployment in South Africa, we decided to visit the sharing economy model to address issues around the sharing and distribution of food. When people get together it becomes beneficial for all parties. (Pasiya 2018)

Aside from providing economic opportunities at a time of scarcity, the app is designed to enable people to share their excess food with neighbors—with or without monetary exchange involved. As Vatsha puts it, "The platform can also be used for social responsibility, allowing people or establishments to share their food at no cost to the under privileged" (Pasiya 2018). On the other side of the world, a food-based social networking app called U Gotta Eat similarly offers a mix of enterprise with social and communitarian values. While Mapha focuses on South Africa's context of economic crisis, U Gotta Eat has a particular emphasis on health and well-being, social justice and reducing waste in an American context where "40% of food in the US goes to waste, yet 1 in 8 Americans face hunger."[6] Developed in Cleveland—a city characterized by significant inequality in terms of access to healthy food—by a couple (one of whom is a chef) U Gotta Eat is a business that has the laudable if ambitious aim of "eliminating food waste and hunger, while bringing communities together" (Pettaway 2017). Like Mapha people can share *or* buy within the network, which again has a community-building focus. Co-founder Tonya Kinlow claims that with the app:

Users will be able to plan meals with other families, and as a result, possibly release the burden and pressure of daily cooking in homes where caregivers have lots on their plates. For her, the app is more than just a food service, it's a movement (Pettaway 2017).

This mixed discourse of enterprise and service provision with the more politically and socially engaged language of "movement" and "social network" characterizes much of the digital meal sharing space. While one could see these claims to social responsibility as purely branding exercises—and as we have discussed, such apps can also promote low-paid and precarious labor practices—there is much more to meet the eye in the larger digital sharing food space than questions of economic exploitation and exchange value. For instance, influential US business scholar Russell Belk argues that much of the sharing and collaborative consumption practices occurring online are underpinned by "non-ownership models of utilizing consumer goods and services" with most people using sharing sites and apps (whether commercial or not) doing so without any expectation of or indeed interest in compensation (Belk 2014: 1596).

Indeed, Belk suggests we have greatly underestimated the role of sharing in general within social relationships, tending to view complex acts of collaborative consumption in terms of reductive models of exchange, a symptom he argues of both the hegemony of rationalist models of consumer behavior and a tendency to marginalize or ignore key non-economic social practices associated with "the interior world of the home rather than the exterior worlds of work and the market" (Belk 2010: 716), such as the routine sharing, caring, connective, and emotional activities that underpin family life. Similarly, as Jarrett notes while women's central role in the household and broader economy needs to be recognized as being part of processes of exchange, much of what women do is "about the freely given labor (a distinction usefully made by Andrejevic 2009), the gifts of affect, and personal and domestic maintenance that reflect, reproduce, and/or transgress the social order, but which are framed as merely economic inputs to their detriment" (Jarrett 2014: 18).

As Haynes comments about the Chilean families (discussed before) who use social media to share and sell meals to neighbors, the women who largely manage these home "businesses" do not necessarily see what they do as "work" but rather see themselves as "caretakers of the community" (Haynes 2016: 131). As she puts it, "While women often say that they enjoy administering these types of businesses, it is clear that they are not central to their self-understanding—despite the labour they put into these operations, they continue to report their occupations as homemaker or nonworking" (131).

For Belk (2010) then, a key way to understand sharing on the internet is as an extension of familial practices of "caring and sharing" but turned outwards and extending into the world of strangers.

Reading the profiles of the many cooks, hosts, and chefs offering their services on meal sharing apps and platforms, another key and related theme is connecting with and recognition by a larger critical food community. A host in Melbourne on the meal sharing platform www.mealsharing.com, for instance, describes his interest in participating in the "home cooking" community as follows:

> I am a Malaysian who migrated to Melbourne in 2013. During the day, I am an accountant and when I have spare time, I am a self-taught cook. I am practicing to enter "My Kitchen Rules". In my quest to practice, I make a lot of food that I am unable to finish and would love it if someone else would help me eat it and give me constructive feedback. You can also have bragging rights to tell anyone you met me and had a meal made by me once I win the show :) I look forward to having you at my table for a meal.[7]

Meanwhile, in New York, "pop-up dinner" host Zuhra Abdullahi, a chef specializing in Nigerian French Fusion cuisine describes her website XuhsWorld (which includes a blog, recipes, and menus for potential hosted dinners), as a "platform to build and spread northern Nigerian gastronomy" (www.xuhsworld. com/about1). Cooking for and sharing food with "others"—strangers united by a love of all things culinary—marks the way that the practices of meal sharing can be seen as what David Gauntlett describes in his book *Making Is Connecting* (2018) as "creative social acts" rather than purely forms of work (166). As Gauntlett argues, much of the exchange occurring via the internet is of a social rather than an economic nature. Of particular relevance for thinking about cooking and meal sharing, Gauntlett contends that processes and practices of "making" online exemplify Ivan Illich's concept of conviviality as "a meaningful kind of communication and engagement between people" who are enabled to live creative and autonomous lives (150).

Conclusion

In this chapter, I have used the emergent space of digital meal sharing to examine some of the ways in which the labor and social practices once associated with the largely invisible and feminized space of the home are beginning to enter into new relationships with, and in turn are reshaping, not only the world of work but also broader social and community relations, including the role of the household in civic society. Gender, work, and questions of value are central to this transition. On the one hand, we are seeing something of a shift in the gendering and revaluing of what was once relegated to the realm of "women's work," in terms of a recognition of the material and creative labor of cooking and of the emotional and expressive work associated with social reproduction and the maintenance of social bonds. At the same time, the digital sharing economy can also be seen to reproduce and extend upon some of the more problematic elements of feminized labor—precarious, underpaid, and unregulated. While new media platforms have enabled web users a tremendous degree of creativity and interactivity and of course the capacity to create and share content, the flipside of this is that digital engagement can be seen as providing a kind of incidental, free form of labor for commercial interests (Terranova 2000; van Dijck 2013) or "estranged free labour" as Mark Andrejevic (2013) puts it; i.e., creating forms of value that can be monetized but without direct recompense to users. As theorists like Fuchs argue, beyond narrow notions of work, the emotional and intellectual practices engaged in by online foodies, that is, the act of sharing and caring itself, can also be potentially converted into valuable affective or cognitive commodities that are exchanged between digital media companies and advertisers (Fuchs 2013).

Alongside these powerful economic and labor-based critiques, a range of scholars have instead foregrounded the participatory, connective, and collaborative dimensions and potential of digitized social relations. Theorists of sharing and collaborative consumption such as Belk, and those interested in creativity, "making" and connecting online, such as Gauntlett, are concerned with moving away from a focus on monetary and capital exchange to a recognition of a range of other systems of value at play in digital sharing spaces—civic, communitarian, convivial. Within this paradigm of connected conviviality, the space of domestic food preparation, serving and sharing meals with others, via the affordances of digital technology, is an exemplary space in which to think about new experiments in collectivized ways of living, caring, sharing, and working in otherwise privatized societies. As we have discussed in the book thus far, householders rather than commercial and/or professional players are providing much of the content available on and shared via the internet. They are also connecting with other households, communities, businesses, and other actors in ways that are arguably reframing the role of the domestic in relation to civic life, something I discuss further in the chapters on food politics online and on digitally enabled forms of ethical consumption.

While, as we have seen, much of the meal sharing economy works along a social enterprise model (mixing social justice, community support, and economic concerns but at a small scale and local economic level), for those keen to support digital collaborative sharing communities that are not exploitative and that prize and support the work of their users there are understandable concerns about the uberization of the digital economy. As Bradley and Pargman note, the movement toward a shared digital "commons" represents:

> A reaction against the global contemporary for-profit sharing economy platforms, which build on peer-to-peer production and sharing of resources, whilst the expansion of the platforms primarily benefit the corporate shareholders, and to little extent the millions of users who in fact "build" the content of the platform (Bradley and Pargman 2017: 245).

How do we ensure that non-profit-oriented or post-capitalist modes of sharing are able to flourish within online communities? How might we shift from focusing primarily on platform economies to also enabling forms of "platform cooperativism, where sharing platforms are turned into cooperative structures where the former platform 'users' also become owners and decision-makers and gain parts of their livelihood from the platform" (Bradley and Pargman 2017: 245). This means actively building and protecting spaces on the web that can hold their own alongside large-scale commercial players. Bradley and Pargman point to Wikipedia here as the obvious example of a large "for-benefit" centralized commons that has had mainstream success (2017: 245). As I discuss in the chapter on food politics and ethical consumption, there are many other examples of open source platforms that are enabling the civic and social dimensions of what we might term "sharing ecologies" rather than economies to challenge overly marketized forms of digital social relations.

Finally, crucial here is the need to ensure our informational infrastructures are not monopolized by global commercial players. As Berners-Lee (2007) concludes in his testimony before the United States House of Representatives Committee on Energy and Commerce Subcommittee on Telecommunications and the Internet Hearing on the "The Future of the World Wide Web," the importance of open information networks to democratic processes means:

> We ensure that both technological protocols and social conventions respect basic values. That the Web remains a universal platform: independent of any specific hardware device, software platform, language, culture, or disability. That the Web does not become controlled by a single company—or a single country. (8)

In Chapter 6 and the concluding chapter I discuss questions of food futures, platform cooperativism and data governance in more detail. The next chapter examines the rise of ethical consumption online.

Notes

1   https://www.airbnb.com.au/experiences/322725?source=p2¤tTab=experience_tab&searchId=d1a87d13-5573-4c9d-b746-49fcef4273d8&federatedSearchId=38b4b3 2b-e3c5-4320-9252-655654960bf5§ionId=41f075a7-f87a-4700-ac0b-cea2b10272aa

2   https://cafebazaar.ir/app/com.mamanpaz.chef.android/?l=en

3   lapiat.com/how-it-works-the-chefs-caterers.

4   Ibid.

5   This household study of digital media use in Australia conducted from 2014 to 2016 was led by Jo Tacchi and Tania Lewis and funded by KPMG and RMIT University. Along with the lead investigators, the following researchers were involved in data collection and/or analysis at various points in the study: Dr. Tripta Chandola, Dr. Victor Albert, Shae Hunter, Dr. Jacinthe Flore, and Dr. Jolynna Sinanan.

6   See www.ugottaeat.com/about-2/

7   https://www.mealsharing.com/users/thivya-m

5

The Shopping Complex: Food, Ethical Consumption and Apptivism

Introduction

When *Time* magazine named the top ten things that "broke the internet" in 2014, in between Kim Kardashian's butt on the cover of *Paper* magazine and the new iPhone 6 release was a Kickstarter for potato salad. As the story goes, when all round ordinary guy (and very ordinary cook), Zack "Danger" Brown got a craving for potato salad, he initiated a Kickstarter campaign to try and raise the $10 needed to purchase the ingredients, along with winning quips for pledgers such as "The internet loves potato salad! Let's show them that potato salad loves the internet!"[1] While the Kickstarter may have started as something of a prank, Brown (recent co-author of *The Peace, Love and Potato Salad Cookbook*, given free to pledgers) ended up raising US$55,000, going on to fund a free community festival called Potato Stock and raising money for and partnering with a local nonprofit organization in his state of Ohio to support charities fighting hunger and homelessness.

As a home cooking moment that turned into an act of food justice, the Potato Salad Kickstarter is a particularly generative example for thinking about the relationship between food, media, the digital, and the shifting nature of politics and activism today. How has the realm of domestic food purchasing, eating, and cooking—once privatized and largely feminized—become a site of what we might see as an everyday politics? What has shifted in the world of everyday citizenship that ordinary people with no particular expertise or background in food feel they can make an *intervention*, in this case into the realm of food justice? And how might we understand these kinds of acts or practices? Are they a form of politics or civic engagement? Or do they represent, as some have suggested about digital app-tivism, for instance, a market-driven emptying out of activism, i.e., a kind of digital politics-lite?

While one way to read Zack Brown's venture would be as a form of social enterprise—a profit-oriented initiative but one tied to social concerns—here I want to read it in a somewhat different way. I want to suggest we might also understand the potato-salad-as-food-justice example as a form of "ethical" or "responsible" consumption or what Juliet Schor (1999) has termed "the new politics of consumption" whereby everyday acts of purchasing, cooking, and consuming food, as well as goods, energy, and water more broadly, become tied to a sense of global responsibility. The ethical sensibility underpinning Zack Brown's sense of responsibility to his community is one that arguably is shaping the way people around the world, particularly in the Global North but also among the burgeoning middle classes of the South (Gregson and Ferdous 2015) are coming to understand their relationship to food and consumption. If going shopping for food or cooking dinner used to be seen as a fairly mundane act, this ethical turn means that once-ordinary practices such as purchasing eggs (caged or free range?) or chocolate (Fair Trade? Palm oil-free? organic?) or cooking up a large batch of food that one might potentially share with others, have become imbued with broader social and political significance. With the caveat that, as a number of critical commentators have pointed out, the (commonly middle class) ethical foodie engaging in these moral concerns and practices tends to be in a privileged position to do so through possessing certain forms of economic, cultural, and class capital (Bell and Hollows 2011; Littler 2011).

This shift within wealthy capitalist democracies toward seeing everyday household consumer choices or practices as being inseparable from once "distant" issues such as food insecurity, the welfare of so-called food animals, environmental impacts, and the treatment of food producers has been referred to by social theorist Anthony Giddens as the rise of "life politics" (1991). While politics is often purely associated with the public or civic realm, the concept of life or lifestyle politics refigures the private sphere—domestic and everyday life—as a site of politically inflected practices, while also invoking a kind of DIY ethic. In the process, everyday life becomes a site of potential experimentation around ways of living and being, consuming and producing, where the simple act of making an ordinary meal can be turned into a moment of larger social connection and an opportunity to make money for social causes.

There has been considerable critique of the rise of the "intimate" forms of everyday political engagement that we associate with the digital realm—for instance, modes of civic engagement such as online petitions launched by concerned parents calling for the banning of certain kinds of food additives in children's sweets have been seen as reducing political protest to a form of "clicktivism." American cultural theorist Lauren Berlant, in her work on intimate publics, talks rather scathingly of the way in which the center of political life has shifted toward the private sphere with citizenship increasingly seen as being "produced by personal acts and values" (1997: 5). This shift, for Berlant, constitutes "downsizing citizenship to a mode of voluntarism" (1997: 5). In contrast, Swedish political scientist Michele Micheletti—writing and researching from the social democratic setting of Scandinavia rather than the neoliberal United States—argues that political consumerism is in itself a form of civic engagement, with the many and varied ethical and political "choices" of individual consumer-citizens contributing en masse to what she sees as "individualized collective action" (2003).

Whether we view these developments in positive or negative terms, it is clear that the digital realm is a space in which a growing range of forms of participation that we might understand as political and ethical are taking place. As José van Dijck argues in *The Culture of Connectivity*, "Within less than a decade, a new infrastructure for online sociality and creativity has emerged, penetrating every fiber of culture today" (2013: 4) while shaping the landscape of civic and political engagement in a range of unforeseen and unpredictable ways. The participatory and interactive affordances of the digital realm, and in particular its ability to connect once distant actors, are arguably enabling a range of forms of ethical consumption and life (or lifestyle) politics around food to flourish. From crowdfunding platforms such as Kickstarter and apps that enable people to share and distribute excess food to shopping websites where consumers can tailor their purchases to particular political or personal concerns (choosing to tick the animal welfare box and food justice but not environmentalism for instance), the just-in-time, routine affordances of smartphones and domestic digital advices are creating an arena in which consumers are potentially able to convert their daily practices around food—from shopping, cooking, and eating—into forms of what might be understood as everyday individualized modes of "activism."

This chapter discusses the growing practice of ethical consumption online, examining the potential and limitations that this mode of lifestyle-led political consumerism might offer for the broader realm of food politics. Mapping the rise of the political or ethical consumer, I discuss the key role in recent years of mainstream media in the Global North, in particular documentaries and food television, in paving the way for the recognition of the consumer-citizen as an important social actor. My argument, then, is that the practices and politics of today's online food citizen—while articulated to contemporary issues and tied to particular digital affordances—can be seen to have a range of connections to, and ongoing links with, a broader process of media mainstreaming of ethical and political consumerism that has occurred over the past three decades. Within and through these various media framings, the ethical consumer has been constructed as an ethical actor in certain kinds of distinct ways. Food media often operates on the assumption that the provision of knowledge and transparency around food and its origins will somehow empower consumers (and potentially producers and corporates) in the Global North to behave ethically and "responsibly." As Elspeth Probyn has noted in her book *Eating the Ocean* (2016), this often translates to a fairly simplistic focus on eating locally, an ethical "mantra" that as she points out is an increasing impossibility in relation to seafood in a complexly globalized fishing industry. As we will see the ubiquity of digital technology in many people's daily lives has extended upon these media genealogies and added a further range of affordances to the arsenal of the ethical consumer. Apps and platforms, for instance, tend to shape certain kinds of engagements, including more recently enabling shoppers (and other actors) to potentially instantly trace complex pathways of provenance, processing, and production, i.e., the entire supply chain of any food or drink, via blockchain technologies (Pearson et al. 2019).

Indeed one of the main media tropes the chapter discusses is the investigative commodity chain approach or focus on food and traceability and supply chain transparency, which has informed a range of ethical consumption-oriented media, from film documentary, to television, to digital interactive fora. However, as I suggest, a key transition that characterizes the digital turn is from primarily *representing* problematic food practices and *informing* consumers— as per the consciousness raising approach of documentaries such as *Food Inc* (2008)—to a more *practice*-based approach, with "just in time" smartphone apps enabling shoppers in their local grocery store or supermarket to check barcoded information and, in a sense, *intervene* in the commodity chain process, deciding to purchase say that imported Fair Trade product rather than a possibly cheaper local alternative.

As I discuss, however, the smartphone-enabled act of consuming ethically (at least as defined by the consumer's concept of the ethical) can easily become a rather routinized habit where individual consumers "act" without necessarily having a broad critical awareness of the community of consumers, farmers, producers, and/or software designers that are linked to their act of digital engagement. The question of responsibility here is also limited to that of the private concerns of an individual citizen (often in the Global North) in the position to both access and afford to purchase food alternatives, a situation not available to those who live in so-called food deserts, a term often used in the context of the urban United States or United Kingdom regarding areas where one has limited access to relatively affordable and nutritious food (see Wagner et al. 2019, for instance, for a discussion of whether the food desert concept has applicability in the Global South).

In discussing the rise of various different media approaches to ethical consumption over the past three decades, then, my focus is limited primarily to Anglo-American and European contexts and in particular the UK which has been a major pioneer in this field, with a number of supermarkets embracing the ethical consumer movement. Political and ethical consumerism more recently has of course become a global development, though often articulated in distinct ways in local and national contexts. For instance, given China's large and growing urban middle class, there has been increasing interest in "green" and "ethical" consumer markets in the country. In recent years there has been growing media coverage and academic scholarship on consumer-citizen-led initiatives related to food, health, and environmentalism across South-East Asia from rooftop productive gardening in Hong Kong to China's "back-to-the-land" movement and the rise of permaculture in Malaysia (Choong 2014; Live Curiously Magazine 2014; Thompson 2014). However, how notions of green consumption, organic food, or indeed the consumer as citizen/civic actor are framed and understood in say China and Vietnam is often quite different from Anglo-American conceptions, values, and practices. For instance, Chinese consumers have distinctive concerns around risk, food safety, and personal health—including a growing interest in buying "safe" foreign food products—in the face of domestic pollution and a lack of trust in domestic corporate practices while there is a strong emphasis on the need for government (rather than consumers) to be policing and regulating food policy and corporate behavior (Huo 2016). Meanwhile, in Vietnam, the organic food sector targets a small cashed up urban middle class less concerned with "green consumption," environmentalism, and elongated food chains than with the food safety issues that shape a complex food environment impacted by "compressed modernity" (Figuié et al. 2019); in the face of significant food anxieties, well-heeled Vietnamese urbanites tend to eat organic for the well-being of themselves and their loved ones rather than for the good of the planet (Faltmann 2019).

My argument here, then, is that the rise in the twentieth century of an ethical consumer movement linked to personal agency and lifestyle practices has tended to be a development that is articulated in particular to Euro-American social, political, and cultural contexts. In particular, the naming of the ethical consumer as a political actor is arguably a product of a particular co-articulation of Global Northern late liberal democratic capitalism, increasingly privatized (and privileged) lifestyle-driven forms of "civil" society engagement, the growing visibility of the environmental, food (in)justice, animal rights, and health impact of agri-business and the role of key media and political brokers, from consumer organizations to celebrity chefs. This complex origin has led to a similarly complex evolution, with the digital landscape today exhibiting a wide range of spaces and platforms targeted at ethical consumers, many tied to business as usual but some speaking to the civic and connective potential of online engagement, paving the way for the discussion in the following chapter of digital food politics.

Mobilizing the ethical consumer: From *Time* to *Food Inc*

In 2009 the cover of *Time* magazine ran with the banner "The rise of the ethical consumer" and featured an article entitled "The Responsibility Revolution" reporting that, in their poll of 1003 Americans, "nearly 40% said they purchased a product in 2009 because they liked the social or political values of the company that produced it" (Stengle 2009: 24). The *Time* article arguably marked a watershed moment in the growing media visibility of the consumer as a political and ethical actor. From "guilt free" Fair Trade chocolate to palm oil-free products, ethical consumption was becoming an everyday concept (and market category), at least in wealthy capitalist nations around the world (Barnett et al. 2011; Crocker and Linden 1998; Harrison et al. 2005; Lewis and Potter 2011; Littler 2009; Shaw and Newholm 2002).

The founders of the UK *Ethical Consumer* magazine, Mary Rayner, Rob Harrison, and Sarah Irving argue that the early first wave of ethical consumerism started to emerge in a number of Western countries from the 1980s onward, a development they link to the ascendancy of global free market economics and the steady demise of government regulation of corporate activities. Consequently, they suggest, consumers began to become increasing drawn into the role of watchdog and regulator in relation to issues of animal welfare, environmental sustainability, and worker's and human rights. Despite this turn toward deregulation and privatization, in their study of ethical consumption in the UK Barnett and colleagues argue that it wasn't until mainstream media started to become interested in the consumer-citizen as a potentially newsworthy figure, from the late 1990s onward, that notions of ethical, responsible, and green consumerism began to gain broader traction in the public sphere (Barnett et al. 2005).

While Rayner and colleagues see the seeds of ethical consumption as being sown in a distinctly neoliberal moment, other more critical discourses, some Marxist inspired, also began to emerge at this time, particular in the documentary space. Here I want to discuss some of the various genres of critical media representation that emerged in the 2000s—from a growing ideological critique of overconsumption to an emphasis on the role of consumer-citizens as potential agents of transformation—that paved the way for the more recent mainstreaming of political consumption, and the rise of the online platforms and apps targeting the ethical consumer.

Over the past decade and a half, the media landscape has transformed significantly—particularly in the Global North—in relation to mainstream representations of issues around consumption and the connection between lifestyle, environmentalism, and the plight of workers and producers in the Global South. This period has seen the rise of numerous hard-hitting popular documentaries concerned with the impact and risks of capitalist modernity, particularly in relation to global warming (Lewis 2008b), including Al Gore's *An Inconvenient Truth* (2006) and Leonardo di Caprio's *The 11th Hour* (2007), the latter also marking the growing entry of celebrities into the global political arena (Goodman 2018).

Closely linked to and overlapping with these environmental critiques of modern living, a range of critical revelatory food commentaries with a critical focus on materialism and "affluenza" in wealthy developed nations have made their presence felt in the mainstream cultural and media landscape (De Graaf et al. 2005). These have ranged from media coverage of global anti-consumerist activism around corporate practices, particularly the targeting of major transnational food corporations such as McDonald's (from the 1997 documentary *McLibel*, to PETA's recent "McCruelty: I'm Hating It" campaign[2]) to popular cultural critiques of overconsumption, such as those offered up in high-profile US documentaries *Super Size Me* (2004), *Food Inc* (2008), and the more recent and much-discussed Australian production *That Sugar Film* (2014).

While both Gore's and di Caprio's offerings foregrounded the anthropogenic dimensions of climate change—*The 11th Hour*'s key evocative images are of a planet earth marked by a giant human footprint and sitting in a sea of garbage—they were also strongly pedagogical, emphasizing the role of consumers as potential change agents in the battle against modernity's excesses. On *Super Size Me*, and its more recent variation *That Sugar Film*, the consumer is positioned rather differently. The consuming, ingesting body, here, becomes a literal site of experimentation vis-à-vis the risks and excesses of consumer capitalism. Nevertheless, these diverse critiques all position the food citizen as a potentially political agent, whose engagement in embodied and material life practices and modes of consumption is key to transformation: as *The 11th Hour*'s byline says "This generation gets to completely change the world."

Alongside these broad media critiques of hyperconsumerist modes of modernity, we also began to see the emergence in the 2000s of a new genre of popular food documentary specifically aimed at the consumer-citizen in the Global North as a key player in questions of social justice and rights for third world producers. If the affluenza debate presented a moral and environmental critique of the impact of capitalist-fueled lifestyles in the Global North, a flurry of popular investigative documentaries such as the 2006 documentary *Black Gold* on coffee production and *The Dark Side of Chocolate* (2010) offered a highly critical view of the globalization of food commodity chains, revealing the uneven global conditions linking privileged consumers in the Global North to often-exploited producers in the South.

As Hughes and Reimer discussed in the introduction to their edited collection *Geographies of Commodity Chains* (2004), the increasing popular interest in the social lives of commodities went hand in hand with a growing academic literature on commodity chain analysis, particularly coming out of cultural and political geography. A range of approaches to mapping the commodity chain have emerged from the field. Classically a global commodity chain approach seeks—rather like the popular exposés of commodity production mentioned above—to reveal the hidden geographies masked within the social relations of contemporary consumption, reflecting a Marxist-inspired concern with commodity fetishism and with foregrounding processes of commodity production in the Global South (Lewis and Potter 2011). The political economy of the global agri-food industry, particularly in relation to meat production, is often seen as exemplary of this disconnect between consumers and the exploitative realities of production. As we will see, one of the perhaps paradoxical affordances of the internet for the food community has been the ability to *re*connect with food producers and to make visible some of the links in often convoluted food commodity chains.

While the academic focus of global commodity chain approaches has tended to be on production, with the role of the consumer and the retail dimension of the commodity processes often treated as relatively marginal matters, the broader mobilization and popularization of this Marxist-inspired critique put the consumer at center stage. Key here has been the role of organizations such as Fair Trade. A poster for the 2008 Fair Trade Fortnight, for instance, depicts three first world consumers respectively drinking coffee, eating pineapple, and purchasing a t-shirt against the backdrop of images of happy third world producers harvesting coffee beans and pineapples and picking cotton. The implications of this "connected consumption" are spelled out in the advert's anchoring text "Picking products with the Fair Trade Mark means farmers and workers in developing countries can improve their future [...] Make change happen, choose Fair Trade."

But if Fair Trade in the 2000s offered a rather positive take on the relationship between ethical consumers and distant producers—a kind of "caring at a distance"—many of the food-oriented pop docs emerging at this time were not so sanguine. The blurb for the 2006 documentary *Black Gold* on coffee production, for instance, reads: "As westerners revel in designer lattes and cappuccinos, impoverished Ethiopian coffee growers suffer the bitter taste of injustice." In a similar vein, the 2010 documentary *The Dark Side of Chocolate* offered a rather sensationalized "undercover investigation" of the cocoa industry a decade after it pledged to end the exploitation of child labor, finding evidence of the ongoing exploitation and slave trading of African children to harvest chocolate.

Through the genre of the investigatory popular documentary film, the 2000s emerged as a time when the production processes behind food goods like coffee and chocolate in particular were put under public scrutiny. And crucially where the links between the fetishized pleasures of consumers in the Global North and the pain and suffering of third world producers or, in the case of *The Dark Side of Chocolate*, the exploitation of child workers were revealed. The defetishization of commodities, here then, were placed side by side with questions of consumer responsibility and moral agency (Goodman 2004). The everyday shopping habits of food consumers were thus put under the spotlight with a consumer's actions in one part of the world being seen to be directly connected to the experience of producers and workers in distant other parts of the world, preempting as we will see, some of the forms of digital engagement that have sought to link consumers to producers, such as National Geographic's interactive food website "A five-step plan to feed the world" (Foley 2017).

Domesticating political consumption:
The ethical turn on food TV

Around the time of these blockbuster critical documentaries, we also started to see the emergence of shows on television in the 2000s, particularly in the space of reality, lifestyle, and social observational television, focused on people experimenting with new ways of consuming and living. If pop docs were concerned with documenting the risks of modern living, these shows often attempted to offer transformational "solutions," through for instance weight loss (*The Biggest Loser*) or radical changes in diet and lifestyle (*Honey We're Killing the Kids*).

This concern with lifestyle transformation manifested itself in a minor but significant subgenre of popular factual or reality shows that saw ordinary people swapping the pressures of modernity for alternate lifestyles or at least attempting to modify the ecological impact of their urban lives. New Zealand's award-winning show *Off the Radar*, for instance, documented the experiences of comedian Te Radar when he decided to "ditch the city and consumer luxuries in an experiment to see if he can live sustainably, for months on a remote patch of land west of Auckland"—learning to shoot and skin animals for instance. Similarly, in the UK lifestyle-oriented "back to nature" popular documentaries like the *River Cottage* series and *It's Not Easy Being Green*—the latter featuring a suburban family uprooting their comfortable middle-class lives to live sustainably on a farm—tapped into an interest in escaping the pressures of modernity through "downshifting" and adopting slow modes of living. Public television producers in Australia also briefly experimented in the 2000s with popular factual environmental programming, producing two reality-style household "eco-makover" shows, *Carbon Cops* and *Eco House Challenge* (Lewis 2008b), in which households underwent dramatic changes in their usual overconsuming lifestyles in order to become more environmentally friendly.

While this "eco" moment on TV in the Global North was short lived, it arguably marked a broader ideological "process of reframing the domestic and the personal as ethico-political sites, [where] the realm of consumption itself has become to a certain extend de-privatized" (Lewis 2008b: 238). Food documentaries and food television more broadly are—and continue to be— one of the key spaces in which domestic consumers are targeted around issues of food justice and insecurity, and the problematic practices of agri-business and the fast food industry (Bell et al. 2017; Lewis and Huber 2015; Phillipov 2016). Indeed, one of the main sites in recent years where questions around the politics and the ethics of the food we buy, eat, and cook on a daily basis became mainstreamed has been via food programming on television and in particular through the figure of the celebrity chef (Bell and Hollows 2011; Goodman et al. 2010; Lewis 2008a).

Much of food television has been softly persuasive on this front. For instance, the hugely popular genre of food tourism programming (*Anthony Bourdain: No Reservations, Rick Stein's Seafood Odyssey*) introduces us to culinary traditions, communities, and local products, while arguably quietly challenging "the massified, supermarketized world of industrial food" (Lewis 2008b: 232). One of the key media spaces where the food consumer has been targeted more aggressively is via social documentary formats or what David Bell and Joanne Hollows refer to as the "campaigning culinary documentary" (Bell et al. 2017), with UK Channel Four's Food Fight series—launched in 2008 with *Hugh's Chicken Run* followed by *Jamie's Fowl Dinners*—representing a major intervention in this space.

Here UK celebrity chefs Hugh Fearnley-Whittingstall and Jamie Oliver played a crucial role in giving heightened visibility to questions of food sourcing, animal welfare, sustainability, and subsequently health and obesity, seeking to recruit consumers, supermarkets, and government to the cause of ethically engaged food consumption and production. Both chefs joined figures like farmer-activist Joel Salatin (made famous by *Food Inc*) and food journalists Michael Pollan and Eric Sclosser as key media actors involved in transforming the politics and ethics of food into an ordinary everyday household issue, shifting from the epic global justice angle of Fair Trade-influenced pop docs to questions of household food consumption, and in turn, to issues of lifestyle, taste, and conceptions of the good life.

If chocolate, coffee, and the plight of third world producers were the focus of the first wave of ethical media, for celebrity chefs, chickens and eggs became a key initial ethical mantra in Channel Four's Food Fight series. In *Jamie's Fowl Dinners* a TV special made for Channel Four, which was aired in 2008, Oliver revealed various unpleasant truths about the chicken industry—including carbon monoxiding "unwanted" male chicks—in front of a visibly shocked "live" audience, which included not just consumers but also a mix of supermarket representatives, farmers, food activists, and government food regulators.[3] Oliver was later joined by a host of other celebrity and professional chefs, including Heston Blumenthal and Gordon Ramsay.

Channel Four's interventions into food politics include a series of 2011 specials on sustainable fishing (*Hugh's Fish Fight, Jamie's Fish Supper, Heston's Fishy Feast*, and *Gordon Ramsay: Shark Bait*). Like Oliver, Hugh Fearnley-

Whittingstall has put the genre of the "campaigning culinary documentary" to good political use. Leveraging his ethical credentials as a food/lifestyle activist-television personality, Hugh Fearnley-Whittingstall has also successfully made use of social media to encourage consumer engagement around ethical fishing practices. In 2010 for instance Fearnley-Whittingstall launched a Fish Fight campaign against the then European practice and policy of discarding up to 50 percent of dead edible fish found in fish catches (www.fishfight.net). Targeting consumers initially in the UK, the website depicts a number of supermarket dockets on hooks featuring the contact details and fish sourcing policies of the major UK supermarkets with the following call to arms:

> The power to protect our oceans is in your hands now, so make sure our supermarkets and our politicians hear your voice. Ask them a question, tell them what you think, and don't give up until they respond to you!

The fish fight campaign spread to other parts of Europe with celebrity chefs and other spokespeople using a mixture of online, TV, radio, and press and social media (for instance, an online tool allowing "Fish Fighters" everywhere to contact their local politicians in their native language) and three years later saw an EU vote against the practice and a change of policy.

Digital tools and platforms: Ethical shopping and apptivism

The important role of social media in the success of the Fish Fight campaign in terms of connecting consumers to politicians, supermarkets, and other social actors provides a useful segue from the space of broadcast television to the digital realm where a number of websites, tools, and technologies have proliferated in recent years which target the ethical consumer. If food documentaries have alerted consumers to the connection between their food practices, the environment and the lives of distant food producers, and celebrity chefs have brought this even closer to home with a focus on how consumers' everyday actions in the supermarket and kitchen might impact on local producers, supermarkets' sourcing policies and animal welfare, the digital realm would appear to take this to the next level. Offering the consumer-citizen a range of tools to customize their personal engagement with issues of responsible and ethical consumption, the digital realm can be seen as enabling a "life politics" that tailors consumption to people's specific lifestyle concerns and needs. In this sense digital ethical consumption takes us from the realm of food and political

Figure 5.1 Virgin mobile and OzHarvest's meal for a meal campaign [Credit: author screen shot].

literacy, i.e., a focus on consciousness raising to enabling *practices* of engagement. A key shift associated with the move to digital platforms for consumers, then, is the connection that everyday digital devices and platforms make with people's actual daily household routines and rhythms, whether when they are making food choices at the grocery store or market, or when they are sharing their food skills and knowledge with others.

For instance, a number of sites have emerged on the web which use interactive platforms and layered info-graphics to enable users to interact with and locate themselves within the larger politics of consumption—to link their experiences and practices to larger global or communal concerns. National Geographic's interactive food website "A five-step plan to feed the world" (Foley 2017) mentioned above, offers a re-visioning of the usual depiction of the elongated exploitative commodity chain associated with agri-business, reconnecting us with the "faces" of small farmers around the world whom the author sees as the new drivers of a green agricultural revolution. Like the pop doc format discussed earlier, the website locates the consumer within an epic, global food landscape but unlike the documentary format the user is free to navigate through the website's various narrative, info-graphic, and pictorial options, choosing to delve (or not) into details about how and where the world might increase its current crop yield for instance or to instead flick through pictures of mass meat production and deforestation. While the scope of this dynamic digital web-based story is global— "A Five Step Plan to Feed the World" it announces in a pull-down banner at the top of the site-it ends on a note of personal responsibility and a food future determined by consumer choice. "As we steer our grocery carts down the aisles of our supermarkets, the choices we make will help decide the future" (Foley 2017).

Similarly, ethical shopping websites like Follow the Things[4] make visible and materialize the politics of production behind the commodity chains or networks that bring us Israeli avocados grown on illegally seized Palestinian land or bananas grown by Nicaraguan workers who have sued Dole, one of the biggest food corporations in the world, for exposing them to a banned pesticide linked to severe health problems. As we see from the Follow the Things mission statement below, again they draw on a similar revelatory, conscious-raising discourse as the food documentaries discussed earlier.

> Who makes the things that we buy? Few of us know. They seem to be untouched by human hands. But news stories, documentary films and artworks showing the hidden ingredients in our coffee, t-shirts, phones and countless other commodities keep appearing. They often "expose" unpleasant working conditions to encourage more "ethical" consumer or corporate behaviour. followthethings. com is this work's "online store". Here you can find out who has followed what, why and how, the techniques they use to "grab" you, the discussions they provoke, the difference they can make, and how to follow things yourself (www. followthethings.com).

Effective as it is, some of the website's information is decidedly dated, illustrating the contrast between a static website with a relative lack of updates, which like the commodity chain-based food documentary, rapidly becomes dated, versus the more dynamic flows of information associated with say crowdsourced and peer-reviewed ethical consumption platforms and apps (Humphrey and Jordan 2018).

In an essay on the digital, political agency and coffee producers, Sarah Lyon (2018) highlights Goodman and colleagues' argument that Fair Trade has been a leading developer of online tools for building interactive connections between consumers and producer communities. As such, Fair Trade has come a long way from the kind of static advertising linking first world consumers to third world producers discussed earlier in this chapter.

> Fair Trade consumers can now use the Internet to research coffee producer organizations in-depth, learning their unique histories and details about local culture. It is usually possible to identify how long an organization has been Fair

Trade certified, other certifications they may have, and the importers who work as intermediaries between producer organizations and coffee roasters. Frequently, specific information about contract negotiations and pricing information is also readily obtainable (Lyon 2018: 75).

All these informational approaches assume that the ethical consumer is a purely rational actor, whose acts of consumption are always planned and conscious (i.e., the habitual aspects of household consumption and the time pressures on householders are seldom taken into account), and who of course have the economic and cultural capital that make them willing to pay the extra cost of a Fair Trade purchase. Further, as Lyon argues, it is solely the consumer here who tends to be granted agency meaning that "this digital transparency remains largely one-sided and highly structured by the power inequities that shape the coffee market itself" (2018: 75).

Which brings us to the growing use of apps in the space of ethical consumption and lifestyle politics, or what has been termed more broadly "apptivism." If, as I have argued in the context of the contemporary globalized foodscape, there has been a growing public and media concern about the disconnection between consumers and the origins of their food, in response to these concerns we have seen a large range of food apps emerge over the past decade. Such apps seek to reconnect consumers to food and food producers through various means, whether enabling individual consumers to access information about the origins of a food product's ingredients or through linking consumers to a broader community of food citizens. Humphery and Jordan (2018) in their systematic research on mobile ethical consumption apps, argue there are three types on the market—the first are largely informational apps (such as The Good Shopping Guide and Shop Ethical!) while the second are apps that reply on barcode technology.

GoodGuide, still one of the more developed online ethical shopping guides, represents the second kind of app. Employing a team of researchers, it offers a range of technological quick fixes for ethical consumers on the go, including, as noted, a mobile phone app that allows you to use barcode technology to get just-in-time information about the environmental, health, and social impacts of companies and products. The mobile app also offers a personal filter option on commodities whereby you can tailor the guide's app to fit your own personal ethical concerns and lifestyle needs (i.e., you might tick the box for animal-cruelty-free products but not for products that minimize their impact on the environment and/or support labor rights), arguably reducing complex interconnected issues around the global ethics and politics of consumption to purely a question of personal taste.

If value-driven acts of consumption have become a new stage for enactments of civil society and political agency, then the just-in-time, connected affordances of personalized digital apps like GoodGuide it would seem are in the vanguard of the new politics of consumption. However, there are obvious limits to this kind of privatized, consumer-driven approach to "revolutionising" food practices. Many of these apps and websites offer a fairly banal ethical "shopping can save the world" message without necessarily challenging the foundations of commoditized food consumption itself.

As Humphery and Jordan point out, in their research on mobile ethical consumption apps, "a key political question to ask is to what extent a given technocultural terrain supports and facilitates the generation—through horizontality and openness—of a community of interest and/or activists" (2018: 524). As they note, rather than producing genuine forms of activism, there is a tendency in the space of apptivism to reify a kind of mobile privatization whereby the act of consuming ethically becomes somewhat mindlessly routinized and where individual consumers have little sense of the broader community of consumers, farmers, producers, and/or software designers that are linked to their act of digital engagement.

The third group of apps they discuss employ crowdsourcing technology, offering some capacity for the community to input to the information shared via apps and to also potentially connect with a network of activists. Examples they discuss include the Buycott app which enable users not only to join consumer campaigns but to also add different causes to the campaigns listed (again, like GoodGuide one can tick one's preferred causes such as animal rights and labor issues and scan products to check the ethical credentials of the brand) while a range of other apps depend on user input regarding products and store locations. These apps offer a very restrictive logic of engagement for users with "community" purely linked through acts of shopping and sharing product information. As Eli and colleagues (2016) in their study of the Buycott app argue:

> Despite the app's reliance on user-generated campaigns and crowd-sourced data, the forms of activism it enables are constrained by the app's binary construction of action as consumption or non-consumption and its ethos of "voting with your wallet". Consumers are thus imagined as wielding political power through retail products and in retail spaces, with action framed as an individual consumption decision, albeit in the context of corporatized campaigns (2016: 71).

Potentially more challenging are those apps that enable consumers to engage with food consumption practices and its impacts beyond the realm of shopping per se.

For instance, Australian website Spare Harvest is concerned with connecting local farmers, gardeners, and cooks around the world (the website has a global map where people can click onto local postings) who want to swap, sell, or share their excess harvest. While people sign up for free, businesses wanting to promote their excess produce pay an annual fee to reach their local community. As the founder puts it, "It's about making sure that all those valuable resources are constantly circulating in our community and don't end up in landfill" (Nichols 2017).

Similarly OLIO, an app created by Brit Tessa Cook and American Saasha Celestial-One, the daughter of "hippy entrepreneurs," is aimed at reducing food waste. Concerned with the huge amount of food that is thrown away by households and businesses on a daily basis in the Global North, the co-founders developed the apps to connect neighbors with each other and/or with local businesses to exchange any surplus food they might have, with app users able to share images of unused food with the OLIO community. OLIO uses can also become Food Waste Heroes, which involves collecting unsold food from local food businesses, bringing the food home, listing it on the OLIO app, and redistributing to their neighbors, who pick up the food. OLIO thus emphasizes a civic-minded digital engagement with a commercial edge where the act of sharing leftover food is framed as a potentially collective and transformative act ("a food sharing revolution") but with potential personal and business benefits. As they state on their website, "Our vision is for millions of hyper-local food sharing networks all around the world. We believe OLIO can help create a world in which nothing of value goes to waste, and every single person has enough to eat—without destroying our planet in the process".[5]

Connected consumption: Beyond ethical consumption as transaction

While not focused on ethical consumption per se, apps such as OLIO suggest the ways in which the digital realm is enabling food citizens not just to make connections between what they buy and how it impacts on various "others," but to locate themselves within a broader food ecology and economy, in this case the food consumption and production of local households and businesses. Furthermore, OLIO enables users to actively intervene in the process of

Figure 5.2 Facebook page of Alternative Food Group: Deep Winter Agrarians [Credit: author screen shot].

managing community food waste through redistributing food and to do so through connecting and acting with others. What OLIO is not concerned with is how food is produced and where it is sourced.

However, the digital space has seen the emergence of more critical uses of interactive platform technology that aim to connect ethically minded consumers to a range of actors and groups concerned with offering genuine alternatives to global agri-business. One key area here is the rise of digital food networks. While still a nascent area of research, critical scholarship has begun to emerge on the roles of digital platforms in shaping and enabling various virtual, networked alternatives to globalized food (Hearn et al. 2014). For instance, in an article on "the online spaces of alternative food networks in England," Elizabeth Bos and Luke Owen explore the way in which the digital realm offers opportunities for reconnection with the "complex systems of food provisioning" that have worked "to distance and disconnect consumers from the people and places involved in contemporary food production" (2016: 1). Studying eight alternative food networks and twenty-one online spaces, they examine the ways that consumers and producers alike are using digital means to reconnect with local and rural food production to build potential alternatives to global agri-business. As their research on online food hubs suggests, digital networks are as much about strengthening connections to place and the local, as they are about forging global links, and often involve a complex co-articulation of practices and connections between consumers and producers through both offline and online spaces and practices.

Another example of an ethical consumer-based network that has sought to forge a genuine participatory community is the Open Food Network (openfoodnetwork.org), an originally Australian (now global) online collective and software platform. The approach to the development of this marketplace software platform was informed by many previous activities worldwide, with particular influence from open source technology developed by US food hub the Oklahoma Food Coop (see Figure 5.3) and the networked approach of Local Dirt,[6] which is not open source. As Humphery and Jordan (2018) note, one of the very real limits with the predominant forms of purely click and swipe-based apptivism is the reliance on black-boxed technical systems in which users have very little say over design or informational input. While participatory platforms online once represented a relative opening up and democratization of media and communication systems, as we saw in the chapter on YouTube, today digital access and interactivity often comes with an invisible price tag.

Along with the alternative online food hubs foregrounded by Bos and Owens, developments like the Open Food Network take seriously the participatory promise of web 2.0 and attempt to provide open platforms that are built to embrace rather than exploit the knowledge and input of a range of parties including consumers. When Kirsten Larsen and Serenity Hill's Melbourne-based Eaterprises first starting building and trialing a digital platform with various food coops in Melbourne, they used crowdsourcing to develop their multi-user platform which links multiple players from consumers and farmers to various local food enterprises around Melbourne and Melbourne's extensive network of food collectives. This early set of trials eventually developed into the Open Food Network. Linking consumers, food hubs, and farmers to local

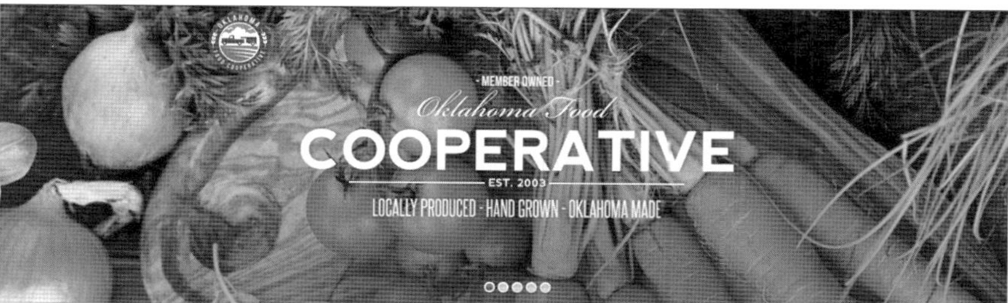

Figure 5.3 Homepage of the Oklahoma Food Cooperative's website, http://oklahomafood.coop/ [Credit: author screen shot].

food enterprises, the Open Food Network has been taken up as a model around the world.

While the Open Food Network, like the apps discussed above, leverages off the notion of the ethical consumer as an informed, change agent who can make a difference through their shopping choices, the focus here is on networking and connectivity at a much broader level, with consumer/users being invited to help build the open source platform itself. The consumer here, though, is not just a prosumer or consumer citizen but rather an actor articulated into a broader socio-technical and political model of connectivity. The networked space afforded here also involves a number of ethical players from community groups, to farmers, to households—and also importantly includes ethical software and technical systems. The kinds of "agency" promoted here, then, are plural and complex—with alternative household consumption tied to practices of participation in the construction of alternative foodways.

Conclusion: Ethical consumption 3.0

In this chapter, I have offered an overview of the role played by media in the past three decades in mainstreaming ethical consumption in the Global North, providing a broader context for understanding the more recent emergence of digital apps and platforms targeting the ethical consumer. We can see some clear links between the ways in which some of today's digital platforms address users as potential political consumers and the earlier media manifestations I've discussed in this chapter. For instance, one of the main media tropes or themes that I have highlighted is the investigative commodity chain approach, which as we have seen has traveled across media spaces, from film documentary, to television, to digital interactive fora. This particular approach shares a concern with *informing* the consumer, i.e., its revelatory, consciousness raising approach assumes that the savvy consumer will take their knowledge and act accordingly. While, as we have discussed, there are major limitations to this kind of privatized politics, a more interesting and critical development within the space of political consumerism has been the media's focus on *connecting* consumer-citizens with various "others," both human and non-human—the environment, producers, farmers, workers, material goods, both distant and local. Household food purchasing and eating practices can become potentially directly linked—via mobile apps and web platforms—to ethical brands, particular political consumer causes and/or to boycotting practices. As discussed, though, the black-boxed nature of many of these digital apps offer major limits for sharing critical concerns and for connecting with wider communities of activism.

Where digital affordances do offer the possibility of a more progressive politics is through enabling a broader engagement with political consumerism, where the commodity chain critique is in a sense put *into action* so that the various actors and processes along the chain are able to potentially connect and engage with one another. The Open Food Network, for instance, exemplifies an evolving digital space (and open socio-technical system) in which producers, consumers, retailers, and other community groups are able to come together to potentially build alternative food systems.

Examples such as the Open Food Network also point to the need to conceptualize notions of ethical consumption in a broader way, moving beyond purely the realm of shopping. If, as Wendell Berry puts it (2009) "eating is an agricultural act," then the act of consumption likewise is automatically a larger social and connected act—one that can never be private or privatized. Furthermore, ethical consumption as a broader "lifestyle" practice is often inextricably linked to a range of other life practices. As Witterhold and colleagues (2017) comment in their qualitative study of European political consumers, "though market-centric practices like product boycotts form an important part of political consumption" (102), their participants engaged in a wide range of activities that involved attempting to live differently, from growing and preserving their own food, to making their own furniture and, interestingly, also writing their own computer programs.

Which brings us to the key question we asked at the outset of this chapter: What might be the political potentials and limits of the digital realm for alternative food activism? One interesting shift that the sheer ubiquity of digital technology has offered the space of ethical and political consumption is that where broadcast and documentary media have tended to focused on *representing* concerns about the impact of consumer practices and on attempting to mobilize consumers as political actors through ideological, consciousness raising processes, the digital realm actually *enables* ethical consumer practices, whether through barcode technology that informs users of the origins of a product or through apps that enable users to share images and details of surplus food to share with others. Again, though these practices and the infrastructures that enable them are far from neutral; as we've seen, the market-driven, algorithmic logics underpinning many of these apps can present substantial limits to building alternative forms of food activism and food communities.

The emergence of open source alternatives to the kind of privatized apps discussed above, such as the Open Food Network, however, speak to a shifting and evolving space that is marked by a plurality of practices and forms of politics. As Mimi Sheller and John Urry argued more than a decade ago in an essay in *Theory, Cultural and Society* on the increasingly intertwined and hybridized nature of public and private life: "The new hybrids of private-in-public and public-in-private do not automatically imply a decline in politics or a collapse of democracy, but may instead point to a proliferation of multiple 'mobile' sites for potential democratization" (2003: 108).

In her discussion of the "McInformation" network[7] and the capacity of digital media to support the work of anti-capitalist food activists, Eva Girard (2018) argues we need to take a more open approach to the potential role of online technology. As she puts it, adopting a predetermined pessimistic or optimistic assumption about digital affordances "neglects the messiness of activists' material engagements with digital media, and all the frictions and unexpected manifestations of agency that go with it" (2018: 140). Instead, it seems we must assess the political potential of digital food activism through researching real-time case studies. As Girard asserts, "The participatory affordances of social media, for example, cannot be assessed through focusing on apparently rigid technical features, or by examining its setting in communicative capitalism. Instead, attention must be paid to how technologies are used and engaged with in practice, as opposed to in idealised ways" (141–142). In the next chapter we will examine a range of different case studies of digital food politics in action from anti-GMO activism via Facebook to Monsanto's engagement with social media. After Girard, my interest is with taking an "ecological" rather than a deterministic approach to digital technology. As we will see digital media, and its potential, can be seen as being articulated via a complex entanglement between a range of actors, where technological affordances are understood not in static terms but in relation to other media and users, and to broader contextual developments.

Notes

1   https://www.kickstarter.com/projects/zackdangerbrown/potato-salad

2   www.mccruelty.com

3   Oliver and Fearnley-Whittingstall's controversial efforts at the time to raise awareness about the conditions in which chickens are kept in the UK were linked to a significant growth in the numbers of free-range products available in British supermarkets as well as decreased consumer demand for factory-based products.

4   http://www.followthethings.com/grocery.shtml (accessed March 20, 2016).

5   https://olioex.com/about/our-impact/

6   Local Dirt is no longer in operation. See https://articles.extension.org/pages/33119/local-dirt:-beyond-marketing-find-buyers-sell-online-source-and-buy-productyourself-webinar

7   The McInformation network consists of volunteers from around the world who compile and share information about the McDonalds corporation, including having a focus on oppositional campaigns.

6

Doing Food Politics in a Digital Era

Introduction

What does it mean to *do* "food politics" today in a digital era? As Peter Dahlgren notes in his discussion of the emergence of the internet as a kind of public space, the online realm has seen the flourishing of a range of spaces and both new and emergent forms of practices we might understand as "civic" (2015: 24). Ordinary householders are now able to virtually connect with distant strangers who might share their concerns around GMO food or the need to support buying local rather than imported produce; to organize "buycotts" and petitions online against corporations who incorporate, say palm oil, in their products; and to protest against food injustice via a Facebook page. On the other hand, we have also seen countries using the internet for decidedly authoritarian ends while the potential for surveillance has become a major concern in what is often now referred to as a "post-privacy" era. Meanwhile, growing concerns around the corporate ownership and logics structuring web platforms have also raised questions about "the character of these civic spaces" (Dahlgren 2015: 26). The advertisements that regularly pop up in social media spaces such as Facebook while one is engaging with food activism online remind us of the compromised nature of our connectivity in commercially supported web spaces.

The previous chapter examined the rise of ethical and political consumerism online—from apps that use barcode technology to assess the ethical credentials of a food product to platforms connecting consumers with local farmers, aiming to bypass the elongated commodity chains of big agribusiness. As I discussed, in the context of a growing emphasis on personal and household practices of consumption and lifestyle as potential sites of political and ethical engagement with food (Goodman et al. 2010; Lewis and Potter 2011), the particular affordances offered up by digital technologies have begun to shape a whole new terrain of engagement and activism around food; not only for consumers but for an array of other actors, from chef-activists, farmers, and alternative food movements to powerful corporate food players (Bos and Owen 2016; Choi and Graham 2014; Peekhaus 2010; Pink and Lewis 2014: 698).

Moving on from the more personalized and individualized politics of apptivism that we discussed in the last chapter, in this chapter I am interested in what it means to engage in more collectivized modes of civic food politics through and within the realm of digital technology. How do we understand practices and processes of political collectivism in the context of internet platforms? How do the connective affordances of web 2.0 translate into forms of political action? How are concerns around political visibility and impact reframed in digital "civic" spaces that are often dependent on commercial infrastructures, with software codes and algorithms attuned to PR and market-oriented rather than deliberative communicative logics?

In this chapter, I discuss a range of examples of diverse digitally enabled civic or public modes of political engagement around food. Using these examples to touch upon some of the key themes and concerns facing food citizens, producers, and activists in a digital age, the chapter examines both the potential and limitations of what Bennett and Segerberg (2012) have called "connective action," and questions about the politics of visibility and transparency, in a post-WikiLeaks era. What do we mean by "transparency" in an era characterized by an increasingly complex politics of information and data management and access? How do we think about questions of visibility without addressing the systems of infrastructure and software logics that enable content distribution and connectivity? The first section of the chapter uses the example of an Australian household-based permaculture movement called Permablitz[1] to discuss the role of online platforms in organizing and scaling up the activities of households, and to critically reflect on what it means to engage in domestically located "civic" food politics in a digitally enabled context. The second section discusses what might be seen as more conventional forms of political engagement, such as organized protest via petitions and street marches but here enacted through online petitions and blogs and via social media. The third section then moves on to a discussion of the case of corporate engagement with social media, focusing in particular on Monsanto. Examining on the one hand Monsanto's use of social media as part of a supposed open dialogue with the community and on the other recent revelations regarding their less than savory behind-the-scenes digital tactics, the case study illustrates the complex and at times paradoxical nature of digital politics today. The conclusion discusses both the affordances and limits of connectivity and tropes of visibility and transparency within increasingly commercial web space, pointing to the growing need for alternative platforms, practices, and models of digital connectivity.

"It's a Village Out There": Digital transformations and household food politics

In the first section of this chapter I offer a discussion of Permablitz Melbourne, a group of volunteers, brought together through a website, who conduct makeovers in ordinary suburban gardens throughout Melbourne following the principles of permaculture, turning leisure-based backyards and gardens into productive sites of home-based agriculture.[2] My interest here is to frame such civic "experiments" in everyday living (Marres 2009)—activities that tend to gain minimal media coverage and little political recognition—as forms of digitally enabled civic activism, thus challenging conventional conceptions of citizen engagement and "heroic," protest-based models of political action. As the previous chapter foregrounded, increasingly much of what we might describe of as civic engagement today in the food sphere is played out in domestic spaces and through personal practices rather than in city squares and streets.

While countries like Australia rate poorly on global sustainability scales and in terms of federal policies on climate change mitigation and food security, a big-picture focus tells us little about what might be happening in towns, neighborhoods, and households. Some of the more progressive initiatives and policies on energy, greenhouse gas targets, and transport policy, for instance, have emerged at the level of cities and local councils, with cities like Melbourne and Vancouver vying for most livable eco-city status and both aiming, at least on paper, to drastically reduce emissions by 2020. Holden and Scerri point to the dramatic differences, however, between the two cities in terms of how they integrate various players and voices in building and imagining a sustainable future. Vancouver, they argue, exhibits much more success in terms of inviting "citizens to imagine and take action toward a sustainable city in a shared context, and to consider common and distributed responsibilities toward a lighter footprint" (Holden and Scerri 2013: 451).

While Melbourne's policymakers may take a "perfunctory" approach to engaging its citizens (Holden and Scerri 2013), this doesn't mean there is not an active citizenry when it comes to issues of food and sustainability. From community gardening and neighborhood food swaps to sustainability streets and food waste sharing initiatives, Melbourne features a rich diversity of initiatives, movements, and practices which can all be grouped under the umbrella of sustainable, civic food politics. While many of these practices are fairly public and visible, much of what I would argue constitutes forms of civic food activism and citizen engagement occurs at a more ad hoc, grassroots level with individuals and/or groups of friends or neighbors, for example, converting conventional suburban backyards into productive food spaces, and sharing skills and knowledges about building chicken sheds and managing backyard beehives.

My interest in this section, then, is in digitally enabled food initiatives that straddle the boundary between civic forms of engagement and more ordinary, everyday lifestyle practices, extending upon some of the practices discussed in the ethical consumption chapter, such as the Open Food Network. These forms of digitally enabled food citizenship can in part be seen as the product of growing cynicism regarding the level of political will toward environmental issues at a state and federal level (a common comment made by community members in my Australian-based research on grassroots green practices).[3] They also suggest the need to shift our conceptions of food activism and citizen engagement to embrace and recognize practices that are transformational and also embedded in household sites and routines.

A group of volunteers who conduct makeovers in ordinary suburban gardens following the principles of permaculture, Permablitz Melbourne is not so much a community in the conventional sense as a fluid network of people, connected primarily via a website. The Permablitz Melbourne case foregrounds in interesting ways how even the most strongly locally rooted forms of food activism have become co-articulated with the digital realm. Since the Melbourne network formed, Permablitz groups have emerged in Sydney, Adelaide, Alice Springs, Darwin, Canberra, Tasmania, the Sunshine Coast, California, Montreal, Istanbul, Jogjakarta, Bali, Uganda, and beyond. While Permablitz is now internationally connected via the global mobility of key knowledge brokers and trained Permaculturalists, with the movement made visible and linked internationally through a strong web presence, membership of the Permablitz community is also a very hands-on and localized affair, as an excerpt from my field notes from a permablitz I participated in suggests.

> I arrived somewhat late in the morning to the Sunday 'blitz', travelling to a part of northern Melbourne I hadn't visited before. Up above the Pentridge jail housing redevelopment into a tiny street just off the mixed industrial northern reaches of multicultural Sydney Rd. The tell-tale signs of a small suburban cul de sac chock a block with cars suggested something was going on behind the blank faced houses. Armed with a shovel, hat and sunscreen I followed a lanky stranger down the side drive of an ordinary brick house to find a good-sized group of people already at work weeding, hacking away at plants and thoughtfully inspecting the various spaces and 'projects' underway in the to my (inner urban) eyes rather huge quarter acre block. Cut to the end of the day and I and others, no longer strangers, are taking photos and videos of the transformation to post

on the Permablitz website. As our collective images will show, in one day with the aid of planning and the labour and skills of many bodies, a large neglected suburban backyard is on its way to turning into an integrated permaculture garden complete with chickens, an urban farm in the making.

My field notes foreground the at once household-based yet communitarian dimensions of this DIY food movement. "Blitzes" are disparate events (usually occurring over one day though with a longer lead time in terms of planning and preparation) that take place in people's backyards around suburban Melbourne. The participants, most of whom are strangers, are put in touch with the particular permablitz organizer in question through a website, often traveling long distances across town to help. While the core members of Permablitz are foundational to its identity as a movement and meet regularly, for the most part, digital technology is key to the formation and maintenance of this "community," as is increasingly common for many food movements and organizations today.

In the case of Permablitz Melbourne, as a collective of essentially like-minded strangers distributed across the city, many of whom may never actually meet, digital technology is pivotal to "connecting" members of the organization and more fundamentally to organizing the city-wide backyard blitzes that are integral to the movement. With no bricks and mortar "clubhouse," Permablitz Melbourne's "home" is essentially a website (www.permablitz.net) with members' back gardens representing ad hoc meeting places for conducting blitzes and holding workshops. During and around the time of the permablitz, the garden in question thus shifts from being a private place to a public and political space of sorts. It also becomes a resource for the permaculture and broader community in terms of being not only a site of potential food production (reflecting the ethos of the website's logo "eating the suburbs—one backyard at a time"), but also a space in which skills and expertise are shared with and passed on to other blitzers via the workshops and talks that are held on the day.

Photographs, and in some cases time release videos, of the transformational gardening process are posted to the website after each permablitz, serving as a way of documenting and publicizing these various backyard endeavors. These images also act as an advertisement to attract potential future blitzers, while also linking Permablitz Melbourne to other Australian and international communities and offering a guide on how to set up a regional Permablitz network.

The Permablitz community and its transformational practices are driven in the first instance by households and localized experts and intermediaries. The community such as it is is also given cohesion and visibility via digital platforms

Figures 6.1, 6.2, and 6.3 Before and after: suburban garden permablitz involving converting lawn into raised beds for growing vegetables [Credit: author photos].

and digital networks, making it a good example of how virtual connectivity can help dispersed groups of actors to engage in what Michele Micheletti refers to as "individualized collectivism" (Micheletti 2003).

Another key generative aspect of the connective action enacted through systems like the Open Food Network and Permablitz is the way it raises questions of *scale*. The development of localized and regional food systems has often been hampered by problems of scale, particularly how to collectivize efforts and scale-up while still adhering to social and environmental drivers. Here the connective affordances of web platforms have greatly bolstered the ability of distributed local systems to expand and collectivize. As I have argued elsewhere in relation to Permablitz Melbourne and the potentially transformative impact of other "local" sustainability enterprises:

> The cascading effects of seemingly small-scale initiatives, such as the role played by local and personal actions in the Arab spring, often in conjunction with networked media, have foregrounded the increasing insufficiency of macro and micro conceptions of scale in relation to theorizing political activism, engagement and transformation (Lewis 2015: 351).

Whether such groups and initiatives scale up or not via digital affordances, however, they represent significant forms of sustainable political engagement, challenging conceptions of personalized politics and lifestyle-driven citizenship as merely forms of armchair politics, or in the digital realm, clicktivism.

Food fights: From social media to the street

Permablitz, like the Open Food Network, are groups concerned primarily with changing food practices, with their use of technology being targeted mainly toward organizing and connecting dispersed stakeholders and actors. One of the potential limitations of such movements however is their relative lack of visibility outside of "alternative" food communities. The grassroots nature of these movements also raises the question as to what extent they challenge broader normative practices and/or potentially impact on food and environmental governance and policy development.

In this next section, I shift from the politics of lifestyle practices around food consumption and production, to discuss some examples of highly visible digitally enabled forms of political protest aimed at producing corporate and policy changes. Beyond the organizational affordances and connectivity enabled by digital platforms and illustrated in the case of Permablitz, the digital realm has seen a proliferation of forms of civic engagement that aim to challenge political and business interests, ironically often through commercially owned platforms such as Twitter and Facebook. Indeed, despite the constraints of social media, political communications theorist Zizi Papacharissi argues:

> These commercially public spaces may not render a public sphere, but they provide hybrid economies of space where individuals can engage in interaction that is civic, among other things. These spaces are essential in maintaining a politically active consciousness that may, when necessary, articulate a sizeable oppositional voice in response to concentrated ownership regulation (2010: 129).

Paradoxically then while the Googles of this world are increasingly monopolizing internet infrastructure and elements of content, the very same platforms they provide for connecting, interpolating, and knowing users *as consumers*, are the same spaces where participants are protesting against big business interest *as civic agents* albeit often as hybridized "consumer-citizens." As Papacharissi notes, in contrast to grassroots movements such as Permablitz, size and scale do often matter in the space of protest and political opposition. The very platforms that aim to capture large numbers of consumers also afford protesters and organizers with the capacity to communicate with and connect a large diversity of players (though often within local or national contexts, with the capacity to jump to other settings depending on key stakeholders).

The fact that so many people are now enmeshed in social media also enables another paradox; the capacity for anyone to take up and pursue a political cause and to potentially have that cause first, recognized by traditional media and other public organizations and secondly, "followed" by a large number of people, potentially mobilizing actors and organizations along the way. Likewise, while skeptical that the networked modes of engagement enabled by the digital realm offer "sustained political mobilization," Nick Couldry concedes that "the internet has made possible new kinds of legitimate political actors" (2015a: 40). As he puts it, in today's digital political realm it is "no longer just the party leader, or the journalist commentator, or the demonstrator in a crowd, but the individual—without any initial political authority—who can suddenly acquire status as a political actor online" (41).

A good example of this is the now-huge number of online petitions circulating in the digital media sphere, often headed up by the most unlikely of "political" brokers, from clued up teenagers to concerned parents. The power and potential impact of these petitions is that while they often represent a larger cause—from food waste to GMO issues—they do so via a specific personalized narrative, which can carry a significant emotional charge as well as authorizing the action via personal experiences with which others can empathize and connect. While the large majority of the petitions flowing through our social media feeds and email suffer the fate of so many social media memes, being ignored or relegated to email bins or spam, a significant number of them do attain some degree of sustained visibility, and political "mobilisation" to use Couldry's term.

In an article discussing ordinary people using social media "as a megaphone to pressure the food industry," the *New York Times* contends that while big food players will not necessarily admit to the power of social media for raising public concerns around food safety, the growing number of consumer "crusades" that have had some kind of impact on corporate practices, speaks to the enabling capacity of online engagement for the average citizen (Strom 2013).

Successful cases however tend to have had something of an online snow ball effect, picking up a range of supporters and stakeholders along the way, with more conventional authoritative figures (such as health specialists, doctors, and food scientists) and organizations in particular enabling online causes to gain a degree of stickiness and clout within mainstream media commentary. An interesting example of one such successful online food campaign, for instance, is one that was spearheaded by "mom on a mission," Renee Shutters, a quality engineering manager at a beverage container manufacturers in Jamestown, New York. Pursuing a long-term concern that her son's health was being affected by artificial food dyes used in sweets such as blue M&Ms, along with a host of testimonials, Shutters presented her case to the US Food and Drug Administration (FDA), who have been approached by a number of major health and science bodies over the years concerned with the potential detrimental health effects of food dyes, many of which have been banned in Europe. As the *New York Times* notes however Shutter's testimony to the FDA fell on deaf ears: "It wasn't until she went online, using a petition [in 2013] with the help of the Center for Science in the Public Interest, that her pleas to remove artificial dyes from food seemed to be heard" (Strom 2013).

In February 2016, Mars put out a press release announcing that they had decided to "remove all artificial colors from its human food products as part of a commitment to meet evolving consumer preferences" (Mars Incorporated 2016)[4], with Change.Org quickly claiming the decision as a consumer-led success: "After more than 200,000 people signed Renee's petition asking M&M's to stop using artificial dyes, Mars announced it was eliminating the dyes from all food products within 5 years" (Change.org 2016). While they also acknowledge the strategic role played by the Center for Science in the Public Interest (the petition has links to the CSPI and their website including scientific research on the health impacts of food dyes[5]), a long-standing independent, science-based consumer advocacy organization, they present the win as one for ordinary consumers. As they put it:

> The power behind Renee's story is the authenticity of her experience. Renee is a working parent from New York who loves her family and wants the best for them. She spends her time and money in ways she feels are best for her family. She's the real deal, and if Renee Shutters can rally 217,124 people around her single Change.org petition, imagine what food manufacturers must be thinking about the future of artificial dyes in their industry. The consumer-led movement is only going to grow (Change.org 2016).

Interestingly the paradoxical aspect to this is that Mars likewise present it as a "consumer issue"—"Our consumers are the boss and we hear them"—while at the same time playing down the science of food dyes (there is no mention in the press release of the Center for Science in the Public Interest or the input of the pediatric lobby[6]). As their press release states, "Artificial colors pose no known risks to human health or safety, but consumers today are calling on food manufacturers to use more natural ingredients in their products" (Mars Incorporated 2016).

While Change.Org uses this victory to celebrate the power of consumers to organize and connect with other consumers online in order to challenge the world's big food players, they also make the passing point that "consumer influence" is "very much a central part of their business model," paradoxically foregrounding the limitations of challenges that result in what one arguably might see as piecemeal approaches to changing the food system. Renee Shutter's intervention is framed (by both Mars and Change.Org) purely in terms of personal consumption issues, putting in the background larger structural questions, for instance, around the manufacture and marketing of sugar-laden foods aimed specifically at children (whether they have artificial or "natural" dyes in them or not).

In contrast to the personalized framing of the M&M food dye campaign, the next example of digitally networked food politics is that of a large collective nationwide protest that occurred via marches in twenty-two US states and forty-two Facebook pages. The example I want to discuss speaks closely to Lance Bennett and Alexandra Segerburg's (2012) argument regarding the shift from more conventional forms of "collective action" associated with coordinated, community-based organizing, often paired with campaigning via broadcast media, to the rise of distributed internet-enabled forms of "connective action" via disseminated practices and sites on social media.

In Lance Bennett's (1998) earlier work, he argued that the rise of identity politics from the 1960s onward saw a shift from a culture of civility to a more individualized mode of politics, and that this legacy has left us not so much with a sense of disengagement (as is often suggested in more conventional political accounts) but rather with the emergence of civics by other means. For instance, in contrast to the kinds of formal organized groups or practices traditionally associated with civic engagement, what we are seeing are "increases in various forms of lifestyle politics," linked to "networks" rather than fixed organizational structures and organized around specific issues and "lifestyle coalitions" (Bennett 1998: 745). Thus, while studies may show that much of the populace is increasingly cynical about the benefits of engaging with formal political processes such as voting, research also indicates an increased interest in broader political concerns, in participating with friends in political discussions and also in involvement in forms of "direct action" such as boycotts and demonstrations (Bennett 1998: 749). Cue the rise of digitally enabled, personalized politics.

Over a decade later, Bennett and Segerburg's (2012) argument regarding "the logic of connective action" emerges out of a context of a range of international protest movements organized via the peer-to-peer sharing logics of social media, from the Arab Spring, and the 2009 Iranian Green Movement, to the Spanish Indignados Movement and subsequently The Occupy movement, a dispersed global international movement against social and economic inequality mobilized around the slogan "We are the 99%" and the #Occupy hashtag format and organized through websites such as Occupy Together. In contrast to conventional protest politics, the post-Occupy political landscape is characterized by:

> Connective action networks [that] are typically far more individualized and technologically organized sets of processes [and] that result in action without the requirement of collective identity framing or the levels of organizational resources required to respond effectively to opportunities (Bennett and Segerburg 2012: 750).

As they argue, technology here is not just an "add on" to politics as usual but rather:

> What we observe in these networks are applications of communication technologies that contribute an organizational principle that is different from notions of collective action based on core assumptions about the role of resources, networks, and collective identity. We call this different structuring principle the logic of connective action. (760)

Ginevra Adamoli's research on the role of commercial social media for the progressive food movement in the United States offers some interesting insights into the complexity of connective action and food politics. Focusing in particular on the "Right to Know Rally" of 2011, she demonstrates the ways in which a long-running online grassroots campaign led to major high-impact offline protests in which activists demanded that the US government introduce genetically modified (GM) food labelling across the country (Adamoli 2012).

Initially launched by the Organic Consumers Association (OCA), an online, grassroots, non-profit organization concerned with "health, justice, and sustainability" a year prior to the street protests, the campaign—protesting the lack of GM food labeling regulations—was picked up by a range of diverse and dispersed social actors. These figures used a variety of online tools not only to communicate, organize, and plan the protests but also to continue anti-GMO activism via social media after the offline protests were over, thus addressing the concerns expressed by scholars such as Couldry concerning the sustainability of digitally enabled social media-based political engagement. Adamoli's research shows the way in which new kinds of leaders and influencers—similar to popular ordinary champions such as Renee Shutters—can emerge as significant actors via social media, people who from the privacy of their own home can engage politically and may not have previous experience in social movements.

It also illustrates the often-complex and shifting co-articulation of social mediatized networking with more conventional forms of political organization that constitutes contemporary political movements. For instance, while the Organic Consumers Association (OCA) set up the main page for the campaign that organized the march to the White House, a range of other players then created their own pages, drawing on and reworking the OCA's text as well as linking the broader movement to local concerns.

Adamoli's research indicates that while social media users were aware of the limitations of Facebook in terms of privacy and data monitoring, the platform had huge benefits in terms of enabling a wide range of actors and networks to organize collectively online, resulting in significant impacts offline including policy change (Adamoli 2012).[7] The success of the Right to Know Rally campaigns illustrates the enabling capacity of new media technologies for would-be activists (Pink and Lewis 2014: 698), offering those with a degree of social capital online, to connect cheaply and easily with a large range of others, in a way that is quick, efficient, decentralized, and flexible.

Complicating communication: Corporate food politics online

While web 2.0 has seen progressive food networks globally connect and scale-up via non-proprietary platforms, as Papacharissi points out, for most web users their main engagement with the digital realm is through "commercially public spaces" (2009: 242). As we have discussed throughout the book, the progressive affordances of the digital realm in terms of participatory capacity thus have to be viewed in the light of online space being increasingly dominated by corporately owned and managed infrastructures and platforms.

Alongside their ownership of platforms and funding of search and algorithmic processes, corporate players are significant and particularly powerful content providers. In the domain of food, the top global agricultural and fast food corporations are all major users of social media (Stevens et al. 2016), with many companies dedicating entire departments of staff and resources to managing their social media presence and strategies, while Facebook and increasingly Instagram draw a significant proportion of their revenue from online advertising (Johnson 2017).

Controversial agricultural corporation Monsanto, described by Bloomberg as America's "Third-Most-Hated Company" (Bennet 2014), for instance have invested heavily in a social media presence. In this last section of the chapter I want to use Monsanto (owned as of 2018 by German multinational pharmaceutical company Bayer) as a brief case study of social media-based corporate food engagement. I am interested here in the ways in which their activities—particular their online practices behind the scenes as it were—further contribute to and complicate our understanding of social media as a "civic" space. What does it mean to be "visible" online and to have a social media presence? Is corporate engagement in social media spaces purely an extension of long-running PR practices concerned with performing brand identity and (degrees of) social responsibility? While corporations are seen as particularly powerful actors online, what are the potential risks of engaging with new media in an age of WikiLeaks and data transparency?

Monsanto's former head of internet PR Jay Byrne—speaking to colleagues outside the corporation—once notoriously characterized the internet as "a weapon on the table. Either you pick it up or your competitor does, but somebody is going to get killed" (Peekhaus 2010). Monsanto's more recent social media-based tactics—at least those that the company has sought to make visible to the public—have been rather less aggressive. In recent years the company has actively attempted to position itself as a responsible corporate player engaged in a "rational" public dialogue around nutrition, sustainable population growth, and environmentalism (see Peekhaus 2010), using the heightened visibility and "spreadability" of social media to use Jenkins, Ford, and Green's term[8] to reframe public debate around biotech as a sustainability issue.

Rebranding itself via Twitter, for instance, using discourses of "sustainable development" and "biological conservation," Monsanto has sought to counter the attacks of anti-GMO activists through a "be part of the conversation" campaign in which members of the public are invited to ask questions about the company and its practices. On Monsanto's "The conversation" webpage we see images of various (apparent) members of the public along with thought bubbles containing questions and answers, positioning the company as an interlocutor in a larger public dialogue around nutrition, health and safety, population growth, and environmentalism (Peekhaus 2010). Meanwhile, the corporation has tried to personalize and humanize its image, with its executives attempting to present a friendly face of Monsanto through personal posts and tweets. For instance, as science writer for *Wired* magazine Sarah Zhang has noted (2016), while she declined to be included in a selfie with now-retired Monsanto Executive Vice President and Chief Technology Officer Robb Fraley, this did not stop him snapping and posting an image in her office on his Twitter account.

In their bid to influence public opinion and to polish up a thoroughly tarnished brand, Monsanto also hired a director of millennial engagement, Vance Crowe, himself a millennial, as well as cofounded a food fellowship for journalists. However, the global publicity given to Monsanto's abuses of social media's civic realm in the United States including gardener Dewayne Johnson's recent court case against Monsanto has framed the corporation's attempts to represent themselves as good online corporate citizens in a very different light indeed. More broadly, it has also foregrounded the gap between the performative, "frontstage" realm of commercial social media activity and practices "backstage" (to use Erving Goffman's terms from his seminal work *The Presentation of Self in Everyday Life* 1971). While of course there is nothing new about corporations operating behind the scenes—whether attempting to influence politicians and interest groups or pushing agendas through putting pressure on mainstream media—the Monsanto–Johnson case has paradoxically foregrounded the ways in which the digital realm on the one hand offers new affordances for corporate abuses of power but on the other hand can also leave corporations vulnerable, with once-discrete conversations held behind closed doors now "discoverable" via mobile texts and emails.

In making a systematic case against Monsanto, a significant aspect of the court proceedings was a reliance on these digital traces—particularly emails, but also PowerPoint documents, and mobile texts. As press coverage highlighted, Johnson's lawyers Baum Hedlund were able to show that, despite Monsanto's claims that they had seen no scientific evidence to link the glyphosate used in their trademark herbicide RoundUp to cancer, years of internal emails indicated the opposite was the case; that despite receiving research and expert warnings the company "spent decades hiding the cancer risks of its herbicide" (Levin 2018). On August 1, 2017, Baum Hedlund released dozens of Monsanto emails revealing how the company's employees had edited and drafted "scientific reviews" on glyphosate that were presented as "independent" (Baum Hedlund 2017a). On the firm's website, on which one can find (and share via social media) all of the court documents related to the trial, Baum Hedlund also states that the documents show Monsanto has been accused of employing "an army of internet trolls to post positive comments on websites and social media about Monsanto, its chemicals and GMOs, and downplay the potential safety risks surrounding the company's popular glyphosate herbicide" (Baum Hedlund 2017b).

Revealing that Monsanto had created a program called "Let Nothing Go," the documents show that Monsanto paid individuals who seemed to have no link to the company, for instance, to write positive Facebook posts and news articles on its behalf. A Ring of Fire article—a left-wing radio talk show syndicated throughout the United States and co-hosted by Robert F. Kennedy who is co-counsel on the Monsanto Roundup Cancer litigation—claimed:

> The program has become so prevalent that concerned citizens on social media have had to purposefully misspell the company's name to thwart the online trolls. One of the top comments on a Reddit discussion thread highlights the practice: "Everyone should spell Monsant0 with a zero, it allows rational discussion without the Monsant0 shills showing up." (Gay 2017)

The Monsanto–Johnson case is a fascinating one, pointing to the complex, convoluted, and at times paradoxical nature of the realm of digital politics today. Monsanto's cynical use of its "the conversation" website and its executives' engagement with Twitter as part of a supposed open dialogue with the community foregrounds what Couldry describes as the seductive "myth of natural collectivity" (2015b: 620) associated with social media. Here, communicative power asymmetries appear magically erased by the apparently flat networks that circulate the tweets of teenagers and those of global corporate CEOs. Behind the scenes, however, we see the reality of a new media landscape in which corporations seek to use their considerable political clout and resources to channel, control, and shape content and communication flows, as well—as we have discussed elsewhere—to surveil the connective engagement of digital participants and, in particular in Monsanto's case, critics.

In a heartening turnaround from the usual message of corporate hegemony in online space, Monsanto's manipulative online tactics became part of the ammunition central to the legal win against them, a win though that is hard to imagine without the coalition of powerful opponents, including figures like Kennedy, that shored up the Monsanto–Johnson case. It is also hard to imagine the case succeeding without social media and the role that is now played in the contemporary realm by the kind of "radical transparency" associated with WikiLeaks (Ioffe 2017).

From connectivity to transparency: Governing and decoding digital foodscapes

While I have presented the various case studies in this chapter as examples of a kind of digital civics, they clearly represent quite different kinds of engagement and practices, framed by a diversity of understandings of civic politics. As I suggested in the introduction, while digital food politics is a large shifting terrain there are certain key themes that recur in this space, in particular around questions of connectivity as well as concerns around visibility and transparency.

The first two sections of the chapter—on the online community of household-based backyard food producers that constitutes Permablitz, and the protest politics of online petitions and social media-enabled food movements—both foreground the way in which digital connectivity has become an important component of contemporary food politics and activism. The membership of Permablitz is shifting and fluid and is based around particular households using the website's networks to recruit and mobilize participants for garden transformations, i.e., there is a kind of organizational instrumentalism behind the need for digital connectivity (though there is also something of a persuasive political visual rhetoric to the webpage which pictures, via photos and videos, people in action transforming gardens into sites of urban food production).

The case of Renee Shutter's Change.Org petition against the use of food dyes in children's sweets sees the use of digital connectivity as a performative enactment of consumer power. While in reality Shutter's campaign relied on a range of influential organizational actors and lobby groups including the US Center for Science in the Public Interest, pediatric organizations, etc., and battles played out behind the scenes in courtrooms, Change.Org presented her success primarily as a win for "the consumer-led movement" and consumer collectivity.

Thirdly, the Right to Know campaign offers a rich example of Bennett and Segerburg's (2012) "logic of connective action" as a distributed internet-enabled form of "connective action" via decentralized and disseminated practices and sites on social media. While it involved conventional political organizations such as the Organic Consumers Association, an online, grassroots, non-profit organization that initially launched the campaign via Facebook, the collective force of the protest both online and offline was the outcome of a range of diverse and dispersed social actors. Social media here enabled people—from ordinary householders to GMO activists—to connect cheaply and easily and to mobilize others in local contexts and across the country, in a way that was efficient, decentralized, and flexible. Challenging assumptions that the impact of personalized digital civic actions does not necessarily produce longer term change, Adamoli's research (2012) evidenced the significant policy impact of the online campaigning as well as the sustainability of the online campaigning which continued after the offline protests occurred.

Which brings us to questions of visibility and transparency on the internet. A recurrent trope in food activism oriented toward consumers is a concern with making visible the origins and conditions of global food production, often through the provision of information via apps or interactive online platforms. Political engagement and empowerment is thus equated with informational transparency—that is, with the idea that by making visible some of the questionable production processes adopted by big food players consumers will then choose *not* to buy their products while corporations will be driven to change their practices in the face of such boycotts.

However, the case of Monsanto's strategic engagement with social media both front stage and back, points to the complexity of questions of visibility and transparency and who has and does not have access to "information," while highlighting the oxymoronic nature of terms like corporate social responsibility. As Arthur Mol argues, while the possession of environmental information, for example, in a digital era may enable some degree of democratization of systems of governance and control, the rise of what he terms "a new informational mode of environmental governance" also raises critical concerns about the potential for "new power constellations" (2006: 511) around information access and use. As we have seen, Monsanto's considerable resources have enabled it to engage in long-term and systematic campaigns of dis-information and trolling in the social media arena. While the Monsanto–Johnson case offers a welcome counter-hegemonic moment, with Baum Hedlund's release of dozens of Monsanto emails and many other communications and court documents via its website offering a kind of WikiLeaks moment for GM food, such rare wins only serve to emphasize what could arguably be seen as a growing power gap in the digital domain.

Similarly, whether celebrating the participatory potential of the internet or offering a radical critique of social media connectivity, digital media scholars across the critical spectrum agree that the digitization of everyday life through commercial apps and platforms embedded in an increasingly invisible algorithmic logic and culture point to the increasing need to understand and critically debate the social, cultural, and political economies of digital data processes and infrastructures. As critical technology gurus Arthur and Marilouise Kroker put it:

Technological society is no longer understandable simply in terms of the globalizing spectacle of electronic images but in the more invisible, pervasive, and embodied language of computer codes […] when codework becomes the culture within which we thrive, then we must become fully aware of the invisible apparatus that supports the order of communications within which we live (2013: 7).

In a digital age, food citizens increasingly need to develop critical media literacy as much as food literacy. Finally, more than this, the example of alternative food movements developing and sharing open source software and seeking to build alternative infrastructures for connectivity and sharing points to the pressing need for forms of large-scale development of what Trebor Scholz has termed "platform cooperativism" (2014), a concept I discuss further in my final chapter, Digital Food Futures. While platform cooperativism is offered up as a counterpoint to the labor exploitation of platform capitalism and the corporatist end of the sharing economy, as we have seen with examples such as the Open Food Network, it also represents a space for a collaborative peer-to-peer model of software development and information sharing. Rather than assuming then that digital food activists must necessarily "use the master's tools to dismantle the master's house" (to invert Audre Lorde's oft-quoted phrase (2007)), such developments point to the need to develop new tools and to build new spaces for digital engagement.

Notes

1   A term first invented in Melbourne, a permablitz is an event where a group of volunteers come together to transform a backyard into a food-producing garden drawing upon the principles of permaculture.

2   The idea of permaculture was developed in the mid-1970s by Australians Bill Mollison and David Holmgren as an alternative to industrialized forms of agriculture (Holmgren 2002; Mollison 1988; Mollison and Holmgren 1978). Conceived of as an ethical and holistic design system for sustainable living, land use and land repair, "permaculture has come to mean a design system for taking patterns and relationships observed in natural ecosystems into novel productive systems for meeting human needs" and has been embraced by individuals, groups and communities worldwide (www.permablitz.net/resources/our-principles).

3   While a significant proportion of the participants and groups in my research (from food swappers and gleaners to community gardeners) are actively involved in, and at times supported by local council initiatives, they are also often highly critical

of what they see as a lack of engagement by wider state and federal players in implementing progressive environmental policies.

4   https://www.mars.com/docs/default-source/Press-Releases/mars-incorporated-to-remove-all-artificial-colors-from-its-human-food-portfoliofd1ea65e0e2967c1ba01f f0f007138ba.pdf?sfvrsn=4

5   https://cspinet.org/eating-healthy/ingredients-concern/food-dyes

6   See pediatric website of Dr. Greene and associated blogs https://www.drgreene.com/perspectives/putting-kids-first-on-food-dyes/

7   As Adamoli (2012) notes, while mainstream media largely ignored the protests, this online-enabled activism had a significant policy impact, resulting in the reintroduction of three bills including the Genetically Engineered (GE) Food Right to Know Act, the GE Safety Act, and the GE Technology Farmer Protection Act.

8   Henry Jenkins and colleagues (2013) use the term to capture the way in which digital media's participatory culture enables content to be disseminated widely both through formal, informal and ad hoc networks and processes.

Digital Food Futures: From Smart Kitchens to Culinary Commons

I began this book by referencing the futuristic Jetsons-esque images that often accompany the notion of "digital food"—sci-fi, labor-free imaginings of three-course meals magically produced at the touch of a button. The discussion in much of this book, however, has been grounded in people's rather more messy and often labor-intensive (rather than labor-saving) everyday uses of digital media technologies in relation to eating, cooking, and provisioning. Similarly, the chapters on "ethical" apptivism and the politics of digital food have emphasized the fraught nature of digitally enabled life practices and politics at a time when our "public" media spheres have become dominated by commercial interests at the same time as we are seeing the growing colonization of digital space by "surveillance capitalism" (Zuboff 2019). Despite these complexities, much of the discussion of the potential role of the digital in relation to food futures circulating in media debates, marketing reports and, to a lesser but still significant extent, policy documents is underpinned by a kind of techno-optimism, where technology is seen as the solution to a range of issues. Complex global concerns around say food security and sustainability require similarly complex holistic social, economic, political, and cultural responses. Technology in such contexts can too often become not only a quick fix solution but a distraction from some of the key questions we should be asking about our global food systems.

In the arena of the household and digital food, for instance, a recurrent theme in public discourse is that of the "smart" technologized kitchen. As we have seen in this book, internet-based culinary culture owes much to the "ordinary expertise," and conviviality of home cooks and foodies, i.e, to the communities of users engaging in shared online food practices and discourse. Yet, rather than heralding and harnessing these communities of support, care, and advice, the discourse of the smart kitchen tends to be preoccupied with a world of high-tech appliances and connected devices. A typical scenario is offered by BBC reporter, Matthew Wall, where he tells us that "the kitchen of the future will be your

Figure 7.1 Visitor inspecting a Smart Fridge at the 2018 IFA consumer electronics and home appliances trade fair [Credit: Getty Images/Michele Tantussi/Stringer]

interactive friend, helping you cook, shop and eat with optimum hygiene and efficiency" (Wall 2013). Aside from the usual references to smart fridges (see Figure 7.1) and 3D food printers in the home, the article suggests that indeed most of our kitchen tools "are getting brainier." Discussing "intelligent gadgets" currently being proto-typed such as a fork that monitors how fast we eat (eating too quickly has been linked to obesity) and a Wi-Fi-enabled chopping board that can weigh ingredients, suggest recipes, and scale the quantities up or down according to the number of diners, the article predicts an internet of things-style kitchen where "it might not be too long before all our gadgets are talking wirelessly to each other as well" (Wall 2013).

While such digital dreaming may seem harmless enough, these techno-utopian images of the home largely frame our future in individualized, consumerist terms. In this context, digital technology is seen as enabling private individuals to take on responsibility for public or social concerns such as obesity, through using a "smart" fork, or to live more "sustainability" as a household by purchasing "green" energy-efficient gadgets. The focus on speed and efficiency underpinning the smart home is similarly reflected in much of the discourse of convenience associated with digital food—online grocery shopping, for instance, is seen as a key benefit of the digital food economy while digital profiteers ultimately dream of a world where (already precariously employed, low-paid) human food deliverers are replaced with drones.

This emphasis on hi-tech, automated living is not a new development but has links to longer term shifts in consumer culture. As social practice theorist Elizabeth Shove argues in her book *Comfort, Cleanliness and Convenience* (2003), today in many late consumer societies our everyday lives are organized socially and economically to support "convenient" yet highly carbon-intensive ways of living and consuming. Contemporary norms of ease and "quality" of living here translate into expectations around a high level of everyday bodily comfort (from air-conditioned and heated cars, homes and offices to constant access to and snacking on food items), cleanliness (from an expectation of daily showering to antiseptic hand washing and kitchen cleaning products), and a lifestyle of absolute convenience (from privatized transport to access to global, trans-seasonal foods). However, Shove points out that, despite the fact that these lifestyle practices have become accepted social norms in wealthy capitalist societies over the past few decades, there is nothing necessarily inevitable about these highly consumptive, fossil-fuel-driven practices. Indeed, for many people raised in the Global North they can look back just two or three decades to remember a time when social and technical regimes supported and naturalized quite different practices and assumptions around lifestyle and consumption, such as weekly bathing, sharing bath water, walking and cycling, drinking water out of a tap rather than a plastic bottle, minimal meat consumption due to cost, seasonal food access and choice.

Digital media use likewise tends to be embedded in and to naturalize and normalize a late modern, consumerist culture of convenience. However, as I've discussed in the book, there is a substantial price to pay for our everyday digital transactions. For instance, while "smart" kitchens, homes, and cities may offer a certain appeal in terms of an apparent efficiency and ease of living, as we've seen, the often, proprietary nature of digital media software and infrastructure means that people's everyday behaviors are increasingly commoditized and exchanged between digital media companies and advertisers (Fuchs 2013; Zuboff 2019). Thus, aside from the labor that users provide as they interact with and upload data online and through daily tech-enabled practices, another key area where the digital realm has converted audience engagement into a resource is through the generation of *data*. As Lupton discusses in relation to digital food, "digital data pertaining to people's everyday food practices and habits are increasingly being perceived by commercial and non-commercial players alike as having significant value" (2018: 74).

The big data economy—an economy marked by a growing IT investment in mapping and selling behavior trends and interactions through analyzing huge data sets (Zuboff 2019)—is a space in which theoretically anyone can play if they have the right tools. As my discussion of Monsanto highlighted though it is the large global commercial food corporations who are, alongside government, best placed in terms of resources, access, and sheer political and economic power to use large-scale data monitoring for their own purposes, foregrounding what Mark Andrejevic calls the "big data divide" (2014). As Stevens, Aarts, Termeer, and Dewulf note in an essay on social media and agro-food:

> The food and beverage industry is at the forefront of interactive marketing and new types of digital targeting and tracking techniques. Food retailers have taken over social media marketing companies to gain more data and enhance their marketing strategies (2016: 103).

Closely related to concerns over the commercialization of personal data is the rise of data monitoring and what has been more negatively termed "dataveillance," i.e., the use of digital forms of connectivity to monitor individuals and groups but also things and processes (Clarke 1998; van Dijck 2014). Yet it is not only corporations (and governments) who capitalize on such forms of surveillance and data monitoring. The traceability movement, with its focus on transparency, is similarly interested in following and tracking the movement of food commodities. Boosted by technologies like blockchain, traceability has been championed by corporates, farmers, NGOs, and ethical consumer groups alike but often for very different ends. Jaz Hee-jeong Choi and Mark Graham (2014) argue for the potential benefits to consumers that might arise from transparency around and access to food data. For instance, innovations like edible QR codes to tell customers where their dish has come from and apps that analyze photographs of food taken with the user's mobile phone to algorithmically identify its caloric content, "have provided novel and richer ways for consumers to understand food" (Choi and Graham 2014: 152). Food technology scholars have argued that the distributed ledger technology associated with for instance blockchain has the potential to transform our capacity to monitor each step along the food supply chain, helping to build trust and security into global food systems and pinpoint the origin of any food safety or trust-related issue (Pearson et al. 2019). Meanwhile, in the realm of agro-business, the rise of "smart" farming is seeing the use of geo-tagged animals, data-driven production techniques, and the use of drones to monitor crops and animals over large distances (Grindlay 2016; Logan 2017).

Terms like traceability, geo-tagging, data surveillance, and data tracing clearly embrace a wide range of applications and practices that cannot necessarily be understood in generic terms. Nevertheless, I would suggest that some of these practices share limitations around the discourses of visibility and transparency that tend to go with these practices. While at the surveillance end, data monitoring can entail a breach of rights to privacy, there is also a tendency to fetishize "data" and to reify notions of "visibility" in such systems, often forgetting that data and data systems are not "clean," transparent, or neutral but are designed and interpreted by humans in cultural and social contexts that may be characterized by exploitation and inequity. In the context of smart farming, data "visibility" is about the rationalization and efficiency of systems (and the maximization of profit)—with potential (though often short term) benefits in terms of food production and food "security"—but (in the case of livestock farming) often at the cost of environmental and ethical scrutiny and sustainable and equitable approaches to land management. Similarly, in relation to the food traceability movement, gleaning a large amount of "data" about where and how food moves through complex food systems doesn't necessarily challenge the foundations of those systems (for instance, the unsustainable global reliance on a primarily meat-based diet). Indeed it may merely shore up large-scale industrial agri-food models while giving a gloss of "trust" and "safety" to food production practices that have long-term health and environmental costs.

The question of environmental cost leads to another key but often ignored issue that is crucial for food activists, consumers, information technologists, supporters of e-democracy and corporates alike, i.e., the negative environmental consequences of a growing reliance on technology. In an article for the online media studies forum *Flow*, Richard Maxwell and Toby Miller ask whether e-waste is "'the elephant in media studies' living room?" (Maxwell and Miller 2008). Proceeding to list the major environmental problems associated with a growing reliance on digital technologies in everyday life, from the toxic pollution produced from today's electronic media, for instance the cadmium contained in mobile phones, and the growing impact of e-waste, much of which is exported to the Global South,[1] to the large amount of energy required both to produce digital technologies and associated infrastructure and to maintain and use said technologies, they conclude with the following call to arms:

> We urge media scholars to take up the challenge of media technology's impact
> on the environment: recycle and rethink the life cycle of media technology
> within its ecological context, from design to disposal (Maxwell and Miller 2008).

Likewise, for alternative food movements and environmental activists alike, it is important, as Sui and Rejeski put it, "not to treat the Internet as the Holy Grail for environmental salvation" (2002: 155). While there is an expanding critical literature on the environmental, resource, social and health implications of the growing reliance of environmental activists and conservationists on digital technology (Arts et al. 2015; Berkhout and Hertin 2004; Parikka 2015; Rudram et al. 2016), such debates can easily be pushed into the background by discourses of techno-optimism. An important task for food and sustainability activists engaging with digital technologies, then, is not only to address the costs and consequences of this, but to begin to imagine and design food futures that take the technological and infrastructural underpinnings of digital activism into account and that aim to develop more sustainable and equitable engagements with the digital realm.

As John Barry argues in his book *The Politics of Actually Existing Unsustainability* (2012) rather than assuming that certain kinds of technological "innovation" often based on growth models of economics, such as "smart" GM foods for instance are "necessary," we can think about alternative forms of "smart" lifestyles that start our transition to ecological futures with existing technologies, and that reduce our energy and resource demands on ecosystems and the planet through a focus on human well-being, low carbon resource use, and low socio-economic inequalities. Here the contributions of and growing work on the digital commons, on peer-to-peer cooperativism (Bauwens and Kostakis 2014; Bauwens et al. 2019; Scholz 2014) and emphasis on open source and non-proprietary approaches, or what Trebor Scholz has termed "platform cooperativism" (2014), suggest the possibility of a different digital future from one dominated by Facebook and YouTube, though again attention needs to be paid to how a digitally enabled commons might be built in an environmentally sustainable manner.

Drawing on nineteenth-century models of worker cooperativism, Scholz, for instance, argues that we can take back the collaborative platform economy from capital and repurpose it for the communal collective benefit. The suggestion here is that app-based "sharing" models such as those underpinning Uber Eats and Deliveroo do not have to be necessarily exploitative and profit driven but rather can be re-engineered for social democratic ends (Bauwens and Kostakis 2014; Scholz 2014). As Scholz contends, discussing platform cooperativism versus the sharing economy, and imagining "a humane alternative" to laissez faire capitalism:

There isn't just one, inevitable future of work. Let us apply the power of our technological imagination to practice forms of cooperation and collaboration. Worker–owned cooperatives could design their own apps-based platforms, fostering truly peer-to-peer ways of providing services and things, and speak truth to the new platform capitalists (Scholz 2014).

Alternative collaborative food platforms such as the Open Food Network (see Figure 7.2) discussed in Chapter 5 represent one example of cooperativism— where the labor of many adds value to the community in a very different way from proprietary platforms. As Bradley and Pargman argue in their work on the broader sharing economy, the rise of platform cooperativism offers a welcome and timely alternative to "for profit" platforms that seek to make money for shareholders from the freely given labour of and creative content provided by ordinary users (2017: 245).

Discussing a range of urban cooperatives including co-working spaces and reuse and recycling-based collectives, Bradley and Pargman note, after Bauwens, the need for "more general structures that can enable for-benefit collaborative economies to scale up and seriously compete with the mainstream market alternatives" (2017: 245). As they point out, in one of the key case studies they discuss in their article, Wikipedia is an exemplar of a peer-to-peer cooperative model that has successfully transitioned "from the margins to the mainstream" (245). The example points to the benefits—in terms of collectivized scale and

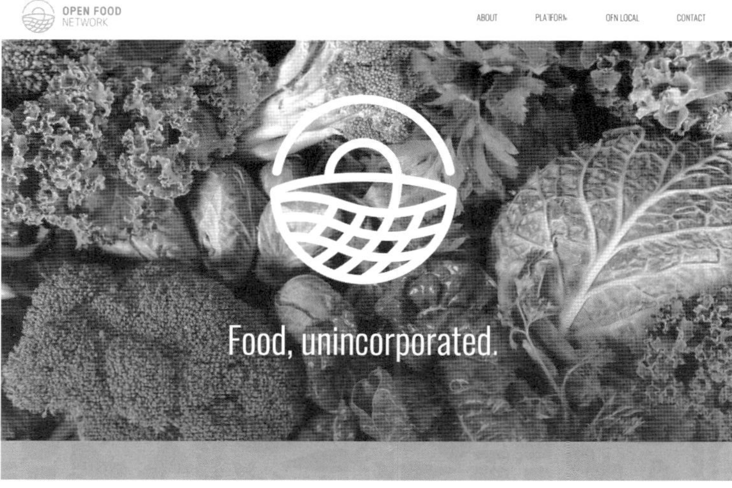

Figure 7.2 Homepage of the open source platform, Open Food Network [Credit: author screen shot].

scope—that digital tools and platforms, under certain conditions and shaped by a particular ethos, can enable.

Much scholarly attention has been paid to the amount of immaterial labor that we as individuals provide to the digital realm and the benefits that commercial players reap from this. In this book, we have also discussed the sheer material and creative labor—growing, provisioning, preparing, cooking, photographing, and videoing food—that shores up the thriving digital culinary realm. Discussing the limitations of digital immaterial labor argument, David Hesmondhaigh points out that we also "have to hold on to the value of work done for its own sake, or as 'gift' labour" (Hesmondhalgh 2010). This kind of labor, alongside the burgeoning open source and peer-to-peer movement, when collectivized offers major possibilities for contributing to and shaping a digital culture that is genuinely cooperative and transparent. As the chapters in this book on ethical consumption and food politics point to, there is a large amount of progressive and communitarian activity occurring around the world that draws on a commons-oriented ethos. What is required is a shift then from privatized approaches to a digital culture where users are viewed as owning their own data and labor and where collectivized cooperativist entities, beyond the monopolized platforms of social media, become the norm rather than the exception.

The considerable media debate and excitement about Internet 3.0 not just in IT circles but in more mainstream media and policy spaces suggests a positive way forward for digital food culture and for a digital commons more broadly. As Jutta Steiner—CEO of Parity Technologies and advocate for a decentralized web—comments in a piece on Internet 3.0 (perhaps somewhat ironically for business magazine *Forbes*), while not long ago it was hard to imagine a web that wasn't dominated by centralized corporate players, today "a new wave of networking technologies, also known as Web 3.0, promises to return the internet to the hands of users" (Steiner 2018). In the food space we are seeing new peer-to-peer platforms such as opencollective.com support a range of transparent and open source food communities and local food systems, while key foundational work on building a digital commons more broadly is being supported by global networks such as the P2P Foundation (p2pfoundation.net/) co-founded by Michel Bauwens and James Burke in 2005. This has occurred alongside the burgeoning of a large range of non-proprietary apps (such as the web browser Brave) that offer the possibility of shifting away from a dependence on commercial social media. Instead of futuristic visions of smart kitchens and privatized consumerist citizens, in a 3.0 scenario, future food imaginings would embrace more global and collective opportunities for sharing culinary knowledge, pleasure, and skills. As *Digital Food* has suggested, peer-to-peer-driven and -supported, wiki-style food platforms are not at all an unimaginable scenario in today's online culinary culture, a culture which is founded largely on the creative labors, passions, and concerns of ordinary householders like you and me.

Note

1   For instance, Caravanos and colleagues' (2014) investigation of the impact of toxic waste on disability-adjusted life-years (DALYs), such as Chromium VI in India, indicates a higher burden of disease expressed in DALYs than other public health threats.

Bibliography

Abbar S., Mejova Y. and Weber I. (2015) You tweet what you eat: Studying food consumption through Twitter. *Proceedings of the 33rd Annual ACM Conference on Human Factors in Computing Systems*. Seoul, Republic of Korea: ACM, 3197–3206.

Abraham A. (2018) Why China has banned videos of people whispering. Available at: https://www.theguardian.com/world/2018/jun/22/china-asmr-videos-ban-censorship-why-reasons-explained (accessed November 23, 2018).

Adamoli G. (2012) *Social media and social movements: A critical analysis of audience's use of Facebook to advocate food activism offline*. Dissertation: Florida State University, Florida. Available at: http://diginole.lib.fsu.edu/islandora/object/fsu%3A183217 (accessed May 20, 2016).

Ahmed N. (2014) Remembering the "home" through YouTube cooking videos: Sensory evocations, cultural negotiations and the diasporic kitchen. *Faculty of Arts and Sciences*. Peterborough, Ontario, Canada: Trent University.

Alleyne R. (2006) How I reduced Ramsay to a blubbering wreck. *The Telegraph*. Available at: https://www.telegraph.co.uk/news/1525100/How-I-reduced-Ramsay-to-a-blubbering-wreck.html (accessed January 28, 2019).

Altintas E. and Sullivan O. (2016) Fifty years of change updated: Cross-national gender convergence in housework. *Demographic Research* 35(16): 455–469.

Andersen J. (2015) Now you've got the shiveries: Affect, intimacy, and the ASMR whisper community. *Television & New Media* 16(8): 683–700.

Anderson M. (2013) At newspapers, photographers feel the brunt of job cuts. *Pew Research Centre*. Available at: https://www.pewresearch.org/fact-tank/2013/11/11/at-newspapers-photographers-feel-the-brunt-of-job-cuts/ (accessed May 2, 2019).

Andrejevic M. (2013) Estranged free labor. In: Schulz T. (ed.) *Digital Labor: The Internet as Playground and Factory*. New York: Routledge, 149–164.

Andrejevic M. (2014) The big data divide. *International Journal of Communications* 8: 1673–1689.

Arts K., Van der Wal R. and Adams W.M. (2015) Digital technology and the conservation of nature. *Ambio: A Journal of the Human Environment* 44(Suppl 4): 661–673.

Attwood F. (2005) Inside out: Men on the "home front." *Journal of Consumer Culture* 5(1): 87–107.

Banerjee J. (2017) Shoots, eats and leaves: The changing frames of food photography. *Forbes India*. Available at: http://www.forbesindia.com/article/recliner/shoots-eats-and-leaves-the-changing-frames-of-food-photography/46393/1 (accessed October 17, 2018).

Banet-Weiser S. (2012) *Authentic™: The Politics of Ambivalence in a Brand Culture*, New York: New York University Press.

Barnett C., Cloke P., Clarke N., et al. (2011) *Globalizing Responsibility: The Political Rationalities of Ethical Consumption*, Malden, MA: Wiley-Blackwell.

Barnett C., Clarke N., Cloke P. and Malpass A. (2005) The Political Ethics of Consumerism. *Consumer Policy Review* 15(2): 45–51.

Barry J. (2012) *The Politics of Actually Existing Unsustainability. Human Flourishing in a Climate-Changed, Carbon-Constrained World*, Oxford: Oxford University Press.

Baum Hedlund. (2017a) Internal Monsanto emails show company altered "independent" papers. *baumhedlundlaw.com*, September 11 Available at: https://www.baumhedlundlaw.com/internal-monsanto-emails-editing-science/ (accessed January 2, 2019).

Baum Hedlund. (2017b) Monsanto paid internet trolls to counter bad publicity. *baumhedlundlaw.com*. Available at: https://www.baumhedlundlaw.com/monsanto-paid-internet-trolls/ (accessed January 2, 2019).

Bauwens M. and Kostakis V. (2014) From the communism of capital to capital for the commons: Towards an open co-operativism. *Triple-C: Communication, Capitalism & Critique* 12(1): 356–361.

Bauwens M., Kostakis V. and Pazaitis A. (2019) *Peer to Peer: The Commons Manifesto*, London: University of Westminster Press.

Belk R. (2010) Sharing. *Journal of Consumer Research* 36(5): 715–734.

Belk R. (2014) You are what you can access: Sharing and collaborative consumption online. *Journal of Business Research* 67(8): 1595–1600.

Bell D. and Hollows J. (2005) *Ordinary Lifestyles: Popular Media, Consumption and Taste*, Maidenhead, England: Open University Press.

Bell D. and Hollows J. (2011) From river cottage to chicken run: Hugh Fearnley-Whittingstall and the class politics of ethical consumption. *Celebrity Studies* 2(2): 178–191.

Bell D., Hollows J. and Jones S. (2017) Campaigning culinary documentaries and the responsibilization of food crises. *Geoforum* 84: 179–187.

Bennet D. (2014) Inside Monsanto, America's third-most-hated company. *Bloomberg*. Available at: http://www.bloomberg.com/news/articles/2014-07-03/gmo-factory-monsantos-high-tech-plans-to-feed-the-world (accessed September 22, 2016).

Bennett W.L. (1998) The uncivic culture: Communication, identity, and the rise of lifestyle politics. *PS, Political Science and Politics* 31(4): 740–761.

Bennett W.L. and Segerberg A. (2012) The logic of connective action: Digital media and the personalization of contentious politics. *Information, Communication & Society* 15(5): 739–768.

Berkhout F. and Hertin J. (2004) De-materialising and re-materialising: Digital technologies and the environment. *Futures* 36(8): 903–920.

Berlant L.G. (1997) *The Queen of America Goes to Washington City: Essays on Sex and Citizenship*, Durham, NC: Duke University Press.

Berners-Lee (2007) Testimony of Sir Timothy Berners-Lee CSAIL Decentralized Information Group Massachusetts Institute of Technology before the United States House of representatives. *Committee on Energy and Commerce Subcommittee on*

Telecommunications and the Internet. Cambridge, MA: Massachusetts Institute of Technology, 1–9.

Berry W. (2009) Wendell Berry: The pleasures of eating. *Centre for Ecoliteracy*. Available at: https://www.ecoliteracy.org/article/wendell-berry-pleasures-eating (accessed January 28, 2018).

Beuscart J.-S., Cardon D., Pissard N., et al. (2009) Pourquoi partager mes photos de vacances avec des inconnus? *Réseaux* 154(2): 91–129.

Bos E. and Owen L. (2016) Virtual reconnection: The online spaces of alternative food networks in England. *Journal of Rural Studies* 45: 1–14.

Botsman R. and Rogers R. (2010) *What's Mine Is Yours: The Rise of Collaborative Consumption*, New York: HarperBusiness.

Bourdieu P. (1984) *Distinction: A Social Critique of the Judgement of Taste*, London: Routledge & Kegan Paul.

Bourdieu P., with Boltanski L., Castel R., et al. (1990) *Photography: A Middle-Brow Art*, Cambridge: Polity Press.

Bradley K. and Pargman D. (2017) The sharing economy as the commons of the 21st century. *Cambridge Journal of Regions, Economy and Society* 10(2): 231–247.

Burgess J. and Green J. (2018) *YouTube: Online Video and Participatory Culture [2nd Edition]*, Cambridge and Medford, MA: Polity Press.

Burgess J., Green J., Jenkins H., et al. (2009) *YouTube Online Video and Participatory Culture*, Cambridge: Polity Press.

Butler J. (1988) Performative acts and gender constitution: An essay in phenomenology and feminist theory. *Theatre Journal* 40(4): 519–531.

Byrnes P. and Sharma N. (2016) Nik Sharma painted by Patrick Byrnes. *Jarry*. Available at: http://www.jarrymag.com/niksharma/ (accessed January 28, 2019).

Campbell C. (1987) *The Romantic Ethic and the Spirit of Modern Consumerism*, Oxford: B. Blackwell.

Campbell C. (2005) The craft consumer: Culture, craft and consumption in a postmodern society. *Journal of Consumer Culture* 5(1): 23–42.

Caravanos J., Gutierrez L.H., Ericson B., et al. (2014) A comparison of burden of disease from toxic waste sites with other recognized public health threats in India, Indonesia and the Philippines. *Journal of Health and Pollution* 4(7): 2–13.

Carman A. (2018) Instagram now has 1 billion users worldwide. *The Verge*. Available at: https://www.theverge.com/2018/6/20/17484420/instagram-users-one-billion-count (accessed May 2, 2019).

Change.org. (2016) How passionate consumers are changing the food industry. *change. org*. Available at: https://www.change.org/l/us/how-passionate-consumers-are-changing-the-food-industry (accessed December 31, 2018).

Chayko M. (2016) *Superconnected: The Internet, Digital Media and Techno-Social Life*, Los Angeles, CA: Sage.

Chen C. (2017) "Let's hail a meal": China's Home Cook offers a sharing economy solution for the kitchen. *South China Morning Post*, April 4, 2017. Available at:

https://www.scmp.com/directories/article/2084737/lets-hail-meal-chinas-home-cook-offers-sharing-economy-solution-kitchen (accessed December 15 2018).

Choi, J. H., Foth, M., & Hearn, G. (eds). (2014). Eat, cook, grow: Mixing human-computer interactions with human-food interactions. Cambridge, MA: MIT Press.

Choi J.H. and Graham M. (2014) Urban food futures: ICTs and opportunities. *Futures: The Journal of Policy, Planning and Future Studies* 62(Part B): 151–154.

Choong M.Z. (2014) Duo turns bungalow's grounds into permaculture "classroom." Available at: http://www.thestar.com.my/News/Community/2014/08/22/Their-educational-garden-Duo-turn-bungalows-grounds-into-permaculture-classroom/ (accessed September 17, 2015).

Clarke R.A. (1988) Information technology and dataveillance. *Communications of the ACM* 31(5): 498–512.

Cooper D. (2012) Toshiba builds scanner that can identify fruit without a barcode, yup (video). *Engadget*. Available at: https://www.engadget.com/2012/03/08/toshiba-fruit-scanner/ (accessed October 25, 2018).

Cooper J. (2015) Cooking trends among millennials: Welcome to the digital kitchen. Available at: https://www.thinkwithgoogle.com/consumer-insights/cooking-trends-among-millennials/ (accessed November 29, 2018).

Couldry N. (2004) Theorising media as practice. *Social Semiotics* 14(2): 115–132.

Couldry N. (2015a) The social foundations of future digital politics. In: Coleman S. and Freelon D. (eds) *Handbook of Digital Politics*. Cheltenham, UK: Edward Elgar Publishing, 35–50.

Couldry N. (2015b) The myth of "us": Digital networks, political change and the production of collectivity. *Information, Communication & Society* 18(6): 608–626.

Couldry N. and Mejias U. (2019) *The Costs of Connection: How Data Is Colonizing Human Life and Appropriating It for Capitalism*, Stanford, CA: Stanford University Press.

Crabbe L. (2012) Photographing food? It's as easy as pie. *Macworld* 29(6): 76–77.

Crocker D.A. and Linden T. (1998) *Ethics of Consumption: The Good Life, Justice, and Global Stewardship*, Lanham, MD: Rowman & Littlefield.

Crowley C. (2018) The World's best cookbook is actually YouTube. Available at: https://www.saveur.com/best-youtube-cooking-channels (accessed November 23, 2018).

Cunningham S. and Craig D. (2017) Being "really real" on YouTube: Authenticity, community and brand culture in social media entertainment. *Media International Australia* 164(1): 71–81.

Cunningham S. and Craig D. (2019) *Social Media Entertainment: The New Intersection of Hollywood and Silicon Valley*, New York: New York University Press.

Dad With A Pan. (2019) Kitchen essentials *Dad With A Pan*. Available at: www.dadwithapan.com/kitchen-essentials (accessed January 28, 2019).

Dahlgren P. (2015) The internet as a civic space. In: Coleman S. and Freelon D. (eds) *Handbook of Digital Politics*. Cheltenham, UK: Edward Elgar Publishing, 17–34.

Danqi. (2014) What photos are most appealing to Weibo users? *China Internet Watch*. Available at: https://www.chinainternetwatch.com/7745/weibo-photos-marketing/ (accessed October 24, 2018).

de Graaf J., Wann.D, and Naylor T.H. (2005) *Affluenza: The All-consuming Epidemic [2nd edition]*. San Francisco, CA : Berkeley, CA: Berrett-Koehler.

de Solier I. (2013) *Food and the Self: Consumption, Production and Material Culture*, London: Bloomsbury Publishing.

de Solier I. (2018) Tasting the digital: New food media. In: LeBesco K. and Naccarato P. (eds) *The Bloomsbury Handbook of Food and Popular Culture*. London: Bloomsbury Academic, 54–65.

Delgado J., Johnsmeyer B. and Balanovskiy S. (2014) millennials eat up YouTube food videos. Available at: https://www.thinkwithgoogle.com/consumer-insights/ millennials-eat-up-youtube-food-videos/ (accessed November 29, 2018).

Deschamps T. (2018) A home cooked meal for cheap? There's an app for that, but critics are sceptical. *The Canadian Broadcasting Corporation*, March 14, 2018. Available at: https://www.cbc.ca/news/business/home-cooking-apps-1.4575533 (accessed December 15, 2018).

Donnar G. (2017) "Food porn" or intimate sociality: Committed celebrity and cultural performances of overeating in *meokbang. Celebrity Studies* 8(1): 122–127.

Dowling Z. (2017) How consumers watch and share videos. Available at: https:// www.ama.org/publications/eNewsletters/Marketing-News-Weekly/Pages/how-consumers-watch-share-videos.aspx (accessed November 23, 2018).

Dredge S. (2014) Vice aims to disrupt "dull, bland" TV cookery shows with Munchies channel. *The Guardian*. Available at: https://www.theguardian.com/ technology/2014/apr/07/vice-munchies-food-online-video-fremantlemedia (accessed January 28, 2019).

Duggan M. (2013) Photo and video sharing grow online. *Pew Research Centre*. Available at: http://www.pewinternet.org/2013/10/28/photo-and-video-sharing-grow-online/ (accessed November 19, 2017).

Duggan T. (2015) Mr. Wizard's food lab: J. Kenji López-Alt's unlikely path to stardom. *San Francisco Chronical*. Available at: https://www.sfchronicle.com/food/article/Mr-Wizard-s-Food-Lab-J-Kenji-L-pez-Alt-s-6493538.php (accessed January 26, 2019).

Durai A. (2018) Malaysian online cooking stars are on the rise. Available at: https:// www.star2.com/food/2018/08/01/malaysian-online-cooking-stars/ (accessed November 23, 2018).

Eli K., Dolan C., Schneider T., et al. (2016) Mobile activism, material imaginings, and the ethics of the edible: Framing political engagement through the Buycott app. *Geoforum* 74: 63–73.

Esquire. (2018) 10 Instagram accounts that will make you a better chef. *Esquire UK*. Available at: https://www.esquire.com/uk/food-drink/g15926144/best-recipe-instagram-accounts/ (accessed January 28, 2019).

Faltmann Nora K. (2019) Between food safety concerns and responsibilisation: Organic food consumption in Ho Chi Minh City. In: Ehlert J. and Faltmann N.K. (eds) *Food Anxiety in Globalising Vietnam*. Singapore: Palgrave Macmillan, 167–204.

Featherstone M. (1991) *Consumer Culture and Postmodernism*, London; Newbury Park, CA: Sage.

Figuié M., Moustier P., Bricas N., et al. (2019) Trust and food modernity in Vietnam. In: Ehlert J. and Faltmann N.K. (eds) *Food Anxiety in Globalising Vietnam*. Singapore: Palgrave Macmillan, 139–165.

First D. (2017) Instagram is ruining food, and I might be the only one who cares. *The Boston Globe*. Available at: https://www.bostonglobe.com/lifestyle/food-dining/2017/08/07/instagram-ruining-food-and-might-only-one-who-cares/GlZVsoSzmMKRpzrtenjfQN/story.html (accessed October 17, 2018).

Fischler C. (1979) Gastro-nomie et gastro-anomie. *Communications* 31(1): 189–210.

Flanagan F. (2019) Theorising the gig economy and home-based service work. *Journal of Industrial Relations* 61(1): 57–78. DOI: https://doi.org/10.1177/0022185618800518.

Foley J. (2017) A five-step plan to feed the world. *National Geographic: The Future of Food*. Available at: https://www.nationalgeographic.com/foodfeatures/feeding-9-billion/ (accessed December 28, 2018).

Folmer E. and Kloosterman R.C. (2017) Emerging intra-urban geographies of the cognitive-cultural economy: Evidence from residential neighbourhoods in Dutch cities. *Environment and Planning A* 49(4): 801–818.

Food&Wine. (2018) The best of stacked. Available at: https://www.foodandwine.com/fwx/slideshow/best-stacked#chicken-shawarma-sandwiches-garlic-sauce (accessed January 25, 2019).

Foster P. (2016) One in four over-65s use social media, after massive rise in "Instagrans." *The Telegraph*. Available at: https://www.telegraph.co.uk/news/2016/08/04/one-in-four-over-65s-use-social-media-after-massive-rise-in-inst/ (accessed October 17, 2018).

Frankel T. (2018) Why almost no one is making a living on YouTube. Available at: https://www.washingtonpost.com/news/the-switch/wp/2018/03/02/why-almost-no-one-is-making-a-living-on-youtube/?noredirect=on&utm_term=.33bc326b2d1d (accessed November 23, 2018).

Fraser N. (2016) Contradictions of capital and care. *New Left Review* 100 July–August: 99–117.

Fuchs C. (2013) Social media and capitalism. In: Olsson T. (ed.) *Producing the Internet: Critical Perspectives of Social Media*. Göteborg: Nordicom, 25–44.

Gallagher R. (2016) Eliciting euphoria online: The aesthetics of "ASMR" video culture. *Special Guest-Edited Issue: The Aesthetics of Online Videos* 40(2). DOI: http://dx.doi.org/10.3998/fc.13761232.0040.202. (accessed December 11, 2018).

Gander K. (2017) How review sites like Tripadvisor and Yelp can make chefs' lives miserable. *The Independent*. Available at: https://www.independent.co.uk/life-style/food-and-drink/chefs-tripadvisor-yelp-review-sites-restaurants-one-star-online-miserable-a7725541.html (accessed October 24, 2018).

Gauntlett D. (2018) *Making Is Connecting: The Social Power of Creativity, from Craft and Knitting to Digital Everything*, Cambridge: Polity Press.

Gay J. (2017) Monsanto hires internet trolls to cover up Roundup's cancer risk. *Eco Watch*. Available at: https://www.ecowatch.com/monsanto-hires-internet-trolls-2401703407.html (accessed January 2, 2019).

Geissler C. (2010) Pix or it didn't happen: Social networking, digital memory, and the future of biography. *The Book of MPub*. Available at: https://tkbr.publishing.sfu.ca/bookofmpub/2010/03/19/pix-or-it-didnt-happen-social-networking-digital-memory-and-the-future-of-biography-by-cynara-geissler/ (accessed November 12, 2018).

Gesenhues A. (2018) YouTube opens channel memberships to more creators & rolls out new revenue opportunities. Available at: https://marketingland.com/youtube-opens-channel-memberships-to-more-creators-rolls-out-new-revenue-opportunities-243013 (accessed November 23, 2018).

Gibson C. (2016) Is this video of George Hamilton eating fried chicken giving you a tingling feeling? Available at: https://www.washingtonpost.com/news/arts-and-entertainment/wp/2016/07/06/is-this-asmr-video-of-george-hamilton-eating-kfc-giving-you-a-tingling-feeling/?noredirect=on&utm_term=.70d5932c5259 (accessed November 23, 2018).

Giddens A. (1991) *Modernity and Self-Identity: Self and Society in the Late Modern Age*, Cambridge: Polity Press.

Giraud E. (2018) Displacement, "failure" and friction: Tactical interventions in the communication ecologies of anti-capitalist food activism. In: Schneider T., Eli K., Dolan C., et al. (eds) *Digital Food Activism*. London: Routledge.

Goffman E. (1971) *The Presentation of Self in Everyday Life*, Harmondsworth: Penguin.

Gómez Cruz E. (2016) Photo-genic assemblages: Photography as a connective interface. In: Cruz E.G. and Lehmuskallio A. (eds) *Digital Photography and Everyday Life Emperical Studies on Material Visual Practices*, London: Routledge, 228–242.

Gómez Cruz E. and Lehmuskallio A. (2016) *Digital Photography and Everyday Life*: Empirical Studies on Material Visual Practices, London: Routledge, 616–619

Gómez Cruz E. and Meyer E.T. (2012) Creation and control in the photographic process: iPhones and the emerging fifth moment of photography. *Photographies* 5(2): 203–221.

Goodman M. (2004) Reading fair trade: Political ecological imaginary and the moral economy of fair trade foods. *Political Geography* 23(7): 891–915.

Goodman M. (2018) Environmental celebrity. In: Castree N., Hulme M. and Proctor J. (eds) *The Companion to Environmental Studies*. London: Routledge, 616-619.

Goodman M.K., Maye D. and Holloway L. (2010) Ethical foodscapes?: Premises, promises, and possibilities. *Environment and Planning A* 42(8): 1782–1796.

Graham D. (2015) *The chef as an emotional and aesthetic labourer: an employee in transition*. PhD thesis, Sheffield Hallam University.

Gregson N. and Ferdous R. (2015) Making space for ethical consumption in the South. *Geoforum* 67(C): 244–255.

Grindlay, D. (2016) Victorian government mandates electronic ear tags for sheep and goats. *The Conversation*. Available at: http://www.abc.net.au/news/rural/2016-08-24/sheep-electronic-tags-lambs-wool-policy-victoria-biosecurity/7779328 (accessed April 26, 2017).

Gunthert A. (2014) The conversational image. *Études Photographiques* 31. Available at: https://journals.openedition.org/etudesphotographiques/3546?lang=en (accessed October 1, 2018).

Halawa M. and Parasecoli F. (2019) Eating and drinking in Global Brooklyn. Food, Culture & Society 22(4) : 387–406.

Harding J. (2018) Some restaurants are banning cell use at the tables. Available at: https://www.cbsnews.com/news/some-restaurants-banning-cell-use-at-table/ (accessed November 12, 2018).

Harrison R. (2014) Observing, collecting and governing "ourselves" and "others": Mass-observation's fieldwork agencements. *History and Anthropology* 25(2): 227–245.

Harrison R., Newholm T. and Shaw D. (2005) *The Ethical Consumer*, London: Sage.

Haynes N. (2016) *Social Media in Northern Chile*, London: UK: UCL Press.

Healy J., Nicholson D. and Pekarek A. (2017) Should we take the gig economy seriously? *Labour & Industry: A Journal of the Social and Economic Relations of Work* 27(3): 232–248.

Hearn G., Collie N., Lyle P., et al. (2014) Using communicative ecology theory to scope the emerging role of social media in the evolution of urban food systems. *Futures* 62(Part B): 202–212.

Hermelin B., Hinchcliffe G. and Stenbacka S. (2017) The making of the gourmet restaurateur—masculine ideology, identity and performance. *NORMA* 12(1): 48–64.

Hesmondhalgh D. (2010) User-generated content, free labour and the cultural industries. *Ephemera Theory & Politics in Organization* 10(3/4). http://www.ephemerajournal.org/contribution/user-generated-content-free-labour-and-cultural-industries (accessed January 25, 2019).

Hess A. and Waldman K. (2015) Will words soon be replaced by GIFs? A debate in words and GIFs. *Lexicon Valley, Slate*. Available at: http://www.slate.com/blogs/lexicon_valley/2015/05/11/are_gifs_the_future_of_communication_will_they_replace_words.html?via=gdpr-consent (accessed November 29, 2018).

Hesse M. (2011) Vegan Black Metal Chef and others fire up extreme cooking on YouTube. *Washington Post*. Available at: https://www.washingtonpost.com/lifestyle/style/vegan-black-metal-chef-and-others-fire-up-extreme-cooking-on-youtube/2011/06/02/AGzkkYKH_story.html?noredirect=on&utm_term=.b18a439a430b (accessed January 25, 2019).

Hjorth, L. and Hendry, N. (2015). A snapshot of social media: Camera phone practices. *Social Media + Society* 1(1): 1–3.

Hjorthol R. and Gripsrud M. (2009) Home as a communication hub: The domestic use of ICT. *Journal of Transport Geography* 17(2): 115–123.

Hochschild A.R. (1983) *The Managed Heart: Commercialization of Human Feeling*, Berkeley and Los Angeles, California: University of California Press.

Holden M. and Scerri A. (2013) More than this: Liveable Melbourne meets liveable Vancouver. *Cities* 31: 444–453.

Hollows J. (2003) Oliver's twist: Leisure, labour and domestic masculinity in *The Naked Chef. International Journal of Cultural Studies* 6(2): 229–248.

Hollows J. and Jones S. (2010) "At least he's doing something": Moral entrepreneurship and individual responsibility in Jamie's Ministry of Food. *European Journal of Cultural Studies* 13(3): 307–322.

Holmgren D. (2002) *Permaculture: Principles and Pathways beyond Sustainability*, Hepburn: Holmgren Design Services.

Hotrec. (2018) Shedding light on the "meal-sharing" platform economy. *Hotrec 'Meal-Sharing' Platform Policy Paper*. Brussels, Belgium. Available at: https://www.hotrec. eu/wp-content/customer-area/storage/594fb766a2dcc6e45760d7165e7be4a6/Final-meal-sharing-report.pdf (accessed July 15, 2018).

Hughes A., Reimer S. and Editors. (2004) *Geographies of Commodity Chains*, New York: Routledge.

Humphery K. and Jordan T. (2018) Mobile moralities: Ethical consumption in the digital realm. *Journal of Consumer Culture* 18(4): 520–538.

Huo Y. (2016) *Exploring the meaning of ethical consumption: A Chinese perspective.* PhD thesis. Gloucestershire UK.: The University of Gloucestershire. Available at: http://eprints.glos.ac.uk/4406/1/PhD%20thesis%2018th%20November%202016_ Redacted%20for%203%20party%20copyright%20mimages%20and%20signature.pdf (accessed April 12, 2018).

IFCO Systems. (2017) The uberization of food: How the sharing economy is transforming the supply chain for the better. *ifco.com*. Available at: http://blog.ifco. com/the-uberization-of-food-how-the-sharing-economy-is-transforming-the-supply-chain-for-the-better (accessed November 29, 2018).

Ioffe J. (2017) The secret correspondence between Donald Trump Jr. and Wikileaks. *The Atlantic*. Available at: https://www.theatlantic.com/politics/archive/2017/11/the-secret-correspondence-between-donald-trump-jr-and-wikileaks/545738/ (accessed January 2, 2019).

Ito M., Okabe D. (2005) Intimate Connections: Contextualizing Japanese youth and mobile messaging. In: Harper R., Palen L. and Taylor A. (eds) *The Inside Text. The Kluwer International Series on Computer Supported Cooperative Work*, vol 4. Dordrecht: Springer, 127–145. DOI: https://doi.org/10.1007/1-4020-3060-6_7 (accessed November 29, 2018).

Iyer L. (2017) Meet 106-year-old Mastanamma, India's latest YouTube sensation. Available at: https://www.theweek.in/webworld/features/society/mastanamma-cooking-youtube-sensation.html (accessed November 23, 2018).

James. (2014) YouTube's best Vegan Chef: Ryoya Takashima from peaceful cuisine. *The Llama Post*. Available at: https://llamapost.com/2014/12/08/youtubes-best-vegan-chef-ryoya-takashima-from-peaceful-cuisine-%E2%98%86/ (accessed January 25, 2019).

Jarrett K. (2014) The relevance of "women's work": Social reproduction and immaterial labor in digital media. *Television & New Media* 15(1): 14–29.

Jarvey N. (2015) Why vice media is expanding its food-themed programming. *The Hollywood Reporter*. Available at: https://www.hollywoodreporter.com/news/why-vice-media-is-expanding-790223 (accessed January 25, 2019).

Jenkins H. (2006) *Convergence Culture: Where Old and New Media Collide*, New York: New York University Press.

Jenkins H., Ford S. and Green J. (2013) *Spreadable Media Creating Value and Meaning in a Networked Culture*, New York: New York University Press.

Johnson L. (March 14, 2017) U.S. digital advertising will make $83 billion this year. *AdWeek*. Available at: http://www.adweek.com/digital/u-s-digital-advertising-will-make-83-billion-this-year-says-emarketer (accessed January 2, 2019).

Johnston J. and Baumann S. (2010) *Foodies: Democracy and Distinction in the Gourmet Foodscape*, New York: Routledge.

Johnston J., Rodney A. and Chong P. (2014) Making change in the kitchen? A study of celebrity cookbooks, culinary personas, and inequality. *Poetics* 47: 1–22.

Joyce G. (2017) Food influencers: The biggest food trends of 2017. *Brandwatch*, September 7. Available at: https://www.brandwatch.com/blog/react-food-influencers-2017/ (accessed December 15, 2018).

Keen A. (2008) *The Cult of the Amateur: How Today's Internet Is Killing Our Culture and Assaulting the Economy*, London: Nicholas Brealey Publishing.

Kelly C.R. (2015) Cooking without women: The rhetoric of the new culinary male. *Communication and Critical/Cultural Studies* 12(2): 200–204.

Kennedy J., Nansen B., Meese J., et al. (2017) Mapping the Melbourne sharing economy. *Melbourne Networked Society Institute Research Paper 5*. Melbourne: The University of Melbourne.

Kenney M. and Zysman J. (2016) The rise of the platform economy xxxii (3) (Spring). Available at: https://issues.org/the-rise-of-the-platform-economy/ (accessed January 12, 2017).

Kim S.-J. (2017) Day Day Cook founder Norma Chu talks digital success in China, Cantonese cuisine and her midnight cravings. *South China Morning Post*. Available at: https://www.scmp.com/magazines/style/travel-food/article/2095179/day-day-cook-founder-norma-chu-talks-digital-success (accessed November 23, 2018).

Kitchin R. (2014) *The Data Revolution: Big Data, Open Data, Data Infrastructures and Their Consequences*, Los Angeles, CA: Sage.

Kroker A. and Kroker M. (2013) *Critical Digital Studies: A Reader [2nd edition]*, Toronto: University of Toronto Press.

le Grand E. (2018) Representing the middle-class "hipster": Emerging modes of distinction, generational oppositions and gentrification. *European Journal of Cultural Studies*. DOI: 10.1177/1367549418772168. (accessed November 23, 2018).

LeBesco K. and Naccarato P. (forthcoming) The Paradox of the Hungry Hipster: The Representation and Cultural Politics of Hipster Foodways. In: Steinhoff H. and Erbacher E. (eds) *Hipster Culture: A Reader*.

Lee S. (2017) Picture perfect? How Instagram changed the food we eat. *BBC News*. Available at: https://www.bbc.com/news/uk-england-london-42012732 (accessed December 28, 2018).

Levin S. (2018) The man who beat Monsanto: "They have to pay for not being honest." *The Guardian*. Available at: https://www.theguardian.com/business/2018/sep/25/monsanto-dewayne-johnson-cancer-verdict (accessed January 2, 2019).

Lewis T. (2008a) *Smart Living: Lifestyle Media and Popular Expertise*, New York: Peter Lang.

Lewis T. (2008b) Transforming citizens? Green politics and ethical consumption on lifestyle television. *Continuum: Journal of Media & Cultural Studies (Special Issue on Environmental Sustainability)* 22(2): 227–240.

Lewis T. (2011) "You've put yourselves on a plate": The labours of selfhood on *MasterChef Australia*. In: Skeggs B. and Wood H. (eds) *Reality Television and Class*. London: Palgrave Macmillan, 104–116.

Lewis T. (2014) Lifestyle Media. In: Maguire J.S. and Matthews J. (eds) *The Cultural Intermediaries Reader*. London: Sage, 134–144.

Lewis T. (2015) "One city block at a time": Researching and cultivating green transformations. *International Journal of Cultural Studies* 18(3): 347–363.

Lewis T. and Huber A. (2015) A revolution in an eggcup?: Supermarket wars, celebrity chefs and ethical consumption. *Food, Culture & Society* 18(2): 289–307.

Lewis T. and Phillipov M. (2015) A pinch of ethics and a soupçon of home cooking: Soft-selling supermarkets on food television. In: Peri B. (ed.) *Food, Media and Contemporary Culture*. London: Palgrave Macmillan, 105–124.

Lewis T. and Philipov M. (2018) Special Issue: Food/media: Eating, cooking, and provisioning in a digital world. *Communication Research and Practice*. Guest Editors: Tania Lewis and Michelle Phillipov. Available at: https://www.tandfonline.com/toc/rcrp20/4/3.

Lewis T. and Potter E. (2011) Introducing ethical consumption. In: Lewis T. and Potter E. (eds) *Ethical Consumption: A Critical Introduction*. London: Routledge, 12–44.

Lewis T., Flore J. and Tacchi J. (2017) Domesticating the knowledge economy: At home with digital advice, information and expertise. *Paper Presented at the Australia and New Zealand Communications Association Conference*. University of Sydney, July 5–7, 2017.

Lewis T., Martin F. and Sun W. (2016) *Telemodernities: Television, and Transforming Lives in Asia*, Durham, NC: Duke University Press.

Littler J. (2009) *Radical Consumption: Shopping for Change in Contemporary Culture*, Birkshire, UK: Open University Press.

Littler J. (2011) What's wrong with ethical consumption? In: Lewis T. and Potter E. (eds) *Ethical Consumption: A Critical Introduction*. London: Routledge, 27–39.

Littler J. (2018) *Against Meritocracy: Culture, Power and Myths of Mobility*, New York: Routledge.

Live Curiously Magazine. (2014) Growing towards a sustainable lifestyle. Available at: http://livecuriouslymag.com/2014/09/grow-sustainable-lifestyle/-Vfi6r52eDRY (accessed September 16, 2015).

Lobato R. (2016) The cultural logic of digital intermediaries: YouTube multichannel networks. *Convergence: The International Journal of Research into New Media Technologies* 22(4): 348–360.

Lobinger K. (2015) Photographs as things—photographs of things. A texto-material perspective on photo-sharing practices. *Information, Communication & Society* 19(4): 475–488.

Logan T. (2017) Drone mapping in agriculture on the rise. *ABC News*. Available at: http://www.abc.net.au/news/rural/2017-03-07/drone-use-increasing-for-ndvi-mapping/8328456 (accessed April 26, 2017).

Lorde A. (2007) The master's tools will never dismantle the master's house. *Sister Outsider: Essays and Speeches*, Berkeley. (ed) CA: Crossing Press, 110–114.

Luckman S. (2015) *Craft and the Creative Economy*, London: Palgrave Macmillan, iBooks.

Lupton D. (2018) Cooking, eating, uploading: Digital food cultures. In: LeBesco K. and Naccarato P. (eds) *The Handbook of Food and Popular Culture*. London: Bloomsbury, 66–79.

Lyon S. (2018) Digital connections: Coffee, agency, and unequal platforms. In: Schneider T., Eli K., Dolan C., et al. (eds) *Digital Food Activism*. 1st ed. Abingdon: Routledge, 70–88.

Kan Y.M., Sullivan O. and Gershuny J. (2011) Gender convergence in domestic work: Discerning the effects of interactional and institutional barriers from large-scale data. *Sociology* 45(2): 234–251.

Manovich L. (2000) Database as a genre of new media. *The Journal of Human-Centred Systems* 14(2): 176–183.

Markham D. (2013) This app turns your produce barcode into the extended label. *Treehugger*. Available at: https://www.treehugger.com/gadgets/app-turns-your-produce-barcode-extended-label.html (accessed October 25, 2018).

Marres N. (2009) Testing powers of engagement: Green living experiments, the ontological turn and the undoability of involvement. *European Journal of Social Theory* 12: 117–133.

Mars Incorporated. (2016) Mars, Incorporated to remove all artificial colors from its human food portfolio. Available at: https://www.mars.com/news-and-stories/press-releases/remove-artificial-colors (accessed February 14, 2018).

Marwick A.E. (2015) You may know me from YouTube: (Micro-)celebrity in social media. In: Marshall P.D.R., Sean (ed.) *A Companion to Celebrity*. West Sussex UK: John Wiley & Sons inc., 333–350.

Maxwell R. and Miller T. (2008) E-waste: Elephant in the living room. *Flow*. Available at: https://www.flowjournal.org/2008/12/e-waste-elephant-in-the-living-room-richard-maxwell-queens-college-cuny-toby-miller-uc-riverside/ (accessed April 26, 2017).

McCormack W. (2018) Social dining app Homecooked gains momentum. Available at: https://yaledailynews.com/blog/2018/09/09/social-dining-app-homecooked-gains-momentum/ (accessed December 13, 2018).

McGuire S. (2015) 88.2% of people travel the world to get their hands on this …. *Vengage*. Available at: https://venngage.com/blog/88-2-of-people-travel-the-world-to-get-their-hands-on-this-infographic/ (accessed October 25, 2018).

McGuire S. (2017) Food photo frenzy: Inside the Instagram craze and travel trend. *Business.com*. Available at: https://www.business.com/articles/food-photo-frenzy-inside-the-instagram-craze-and-travel-trend/ (accessed October 24, 2018).

Meah A. and Jackson P. (2013) Crowded kitchens: The "democratisation" of domesticity? *Gender, Place & Culture* 20(5): 578–596.

Mediakix. (2017) Influencer spotlight: Exclusive interview with YouTuber behind cooking channel SORTEDfood. Available at: http://mediakix.com/2017/06/sortedfood-interview-youtube-cooking-channel/#gs.qkHU43E (accessed November 29, 2018).

Micheletti M. (2003) *Political Virtue and Shopping: Individuals, Consumerism, and Collective Action*, New York and Basingstoke: Palgrave Macmillan.

Middha B. (2018) Everyday digital engagements: Using food selfies on Facebook to explore eating practices. *Communication Research and Practice* 4(3): 291–306.

Miller V. (2008) New media, networking and phatic culture. *Convergence: The International Journal of Research into New Media Technologies* 14(4): 387–400.

Miller D. (2011) *Tales from Facebook*, Cambridge: Polity Press.

Miller D. and Sinanan J. (2014) *Webcam*, Cambridge: Polity Press.

Miller D. and Slater D. (2000) *The Internet: An Ethnographic Approach*, Oxford: Berg.

Miller D., Costa E., Haynes N., et al. (2016) *How the World Changed Social Media*, London: University College London Press.

Mol A.P.J. (2006) Environmental governance in the information age: The emergence of informational governance. *Environment and Planning C: Government and Policy* 24(4): 497–514.

Mollison B. (1988) *Permaculture: A Designer's Manual*, Tyalgum: Tagari Publications.

Mollison B. and Holmgren D. (1978) *Permaculture One: A Perennial Agriculture for Human Settlements*, Tyalgum: Tagari Publications.

Mooney A. and Klein J. (2016) ASMR is the biggest trend you've never heard of. Available at: https://www.thinkwithgoogle.com/consumer-insights/asmr-videos-youtube-trend/ (accessed November 23, 2018).

Moores S. (2014) Digital orientations: "Ways of the hand" and practical knowing in media uses and other manual activities. *Mobile Media & Communication* 2(2): 196–208.

Moores S. (2018) *Digital Orientations: Non-Media-Centric Media Studies and Non-Representational Theories of Practice*, New York: Peter Lang.

Morley D. (2009) For a materialist, non-media-centric media studies. *Television and New Media* 10(1): 114–116.

Morley J., Widdicks K. and Hazas M. (2018) Digitalisation, energy and data demand: The impact of Internet traffic on overall and peak electricity consumption. *Energy Research & Social Science* 38: 128–137.

Moseley R. (2000) Makeover takeover on British Television. *Screen* 41(3): 299–314.

Murphy K. (2010) First Camera, Then Fork. *New York Times*, April 6. Available at: https://www.nytimes.com/2010/04/07/dining/07camera.html (accessed October 17, 2010).

Naccarato P. and LeBesco K. (2012) *Culinary Capital*, London: Berg. Available at: https://www.bloomsbury.com/au/culinary-capital-9780857854155/.

Nichols J. (2017) Spare harvest battles food waste by swapping, selling and sharing excess produce. *Australian Broadcasting Corporation—ABC Rural.* (accessed December 29, 2018).

Nicklas N., Lucas G. and Christina F. (2017) Narratives of progress: Cooking and gender equality among Swedish men. *Journal of Gender Studies* 26 (2): 151–163.

O'Donoghue J.J. (2018) YouTube: Picking up where TV cooking shows left off. Available at: https://www.japantimes.co.jp/life/2018/06/02/food/youtube-picking-tv-cooking-shows-left-off/#.W_hshC1L0Wp (accessed November 23, 2018).

Omnicore Agency. (2019) Instagram by the numbers: Stats, demographics & fun facts. Available at: https://www.omnicoreagency.com/instagram-statistics/ (accessed January 25, 2019).

Paley R.T. (2015) Meet the dad who likes to keep food blogging in the family. *Yahoo! Lifestyle.* Available at: https://www.yahoo.com/lifestyle/meet-the-dad-who-likes-to-keep-food-blogging-in-121301283726.html (accessed January 25, 2019).

Pansino R. (2014) How to make a Frozen princess cake—Nerdy Nummies. YouTube. https://www.youtube.com/watch?v=q53HUAKB9oU (accessed March 15, 2018).

Papacharissi Z. (2009) The virtual sphere 2.0: The internet, the public sphere and beyond. In: Howard P.N. and Chadwick A. (eds) *The Routledge Handbook of Internet Politics.* Abingdon: Routledge, 230–245.

Papacharissi Z. (2010) *A Private Sphere: Democracy in a Digital Age,* Cambridge: Polity Press.

Parag Y. and Sovacool B.K. (2016) Electricity market design for the prosumer era. *Nature Energy* 1(4). DOI: 10.1038/nenergy.2016.32 (accessed January 25, 2019).

Parikka J. (2015) *A Geology of Media,* Minneapolis: University of Minnesota Press.

Parisi D., Paterson M. and Archer J.E. (2017) Haptic media studies. *New Media & Society* 19: 1513–1522.

Pasiya L. (2018) Mapha Food Share is a homegrown app. *Independent Online.* Available at: https://www.iol.co.za/lifestyle/food-drink/mapha-food-share-is-a-homegrown-app-14486892 (accessed December 15, 2018).

Pearson S., May D., Leontidis G., et al. (2019) Are distributed ledger technologies the panacea for food traceability? *Global Food Security* 20: 145–149.

Peekhaus W. (2010) Monsanto discovers social media. *International Journal of Communication* 4: 955–976.

Peng Y. (2017) Sharing food photographs on social media: Performative Xiaozi lifestyle in Young, middle-class Chinese urbanites' WeChat "Moments." *Social Identities* 25 (2): 269–287.

Pettaway J. (2017) Local couple launches social networking food sharing app. *News 5 Cleveland.* Available at: https://www.news5cleveland.com/lifestyle/food/local-couple-launches-social-networking-food-sharing-app (accessed December 15, 2018).

Petter O. (2017) How Instagram has ruined restaurants. *The Independent,* December 1. Available at: https://www.independent.co.uk/life-style/food-and-drink/instagram-restaurants-how-change-photos-food-meals-interior-design-social-media-ban-images-a8080416.html (accessed October 17, 2018).

Phillipov M. (2016) The new politics of food: Television and the media/food industries. *Media International Australia* 158(1): 90–98.

Pine J. and Gilmore J. (1999) *The Experience Economy*, Boston, MA: Harvard Business School Press.

Pink S., Horst H., Postill J., Hjorth, L, Lewis, T, Tacchi, J. (2016) *Digital Ethnography: Principles and Practice*, London: Sage.

Pink S. and Lewis T. (2014) Making resilience: Everyday affect and global affiliation in Australian slow cities. *Cultural Geographies* 21(4): 695–710.

Probyn E. (2016) *Eating the Ocean*, Durham, NC: Duke University Press.

Rath J. (2017) Tastemade wants to shift from making popular foodie videos to becoming a lifestyle brand. Available at: https://www.businessinsider.com.au/tastemade-looks-to-new-countries-and-categories-2017-2?r=US&IR=T (accessed November 24, 2018).

Redrup Y. (2013) Restaurants and cafés rejoice: Industry exempt from providing separate menus with surcharges. *SmartCompany*. Available at: https://www.smartcompany.com.au/finance/economy/restaurants-and-caf-s-rejoice-industry-exempt-from-providing-separate-menus-with-surcharges/ (accessed December 15, 2018).

Rezeanu C.-I. (2015) The relationship between domestic space and gender identity: Some signs of emergence of alternative domestic femininity and masculinity. *Journal of Comparative Research in Anthropology and Sociology* 6: 9–29.

Roquet P. (2016) *Ambient Media: Japanese Atmospheres of Self*, Minneapolis: University of Minnesota Press.

Rose, N. (1989) *Governing the soul: The shaping of the private self*, London: Routledge.

Rousseau S. (2012) *Food and Social Media You Are What You Tweet*, Lanham, MD: AltaMira Press.

Rubery J. (2015) Change at work: Feminisation, flexibilisation, fragmentation and financialisation. *Employee Relations* 37(6): 633–644.

Rudram B., Faith B., Prieto Martín P., et al. (2016) The impact of digital technology on environmental sustainability and resilience: An evidence review. *IDS Evidence Report 209*. Brighton: IDS. Available at: http://www.ids.ac.uk/publication/the-impact-of-digital-technology-on-environmental-sustainability-and-resilience-an-evidence-review (accessed April 26, 2017).

Ruppanner L. (2017) Census 2016: Women are still disadvantaged by the amount of unpaid housework they do. *The Conversation*. Available at: https://theconversation.com/census-2016-women-are-still-disadvantaged-by-the-amount-of-unpaid-housework-they-do-76008 (accessed December 15, 2018).

Salazar M.L. (2012) Visualising 21st-Century Foodscapes: Using Photographs and New Media in Food Studies. In: Williams-Forson P.A. and Counihan C. (eds) *Taking Food Public: Redefining Foodways in a Changing World*. New York: Routledge, 322–339.

Salt B. (2016) Moralisers, we need you! I belong to a secret society and I am looking for new recruits. *The Weekend Australian Magazine. The Australian*, October

15–16. Available at: https://www.theaustralian.com.au/life/weekend-australian-magazine/moralisers-we-need-you/news-story/6bdb24f77572be68330bd306c14ee8a3#itm=taus%7Cnews%7Caus_authors_index%7C1%7Cauthors_storyBlock_headline%7CMoralisers%2C_we_need_you!%7Cindex%7Cauthor&itmt=1476580893995 (accessed November 28, 2018).

Sarvas R. and Frohlich D.M. (2011) *From Snapshots to Social Media: The Changing Picture of Domestic Photography*, New York: Springer.

Schneider T., Eli K., Dolan C., et al. (2018) *Digital Food Activism*, London: Routledge.

Scholz T. (2014) Platform cooperativism vs. the sharing economy. *Medium*. Available at: https://medium.com/@trebors/platform-cooperativism-vs-the-sharing-economy-2ea737f1b5ad (accessed January 2, 2019).

Schor J. (1999) The new politics of consumption. *Boston Review* Available at: http://bostonreview.net/archives/BR24.3/schor.html (accessed December 28, 2018).

Sedacca M. (2017) Why restaurants ban cell phones. Available at: https://www.eater.com/2017/11/30/16672378/cell-phone-ban-restaurant (accessed November 12, 2018).

Sen M. (2018) An Indian food writer breaks free from tradition. *New York Times*. Available at: https://www.nytimes.com/2018/10/02/dining/nik-sharma-season-cookbook.html (accessed January 25, 2018).

Sharma N. (2018) A brown kitchen: An upside-down fig cake to celebrate gay rights in India. *San Francisco Chronical*. Available at: https://www.sfchronicle.com/recipes/article/A-Brown-Kitchen-An-upside-down-fig-cake-to-13221663.php (accessed January 25, 2019).

Sharma S.S and Choudhury M.D. (2015) Measuring and characterizing nutritional information of food and ingestion content in Instagram. *Proceedings of the 24th International Conference on World Wide Web*. Florence, Italy: ACM, 115–116.

Shaw D. and Newholm T. (2002) Voluntary simplicity and the ethics of consumption. *Psychology and Marketing* 19(2): 167–185.

Shea C. (2016) The ravages of Matty Matheson. *Toronto Life*. Available at: https://torontolife.com/food/chef-matty-matheson-vice-canada-parts-and-labour-dead-set-on-life/ (accessed January 25, 2019).

Sheller M. and Urry J. (2003) Mobile transformations of 'public" and "private" life. *Theory Culture and Society* 20(3): 107–126.

Sherman E. (2018) If you're not watching "home: A queer cooking series," You should be. *Food&Wine*. Available at: https://www.foodandwine.com/news/home-queer-cooking-youtube-series (accessed January 28, 2019).

Shove E. (2003) *Comfort, Cleanliness and Convenience: The Social Organization of Normality*, Oxford: Berg.

Smithers R. (2016) Hawaiian salad and watermelon juice "to be 2017 food trends." *The Guardian*, November 2, 2016. Available at: https://www.theguardian.com/business/2016/nov/02/hawaiian-salad-watermelon-juice-2017-food-trends-waitrose (accessed October 17, 2018).

SORTEDfood. (2016) Available at: https://sorted.club.

Sparks J. (2018) This queer cooking show reinvigorated my pride in home cooking. *Bon Appétit!*. Available at: https://www.bonappetit.com/story/home-queer-cooking-series (accessed January 28, 2019).

Stalder F. (2017) *The Digital Condition*, Cambridge: Polity Press.

Steiner J. (2018) What the heck is Web 3.0 anyway? *Forbes*. Available at: https://www.forbes.com/sites/juttasteiner/2018/10/26/what-the-heck-is-web-3-0-anyway/#306d79dc6614 (accessed January 31, 2019).

Steinmetz K. (2015) The dad 2.0 summit: Making the case for a new kind of manhood. *Time*. Available at: http://time.com/3717511/dad-summit-manhood/ (accessed January 25, 2019).

Stengle R. (2009) The responsibility revolution. *Time*, 174: 24–27.

Stevens T.M., Aarts N., Termeer C., et al. (2016) Social media as a new playing field for the governance of agro-food sustainability. *Current Opinion in Environmental Sustainability* 18(C): 99–106.

Strange N. (1998) Perform, educate, entertain: Ingredients of the cookery programme genre. In: Geraghty C. and Lusted D. (eds) *The Television Studies Book*. London: Arnold Publishing, 301–312.

Strangelove M. (2010) *Watching YouTube—Extraordinary Videos by Ordinary People*, Toronto: University of Toronto Press.

Strengers Y. and Nicholls L. (2017) Convenience and energy consumption in the smart home of the future: Industry visions from Australia and beyond. *Energy Research & Social Science* 32: 86–93.

Striphas T. (2015) Algorithmic culture. *European Journal of Cultural Studies* 18(4–5): 395–412.

Strom S. (2013) Social media as a megaphone to pressure the food industry. *New York Times*. Available at: https://www.nytimes.com/2013/12/31/business/media/social-media-as-a-megaphone-to-push-food-makers-to-change.html (accessed December 31, 2018).

Sui D.Z. and Rejeski D.W. (2002) Environmental impacts of the emerging digital economy: The e-for-environment e-commerce? *Environmental Management* 29(2): 155–163.

Szabo M. (2013) Foodwork or foodplay? Men's domestic cooking, privilege and leisure. *Sociology* 47(4): 623–638.

Szabo M. (2014) Men nurturing through food: Challenging gender dichotomies around domestic cooking. *Journal of Gender Studies* 23(1): 18–31.

Szewczyk J. (2017) 18 Foodie Instagram accounts every serious cook should follow. *BuzzFeed*. Available at: https://www.buzzfeed.com/jesseszewczyk/food-instagram-accounts-to-follow (accessed January 25, 2019).

Taillie L.S. (2018) Who's cooking? Trends in US home food preparation by gender, education, and race/ethnicity from 2003 to 2016. *Nutrition Journal* 17(41): 1–9.

Tandoh R. (2016) Click plate: How Instagram is changing the way we eat. *The Guardian*. Available at: https://www.theguardian.com/lifeandstyle/2016/nov/02/click-plate-how-instagram-changing-way-we-eat-food (accessed October 24, 2018).

Terranova T. (2000) Free labor: Producing culture for the digital economy. *Social Text* 18(2): 33–58.

Thompson L. (2014) A map of China's back-to-the-land efforts. Available at: http://www.chinafile.com/reporting-opinion/earthbound-china/map-chinas-back-land-efforts (accessed December 28, 2018).

Thompson R. (2018) The secret sauce behind 11 of Etsy's top sellers. *SmartCompany*. Available at: https://www.smartcompany.com.au/industries/retail/the-secret-sauce-behind-11-of-etsy-s-top-sellers/ (accessed December 15, 2018).

Ticona J., Mateescu A. and Rosenblat A. (2018) Beyond disruption: How tech shapes labor across domestic work & ridehailing. *Data & Society* (online report). Available at: https://datasociety.net/output/beyond-disruption/.

Tolson A. (2010) A new authenticity? Communicative practices on YouTube. *Critical Discourse Studies* 7(4): 277–289.

Turner G. (2016) *Re-Inventing the Media*, London: Routledge.

Unni J. (2001) Gender and informality in labour market in South Asia. *Economic and Political Weekly* 36(26): 2360–2377.

van Dijck J. (2013) *The Culture of Connectivity a Critical History of Social Media*, New York: Oxford University Press.

van Dijck J. (2014) Datafication, dataism and dataveillance: Big data between scientific paradigm and ideology. *Surveillance & Society* 12(2): 197–208.

van Dijck J., Poell T. and de Waal M. (2018) *The Platform Society: Public Values in a Connective World*, New York: Oxford University Press.

Van House N.A. (2009) Collocated photo sharing, story-telling, and the performance of self. *International Journal of Human-Computer Studies* 67(12): 1073–1086.

Van House N.A, Davis M., Ames M., et al. (2005) The uses of personal networked digital imaging: An empirical study of cameraphone photos and sharing. *CHI '05 Extended Abstracts on Human Factors in Computing Systems*, Portland, OR: ACM, 1853–1856.

Viceland. (2018) Oh, banh mi! It's a Vietnamese sandwich. *It's Suppertime!* S1 EP2. Available at: https://www.viceland.com/en_us/video/its-suppertime-oh-banh-mi-its-a-vietnamese-sandwich/5a14b1bb177dd4119d2fb2a3.

Villi M. (2012) Social curation in audience communities: UDC (user-distributed content) in the networked media ecosystem. *Participations: Journal of Audience and Reception Studies* 9 (2): 614–632.

Villi M. and Stocchetti M. (2011) Visual mobile communication, mediated presence and the politics of space. *Visual Studies* 26(2): 102–112.

Wagner J., Hinton L., McCordic C., et al. (2019) Do urban food deserts exist in the global south? An analysis of Nairobi and Mexico City. *Sustainability* 11(7). DOI: https://doi.org/10.3390/su11071963 (accessed December 15, 2018).

Wall M. (2013) Food bytes: The kitchen goes digital. *BBC News*. Available at: https://www.bbc.com/news/technology-25041147 (accessed January 30, 2019).

Warman E. (2018) The 11 best cooking channels on YouTube. *Tasting Table*. Available at: https://www.tastingtable.com/cook/national/best-youtube-cooking-channels (accessed January 26, 2019).

Weinstein E. (2015) In "The food lab," the science of home cooking. *New York Times.* Available at: https://www.nytimes.com/2015/09/30/dining/cookbook-review-the-food-lab-j-kenji-lopez-alt.html (accessed January 28, 2019).

Witterhold K. (2017) Political consumers as digital food activists? In: Schneider T., Eli K., Dolan C., et al. (eds) *Digital Food Activism*, 89–109. London: Routledge.

World Economic Forum. (2016) Are you feeling it? Why consumer companies must master the experience economy. Available at: http://reports.weforum.org/digital-transformation/moving-to-the-next-level-the-experience-economy/ (accessed December 29, 2018).

Zhang S. (2016) A Monsanto exec's selfie-snapping, live-tweeting campaign for GMO acceptance. *Wired.* Available at: https://www.wired.com/2016/03/monsanto-execs-selfie-snapping-live-tweeting-campaign-gmo-acceptance/ (accessed November 22, 2018)

Zhuge Y. (2018) Video consumption, social networking, and influence. *Communications of the ACM* 61(11): 76–81. DOI: 10.1145/3239554.

Zuboff S. (2019) *The Age of Surveillance Capitalism: The Fight for a Human Future at the New Frontier of Power*, London: Profile Books.

Index